GCSE
INFORMATION TECHNOLOGY

Tony Rackham

Letts Educational
Aldine House
Aldine Place
London W12 8AW
Tel: 0181 740 2266
Fax: 0181 743 8451
e-mail: mail@lettsed.co.uk

Every effort has been made to trace copyright holders and to obtain their permission for the use of copyright material. The author and publishers will gladly receive information enabling them to rectify any error or omission in subsequent editions.

First published 1995
Reprinted 1996
Revised 1997
Reprinted 1998

Text: © Tony Rackham 1995, 1997
Design and illustrations: © BPP (Letts Educational) Ltd 1995, 1997

All our Rights Reserved. No part of this publication may be reproduced, stored in a retrieval system, or transmitted, in any form or by any means, electronic, mechanical, photocopying, recording or otherwise, without the prior permission of Letts Educational.

British Library Cataloguing in Publication Data
A CIP record for this book is available from the British Library.

ISBN 1 85758 585 2

Acknowledgements
Where examination questions have been used the answers are my interpretation and entirely my responsibility. I have received willing co-operation and advice from staff in different examination boards and am grateful to the Midland Examining Group, the Northern Examinations and Assessment Board, the National Design Technology Education Foundation, RSA Examinations and Assessment Board, the Southern Examining Group, London Examinations, a division of Edexcel Foundation (Edexcel Foundation, London Examinations accepts no responsibility whatsoever for the accuracy or method of working in the answers given) and the Welsh Joint Education Committee/Cyd-Bwyllgor Addysg Cymru for permission to reproduce examination questions.

My thanks to the many companies and organisations who have given their permission for the use of their materials in the applications and examples. Also to a small army of my family and friends who helped to arrange contacts and to make sure that the hardware, the software and the applications described are up-to-date. I wish particularly to thank Betty, Caroline and Steve who helped in so many ways, including organising and producing most of the photographs.

Tony Rackham

Microsoft screen shots reprinted with permission from Microsoft Corporation.

Aldus screen shots used with express permission. Adobe and Adobe PageMaker are trademarks of Adobe Systems Incorporated or its subsidiaries and are registered in certain jurisdictions.

Printed in Great Britain by Ashford Colour Press, Gosport

Letts Educational is the trading name of BPP (Letts Educational) Ltd

Contents

Starting points

Introduction 1
How to use this book 1
The National Curriculum and the GCSE in Information Technology 2
Assessment objectives 3

Syllabus analysis 5

Examination Boards: addresses 18

Revision and examinations 19

Information technology topics

1	Information and data	21
1.1	Introduction	21
1.2	Data types	22
1.3	Data storage in computers	22
1.4	Coding of information	23
1.5	Using codes to simplify data	24
1.6	Processing information	24
Quick test		25
Summary		26

2	Information systems	27
2.1	Information technology	27
2.2	Computers	29
2.3	Information processing systems	30
2.4	Real time processing	31
2.5	Interactive computing	32
2.6	Batch processing	35
2.7	Multiprogramming and multitasking	36
Quick test		37
Summary		37

3	Data capture	39
3.1	Introduction	39
3.2	Design of data capture forms	41
3.3	Questionnaires	43
3.4	User interfaces	45
Quick test		48
Summary		48

4	Input methods	50
4.1	Input from keyboards	50
4.2	OMR, OCR and MICR	51
4.3	Bars and stripes	54
4.4	Point and touch methods	57
4.5	Input of pictures	60
4.6	Input of sound	62
Quick test		63
Summary		63

5	Output of data	65
5.1	Output on screens	65
5.2	Printers	67
5.3	Graphics and plotters	69
5.4	Other output methods	70
5.5	Choice of output method	71
Quick test		72
Summary		72

6	Storage	73
6.1	Introduction to storage	73
6.2	Main store	73
6.3	Backing stores	75
6.4	Magnetic discs	75
6.5	Compact discs	77
6.6	Magnetic tape	78
Quick test		79
Summary		80

7	Data files	81
7.1	Facts about files	81
7.2	Storage of files	83
7.3	Types of file	85
7.4	Updating files	87
7.5	Other operations on files	88
7.6	An application of files – stock control	89
Quick test		91
Summary		92

8	Security and integrity of data	93
8.1	Security problems	93
8.2	Making copies of files	94
8.3	Other ways of looking after data	95
8.4	Integrity of input data	97
8.5	Methods of avoiding input errors	98
8.6	Methods of detecting input errors	99
Quick test		100
Summary		101

9	Software	102
9.1	Programs	102
9.2	Software	103
9.3	Operating systems	104
9.4	Evaluation of applications software	105
9.5	Types of application package	106
9.6	General purpose application packages	107
9.7	Choosing the right package	111
Quick test		111
Summary		111

10	Presenting your work: word processing and desktop publishing	114
10.1	Word processing	114
10.2	Entering, editing and improving text	115

Contents

10.3	Spelling	116
10.4	Tabs, margins and indents	116
10.5	Working with blocks of text	118
10.6	Further word processing techniques	118
10.7	Desktop publishing	120
Quick test		121
Summary		121
11	**Handling information: database programs**	**122**
11.1	Database programs	122
11.2	Planning – how to design a database	123
11.3	Creating a database file	126
11.4	Searches and queries	127
11.5	Statistics and sorts	128
11.6	More about databases	130
Quick test		132
Summary		133
12	**Models of situations**	**134**
12.1	What is a model?	134
12.2	Simulations	136
12.3	Other computer models	137
Quick test		139
Summary		140
13	**Creating models: spreadsheets**	**141**
13.1	Introduction to spreadsheets	141
13.2	Improving the look of a spreadsheet	142
13.3	Formulae	143
13.4	Copying cells	145
13.5	A spreadsheet as a model	147
Quick test		147
Summary		148
14	**Presenting your work: graphics and charts**	**149**
14.1	Graphics	149
14.2	Paint packages	150
14.3	CAD graphics	151
14.4	Graphs and charts	154
14.5	Types of chart	156
Quick test		156
Summary		157
15	**Communications**	**158**
15.1	Introduction to communications	158
15.2	Teletext	159
15.3	Networks	160
15.4	Local area networks	161
15.5	Wide area networks	163
15.6	Public viewdata networks	163
Quick test		166
Summary		166
16	**Measurement and control**	**168**
16.1	Control systems	168
16.2	Sensors and feedback	170
16.3	Process control	172
16.4	Robots	174
16.5	Data logging	176
Quick test		178
Summary		178
17	**Programming for control systems**	**179**
17.1	Controlling a turtle with LOGO	179
17.2	Programming control systems	181
17.3	Solving control problems	184
Quick test		185
Summary		185
18	**Solving problems using IT**	**187**
18.1	Introduction to problem solving	187
18.2	The professional way – the system life cycle	187
18.3	A coursework project – what to do	190
Quick test		192
Summary		193
19	**Documentation**	**194**
19.1	Documentation and diagrams	194
19.2	System flowcharts	195
19.3	Representing algorithms – structure diagrams	198
19.4	Program and algorithm flowcharts	200
19.5	Example comparing a structure diagram and a program flowchart	202
19.6	User documentation	202
19.7	Technical documentation	204
Quick test		205
Summary		206
20	**The implications of IT**	**207**
20.1	Examinations and the implications of IT	207
20.2	The general effect of IT on our lives	208
20.3	Effect of IT on work and unemployment	210
20.4	The effect of IT on personal privacy	212
Quick test		215
Summary		216

Questions and answers

Examination questions	217
Examination answers	238
Answers to quick tests	247
Index to applications	250
General index	251

Starting points

Introduction

This book is a complete revision course for the GCSE in Information Technology. It also contains the work required for many shorter courses on Information Technology. The book contains:
- all the necessary factual material required by the syllabuses,
- a quick self test on each chapter,
- hints on taking examinations and on tackling coursework,
- a bank of sample examination questions and suggested answers.

How to use this book

1. Find out which syllabus you are studying :
   - Your teacher will tell you the Board and syllabus. You may be taking a full GCSE course, a short course or a combined course (see below – Information Technology courses).
   - Discuss with your teacher your level of study. You may be taking Foundation Tier or Higher Tier examinations (see below – Tiers of entry).
2. Use the Syllabus Analysis section of this book to find:
   - the lengths of the papers for each tier;
   - the types of questions which papers will contain;
   - the chapters from the book which you will need to study for your syllabus;
   - the coursework you are required to produce, and the relative marks for coursework and examinations.
3. For your main revision:
   - If you have started your revision in plenty of time, then tackle topics in the order in which they appear in the book. Otherwise, select only ones which you have been taught but are not confident about.
   - Find the appropriate chapter in the main part of the book. Work through it.
   - Do some examination questions for that chapter (you will find examples at the back of the book). The questions are accompanied by a section of hints, references to the text and possible answers. It is best not to look at the answer to a question until you have tried it yourself.
   - If you cannot do a number of the questions, go back and work through the appropriate chapter again. Make a note of any sections you find difficult so that you can do another quick revision of those later on.
4. For a quick revision prior to the examination:
   - select the chapters you need to revise;
   - go through the text just reading the key terms and the advantages and disadvantages;
   - do the quick test and check your answers against those provided;
   - go over the work again by checking through the summary.

Key terms

Throughout the book, when an important computing term is introduced it is highlighted as follows

KEY TERMS

An explanation of the term is then given followed by notes and examples. If you want to know what a term means look it up in the index at the back of this book. Usually one of the page numbers given there will be in bold type. This refers you to the explanation you want.

1

The National Curriculum and the GCSE in Information Technology

The National Curriculum is divided into four Key Stages:
- Key Stage 1 – ages 5 to 7;
- Key Stage 2 – ages 7 to 11;
- Key Stage 3 – ages 11 to 14;
- Key Stage 4 – ages 14 to 16.

After Key Stage 4 pupils can then be assessed by GCSE examinations which are based on their work for the National Curriculum. Thus the GCSE in Information Technology gives you the opportunity to use the work you have done in your National Curriculum programme of study.

This Programme of Study involves:

1. Using computer systems, software packages and other IT:
   - to solve problems;
   - in a variety of situations.
2. Understanding the impact of IT on working life and on society generally.

The work takes place in two main areas or 'strands':

1. Communicating and handling information.
2. Controlling, monitoring and modelling.

Information Technology courses

GCSE Information Technology can be taken as:

1. a short course

   This does not merit a GCSE rating on its own. To gain a GCSE grade students then have to take another short course as well. The two short courses together may be dealt with by the Examination Board and the school as a GCSE course in the combined subject (e.g. Information Technology and Business Studies).

OR

2. a full GCSE course

   This includes the work for the short course but deals with it more deeply. It may also introduce extra work in some areas (see below under Assessment Objectives).

Tiers of entry

You are allowed to enter the GCSE examinations at either of two tiers. Each tier corresponds to a different level of attainment and is aimed at a different range of grades.

The tiers are:
- Foundation Tier – grades C, D, E, F or G
- Higher Tier – grades A★, A, B, C or D.

The Higher Tier consists of difficult questions and unless you are sure that you can cope with it, it would be better for you to enter the Foundation Tier. If you enter the Higher Tier and do not achieve grade D your grade will be recorded as 'U' for 'Unclassified'.

Spelling, punctuation and grammar

A mark is given for the quality of spelling, punctuation and grammar on all written papers and coursework which you do. This is often referred to on mark schemes as SPG and can make up to 5% of the total mark. On written papers this mark is added on by the examiner who marks the paper. For coursework it is added by your teacher and will then usually be checked by a moderator who works for the examining board.

As these marks could make the difference between grades it is important to pay attention to them while not making yourself too anxious about it.

- Work done for coursework should be checked by doing a spell check and a grammar check if there is one.

- Your revision of key computing terms should include checking the spellings, e.g. words like integer, integrated, justify and repetition are easy to misspell.
- Always read what you have written. It is difficult to make yourself do this but it is worth it. See if what you have written looks right and sounds right. In particular make sure that you have made the right choice between the difficult pairs of words such as:

its	it's	their	there
choose	chose	lose	loose

- Avoid long sentences which ramble. Keep them simple. Often two short sentences are better than one long one. If the question says 'discuss', 'describe' or 'explain' then you should write complete sentences. However, in many questions it is acceptable to give answers in note form.

Assessment objectives

Every syllabus is assessed by coursework and by examinations. These are designed and marked to look for certain abilities on the part of the candidate. You have to revise thoroughly and know the facts of the subject. It is also at least as important that you can show the skills required to discuss the ideas and use the techniques you have learnt about.

The tests for these skills are referred to as **assessment objectives**.

These objectives are quite demanding and quite difficult to understand. This book and your course at school are designed to give you these skills almost without your being aware of them. Nevertheless it is useful for you to see what they are. After all, they explain the purpose behind the setting of much of your coursework and many of the examination questions. A summary of these skills follows.

Assessment objectives for Information Technology

For the full GCSE course you must show that you can:
1. apply your knowledge, skills and understanding of IT to a range of situations;
2. analyse, design, implement, test, evaluate and document IT systems for use by others and develop understanding of the wider applications and effects of IT;
3. reflect critically on the way you and others use IT;
4. discuss and review the impact of IT applications in the outside world;
5. consider the social, legal, ethical and moral issues and security needs for data which surround the increasing use of IT.

The short course has basically the same objectives but is slightly less demanding. You must be able to show that you can:
1. apply your knowledge, skills and understanding of IT to a range of situations;
2. analyse, design, implement and test IT systems and develop understanding of the wider applications and effects of IT;
3. reflect critically on the way you and others use IT;
4. consider the impact of IT applications in the outside world;
5. consider the social, legal, ethical and moral issues and security needs for data which surround the increasing use of IT.

Notice that objectives 2 and 4 are not quite so demanding:
- you do not have to be able to evaluate computer systems and document them for other people to use,
- you cover the impact of computer applications on people in less detail.

In any case each Board sets a different syllabus for the short course so that there are not so many topics to deal with.

Most of these objectives are covered during the normal course of your work at school and your revision programme using the whole of this book. However you are

Starting points

advised to read the following chapters as early as possible to help with coursework skills:
1. For evaluation of software – Chapter 9 from Unit 9.4 onwards;
2. For practical techniques in using software – the relevant Units of Chapters 10, 11, 13 and 14;
3. If you intend to do a control project – Chapter 17;
4. For a project which involves describing your solution to a problem – Chapter 18;
5. For documentation of a project – Chapter 19.

Syllabus analysis

Where the knowledge and abilities required by a syllabus have been summarised below they have been simplified. This has been done to help candidates to understand what is required. To obtain fuller information on what is required, consult your teacher or send off to your examining board for your particular syllabus (addresses are given on page 18).

All of the syllabuses analysed require you to study the topics covered by the Information Technology work up to Key Stage 4 in the National Curriculum. Each GCSE Information Technology syllabus then adds work to this based on the assessment objectives given in the Introduction to this book (page 3).

INFORMATION TECHNOLOGY SYLLABUSES

As explained in the Introduction all of the examining boards:
- offer a short course in Information Technology as well as the full GCSE Information Technology,
- allow entry at two tiers – Foundation Tier and Higher Tier.

Candidates for any of the various syllabuses will be set either one or two written papers and some coursework tasks. These are assessed in the ratio:

>   Coursework   60%
>   Written paper 40%

(with the exception of the NEAB Short Course for which the coursework is 55% and the written paper 45%).

City and Guilds (C&G)

The City and Guilds are running both a full course and a short course for examination only in 1998. After that the GCSE in Information Technology is being passed to NEAB.

Information Technology Syllabus 3562 (full course)

The syllabus is described by six main themes:

1. Communicating information
2. Handling information
3. Modelling
4. Measurement and control
5. Design and development
6. Business applications and systems analysis.

Starting points

Assessment

		% Weighting	Duration
Written Paper	Foundation Paper	40	2 hrs
	OR		
	Higher Paper	40	2½ hrs
Coursework	Minimum 4 short tasks + Design assignment + A case study	60 (Total)	–

Information Technology Short Course Syllabus 3561

The syllabus is described by five main themes:
1. Communicating information
2. Handling information
3. Modelling
4. Measurement and control
5. Design and development.

Assessment

		% Weighting	Duration
Written Paper	Foundation Paper	40	1 hrs
	OR		
	Higher Paper	40	1½ hrs
Coursework	Minimum 2 short tasks + Design assignment	60 (Total)	–

Edexcel, London Examinations (London)

Information Technology Syllabus 1984 (full course)

The syllabus covers and goes beyond the Key Stage 4 programme of study and its two strands of progression, which are:
1. Communicating information
2. Controlling, measuring and modelling.

It also encourages candidates to apply Information Technology through activities in all areas of the curriculum.

Assessment

		% Weighting	Duration
Written Paper	Foundation Paper Section A (System Design) Section B	20 20	2½ hrs (Total)
	OR		
	Higher Paper Section A (System Design) Section B	20 20	2½ hrs (Total)
Coursework	Solve FOUR problems	60	–

Section B of the written paper consists of long, structured questions testing beyond the Systems Design of Section A.

Of the four coursework problems:
- ONE must be on file creation and interrogation
- ONE on creation and manipulation of spreadsheets AND

- TWO on data logging and control OR word processing OR desktop publishing OR one or both can be on free choice topics.

Information Technology Short Course Syllabus 3984

The syllabus covers the Key Stage 4 programme of study and its two strands of progression, which are:
1. Communicating and handling information
2. Controlling, measuring and modelling.

It also encourages candidates to apply Information Technology through activities in all areas of the curriculum.

Assessment

		% Weighting	Duration
Written Paper	Foundation Paper	40	$1\frac{1}{4}$ hrs
	OR Higher Paper	40	$1\frac{1}{4}$ hrs
Coursework	Solve TWO problems	60	–

The two coursework problems must be chosen from:
(a) file creation and interrogation
(b) creation and manipulation of spreadsheets
(c) data logging and control
(d) word processing
(e) desk top publishing.
At least one of the problems must be chosen from types (a) and (b).

Midland Examining Group (MEG)

Information Technology Syllabus 1453 (full course)

The subject content of the syllabus is divided into seven main areas:
1. Communicating information including use of word processing, desktop publishing and CAD/graphics applications
2. Handling information including use of database and spreadsheet
3. Measuring including use of data logging and weather satellite system packages
4. Control
5. Modelling including use of spreadsheets and simulations
6. IT systems design
7. Effects of using Information Technology.

The last of these, the effects of using IT, is regarded as by far the most important for the written paper and 50% of the marks are allocated to it.

Assessment

		% Weighting	Duration
Written Papers	Papers 1 & 3 (Foundation)	20, 20	1 hr, 1hr
	OR Papers 2 & 4 (Higher)	20, 20	$1\frac{1}{4}$ hrs, $1\frac{1}{4}$ hrs
Coursework	1, 2 OR 3 pieces of work	60	–

Each of the written papers consists mainly of questions requiring short responses. There will be a few questions needing longer answers to test for the higher grades.

The coursework will be assessed against two of the five strands:
(i) Information handling   (ii) Communicating   (iii) Modelling
(iv) Measuring   (v) Control

If only one piece of coursework is submitted it will have to involve two of these strands.

At least one of the pieces of coursework must involve addressing a problem and solving it. In the solution you must analyse, design, implement and document an IT system for use by others.

Information Technology Short Course Syllabus 3453

The subject content of this syllabus is divided into the same seven main areas as the full course, namely:
1. Communicating information
2. Handling
3. Measuring
4. Control
5. Modelling
6. IT systems design
7. Effects of using Information Technology.

However, less detail is required of a number of topics.

Assessment

		% Weighting	Duration
Written Papers	Paper 1 (Foundation)	40	1 hr
	OR		
	Paper 2 (Higher)	40	$1\frac{1}{4}$ hrs
Coursework	One OR two pieces of work	60	–

The written paper consists mainly of questions requiring short responses. There will be a few questions needing longer answers to test for the higher grades.

The coursework will be assessed against two of the five strands:
    (i) Information handling   (ii) Communicating   (iii) Modelling
    (iv) Measuring   (v) Control

If only one piece of coursework is submitted it will have to involve two of these strands.

Northern Examinations and Assessment Board (NEAB)

Information Technology Syllabus 1442 (full course)

The syllabus content is divided into two main areas:
A. Tools, techniques and systems involving you in
- awareness of the structure of information systems;
- knowledge and understanding of hardware and software;
- evaluation of the suitability of hardware and software;
- describing methods of gathering, storing and processing data and presenting information;
- understanding the system life cycle.

B. Information systems in society dealing with
- communications;
- the Data Protection Act;
- copyright law and anti-hacking legislation;
- growth of information and its effects on society.

Assessment

		% Weighting	Duration
Written Papers	Paper 1 – Foundation +	20	1½ hrs
	Paper 2 - Foundation	20	1½ hrs
	OR		
	Paper 1 – Higher +	20	1½ hrs
	Paper 2 - Higher	20	1½ hrs
Coursework	Board-set Assignment +	25	
	Project	35	–

The board-set assignment will be sent to the school at the start of the course. It will involve using IT to solve problems and producing a report. You will have to show that you have designed, implemented, tested and evaluated the solutions.

The project is also to produce a report on the solution to a problem. The topic can be from any area of interest to illustrate your IT capability.

Information Technology Short Course Syllabus 2442

The syllabus content is divided into two main areas:
A. Tools, techniques and systems involving you in
- awareness of the structure of information systems;
- knowledge and understanding of hardware and software;
- describing methods of gathering, storing and processing data and presenting information.

B. Information systems in society dealing with
- communications;
- the Data Protection Act;
- growth of information and its effects on society.

Assessment

		% Weighting	Duration
Written Paper	Foundation Paper	45	1½ hrs
	OR		
	Higher Paper	45	1½ hrs
Coursework	Board-set Assignment	55	–

The board-set assignment will be sent to the school at the start of the course. It will involve using IT to solve problems and producing a report. You will have to show that you have designed, implemented, tested and evaluated the solutions.

National Design and Technology Education Foundation (NDTEF)

Information Technology (full course)

The syllabus is based on two main areas:
1. The design, development and use of systems:
   - development of systems,
   - analysis,
   - design,
   - implementation and testing,
   - evaluation,
   - documentation.

Starting points

2. Practical activities/systems in society:
   - communicating and handling information,
   - controlling, measuring and modelling,
   - social, moral and ethical aspects,
   - hardware and software.

Assessment

		% Weighting	Duration
Written Paper OR	Foundation	40	1½ hrs
	Higher	40	2 hrs
Coursework	Pupil-selected task	40	–
	Case study	20	

The assessment of both parts of the coursework and of the written paper is divided in the ratio:
    Design, development and use of systems – 60%
    Systems in society – 40%

Information Technology Short Course

The syllabus is based on two main areas:
1. The design, development and use of systems:
   - development of systems,
   - analysis,
   - design,
   - implementation and testing.
2. Practical activities/systems in society:
   - communicating and handling information,
   - controlling, measuring and modelling,
   - social, moral and ethical aspects,
   - hardware and software.

Assessment

		% Weighting	Duration
Written Paper OR	Foundation	40	1 hr
	Higher	40	1½ hrs
Coursework	Pupil-selected task	40	–
	Case study	20	

The assessment of both parts of the coursework and of the written paper is divided in the ratio:
    Design, development and use of systems – 60%
    Systems in society – 40%

RSA Examinations Board (RSA)

Information Technology (full course)

The syllabus demands:
- knowledge of information systems,
- capability in selecting and applying IT to a range of needs for information,
- application of principles to the analysis and evaluation of existing systems and new information needs,

- skill in designing and documenting systems for others to use,
- understanding of the effects of information systems.

Assessment

		% Weighting	Duration
Written Paper	Foundation	40	$1^{1}/_{2}$ hrs
	OR		
	Higher	40	$2^{1}/_{4}$ hrs
Coursework	Practical tasks	45	–
	Case study	15	

There are four assessment objectives:
1. Techniques for communicating and handling information
2. Techniques for measurement, modelling and control
3. Evaluation and problem solving
4. Application and implications of IT.

The case study is a study which tests objective 4.

One of the practical tasks is compulsory and is set by the board. The others may be from optional ones suggested by the board or can be the candidate's own ideas, as long as the practical tasks between them cover assessment objectives 1, 2 and 3.

Information Technology Short Course

The general demands of the syllabus are the same as for the full course but there are fewer assessment objectives (see below). The subject content for the course is correspondingly reduced – see syllabus analysis table (page 14).

Assessment

		% Weighting	Duration
Written Paper	Foundation	40	$1^{1}/_{4}$ hrs
	OR		
	Higher	40	$1^{3}/_{4}$ hrs
Coursework	Practical tasks	60	–

There are three assessment objectives:
1. Techniques for communicating and handling information
2. Techniques for measurement, modelling and control
3. Evaluation and problem solving.

One of the practical tasks is compulsory and is set by the board. The others may be from optional ones suggested by the board or can be the candidate's own ideas, as long as the practical tasks between them cover assessment objectives 1, 2 and 3.

Southern Examining Group (SEG)

Information Technology Syllabus 3460 (full course)

The syllabus content is divided into four main areas, which can be summarised as follows:

1. The use of IT to gather, store, process and present information
2. The function, purpose and organisation of the hardware and software components of standalone and networked computer systems
3. The use of IT to solve problems, including the analysis, design, implementation and documentation of IT systems
4. - The use of IT by themselves and others
   - The social, legal, ethical and moral issues involved in the use of IT.

Assessment

		% Weighting	Duration
Written Papers	Paper 2 (Foundation) OR	40	1½ hrs
	Paper 3 (Higher)	40	1½ hrs
Coursework	Paper 1, task 1	30	–
	Paper 1, task 2	30	–

For each of the Foundation and Higher Tiers the written paper consists of fairly long structured questions.

The two coursework tasks have to be taken one from each of the National Curriculum strands:
- (i) Communicating and handling information,
- (ii) Controlling, measuring and modelling.

Information Technology Short Course Syllabus 1460

The syllabus content of the short course is divided into the same four main areas as the full course. However, a number of the detailed topics are missed out. For example, there is no need to study macros or programs, the stages of the system life cycle or different types of operating system.

Assessment

		% Weighting	Duration
Written Paper	Paper 2 (Foundation) OR	40	1 hr
	Paper 3 (Higher)	40	1 hr
Coursework	One task (Paper 1)	60	–

For each of the Foundation and Higher Tiers the written paper consists of fairly long structured questions.

The coursework task has to be taken from one or other of the National Curriculum strands:
- (i) Communicating and handling information,
- (ii) Controlling, measuring and modelling.

Welsh Joint Education Committee/Cyd-Bwyllgor Addysg Cymru (WJEC/CBAC)

Information Technology Syllabus (Full Course)

The syllabus content consists of a core and an extension. The core is divided into five main strands:
- handling information,
- measuring and control,
- modelling,
- communicating information,
- applications and effects of IT.

The applications include in particular:
- shops and money services,
- the electronic office, and
- implications of the use of IT in the areas – home and leisure, privacy and security of information, crime and education.

The extension involves:
- tools, techniques and systems within applications,
- information systems in society.

Assessment

		% Weighting	Duration
Written Papers	Paper 1 – Foundation +	20	1 hr
	Paper 2 - Foundation	20	1 hr
	OR		
	Paper 1 – Higher +	20	1½ hrs
	Paper 2 - Higher	20	1½ hrs
Coursework	Portfolio of work +	30	
	Project	30	–

Written Paper 1 is the same one which is taken by candidates for the short course and the full GCSE course Design and Technology and Information Technology (Combined). It is designed to test the requirements of the National Curriculum Key Stage 4 Programme of Study in Information Technology.

Written Paper 2 tests the parts of the syllabus not in the short course.

The coursework portfolio should show your achievements in any TWO of the following:
- communicating information,
- handling information,
- controlling and measuring,
- modelling.

The project is your solution to a problem on any suitable topic. It is assessed on the basis of a report which you submit.

Information Technology Short Course

The syllabus is based on the five strands which form the core of the syllabus for the full course, including the applications section.

Assessment

		% Weighting	Duration
Written Paper	Foundation	40	1 hr
	OR		
	Higher	40	1½ hrs
Coursework	Practical tasks	60	–

The written paper is designed to test the requirements of the National Curriculum Key Stage 4 Programme of Study in Information Technology.

The coursework portfolio should show your achievements in any TWO of the following:
- communicating information,
- handling information,
- controlling and measuring,
- modelling.

Syllabus contents

There follow tables showing which units of the book are required for each of the syllabuses listed above.

Starting points

Table of Analysis – GCSE Short Courses

Unit	Topic	C&G	LONDON	MEG	NDTEF	NEAB	RSA	SEG	WJEC
1	**Information and data**								
1.1	Introduction	•	•	•	•	•	•	•	•
1.2	Data types	•	•	•	•	•	•	•	•
1.3	Data storage in computers	•	•	•	•	•	•	•	•
1.4	Coding of information		•	•	•				
1.5	Using codes to simplify data		•	•	•			•	
1.6	Processing information		•	•	•	•		•	
2	**Information systems**								
2.1	Information technology						•	•	
2.2	Computers	•	•	•	•	•	•	•	•
2.3	Information processing systems	•	•	•	•	•	•	•	•
2.4	Real time processing								
2.5	Interactive computing	•	•	•	•	•	•	•	•
2.6	Batch processing								
2.7	Multiprogramming and multitasking								
3	**Data capture**								
3.1	Introduction	•	•	•		•		•	•
3.2	Design of data capture forms	•	•	•		•		•	
3.3	Questionnaires							•	
3.4	User interfaces	•	•	•	•	•	•	•	•
4	**Input methods**								
4.1	Input from keyboards	•	•	•	•	•	•	•	•
4.2	OMR, OCR and MICR		•			•		•	•
4.3	Bars and stripes		•	•	•	•		•	•
4.4	Point and touch methods	•	•	•	•	•	•	•	•
4.5	Input of pictures			•		•		•	•
4.6	Input of sound								•
5	**Output of data**								
5.1	Output on screens	•	•	•	•	•	•	•	•
5.2	Printers	•	•	•	•	•	•	•	•
5.3	Graphics and plotters			•		•			
5.4	Other output methods								
5.5	Choice of output method								
6	**Storage**								
6.1	Introduction to storage	•	•	•	•	•	•	•	•
6.2	Main store	•	•	•	•	•	•	•	•
6.3	Backing stores	•	•	•	•	•	•	•	•
6.4	Magnetic discs	•	•	•	•	•	•	•	•
6.5	Compact discs	•	•	•	•	•	•	•	
6.6	Magnetic tape								
7	**Data files**								
7.1	Facts about files	•	•	•	•	•	•	•	•
7.2	Storage of files	•	•	•	•	•	•	•	•
7.3	Types of file								
7.4	Updating files	•	•	•	•			•	•
7.5	Other operations on files	•	•	•		•	•	•	•
7.6	An application of files – stock control							•	•
8	**Security and integrity of data**								
8.1	Security problems	•	•	•	•	•	•	•	•
8.2	Making copies of files	•	•	•	•	•	•	•	•
8.3	Other ways of looking after data	•	•	•	•	•	•	•	•
8.4	Integrity of input data	•	•	•	•	•	•	•	•
8.5	Methods of avoiding input errors				•			•	
8.6	Methods of detecting input errors	•	•		•	•	•	•	
9	**Software**								
9.1	Programs	•							•
9.2	Software	•	•	•	•	•	•	•	•
9.3	Operating systems								
9.4	Evaluation of applications software	•	•	•	•	•	•	•	•
9.5	Types of application package	•	•	•	•	•	•	•	•
9.6	General purpose application packages	•	•	•	•	•	•	•	•
9.7	Choosing the right package	C&G	LONDON	•	•	•	•	•	•

Syllabus analysis

Unit	Topic	C&G	LONDON	MEG	NDTEF	NEAB	RSA	SEG	WJEC
10	**Presenting your work: word processing …**								
10.1	Word processing	•	•	•	•	•	•	•	•
10.2	Entering, editing and improving text	•	•	•	•	•	•	•	•
10.3	Spelling	•	•	•	•	•	•	•	•
10.4	Tabs, margins and indents	•	•	•	•	•	•	•	•
10.5	Working with blocks of text	•	•	•	•	•	•		•
10.6	Further word processing techniques	•	•	•	•	•	•		
10.7	Desktop publishing	•	•	•	•	•	•	•	•
11	**Handling information: database programs**								
11.1	Database programs	•	•	•	•	•	•	•	•
11.2	Planning – how to design a database	•	•	•	•	•	•		•
11.3	Creating a database file	•	•	•	•	•	•		•
11.4	Searches and queries	•	•	•	•	•	•	•	•
11.5	Statistics and sorts	•	•	•		•	•	•	
11.6	More about databases	•	•	•		•			•
12	**Models of situations**								
12.1	What is a model?	•	•	•	•	•	•	•	•
12.2	Simulations	•	•	•	•	•	•	•	•
12.3	Other computer models	•				•	•	•	
13	**Creating models: spreadsheets**								
13.1	Introduction to spreadsheets	•	•	•	•	•	•	•	•
13.2	Improving the look of a spreadsheet	•	•	•	•	•	•	•	•
13.3	Formulae	•	•	•	•	•	•	•	•
13.4	Copying cells		•			•	•	•	•
13.5	A spreadsheet as a model	•	•	•	•	•	•	•	•
14	**Presenting your work: graphics and charts**								
14.1	Graphics	•	•	•	•	•	•	•	
14.2	Paint packages	•		•		•	•	•	
14.3	CAD graphics	•		•	•		•	•	
14.4	Graphs and charts	•	•		•	•	•	•	
14.5	Types of chart	•	•		•	•	•	•	
15	**Communications**								
15.1	Introduction to communications	•	•	•	•	•	•	•	•
15.2	Teletext	•			•			•	•
15.3	Networks	•	•	•	•	•	•	•	•
15.4	Local area networks	•			•	•	•	•	•
15.5	Wide area networks	•			•	•	•	•	•
15.6	Public viewdata networks	•			•	•	•	•	•
16	**Measurement and control**								
16.1	Control systems	•	•	•	•	•	•	•	•
16.2	Sensors and feedback	•	•	•	•	•	•	•	•
16.3	Process control							•	
16.4	Robots	•		•				•	
16.5	Data logging	•	•	•	•	•		•	•
17	**Programming for control systems**								
17.1	Controlling a turtle with LOGO	•	•	•	•		•	•	•
17.2	Programming control systems	•	•	•	•		•	•	•
17.3	Solving control problems		•	•	•				
18	**Solving problems using IT**								
18.1	Introduction to problem solving	•	•	•	•			•	•
18.2	The professional way – the system life cycle	•		•	•				•
18.3	A coursework project – what to do	•			•			•	•
19	**Documentation**								
19.1	Documentation and diagrams		•					•	•
19.2	System flowcharts		•					•	•
19.3	Representing algorithms – structure diagrams							•	
19.4	Program and algorithm flowcharts							•	
19.5	Example comparing a structure diagram and …							•	
19.6	User documentation	•	•					•	•
19.7	Technical documentation	•	•					•	•
20	**The implications of IT**								
20.1	Examinations and the implications of IT	C&G	LONDON	MEG	NDTEF	NEAB	RSA	SEG	WJEC
20.2	The general effect of IT on our lives	•	•	•	•	•	•	•	•
20.3	Effect of IT on work and unemployment	•	•	•	•	•	•	•	•
20.4	The effect of IT on personal privacy	•	•	•	•	•	•	•	•

Starting points

Table of Analysis – Full GCSE Courses

Unit	Topic	C&G	LONDON	MEG	NDTEF	NEAB	RSA	SEG	WJEC
1	**Information and data**								
1.1	Introduction	•	•	•	•	•	•	•	•
1.2	Data types	•	•	•	•	•	•	•	•
1.3	Data storage in computers	•	•	•	•	•	•	•	•
1.4	Coding of information		•	•	•	•			•
1.5	Using codes to simplify data		•	•	•	•		•	
1.6	Processing information		•	•	•	•		•	
2	**Information systems**								
2.1	Information technology						•	•	
2.2	Computers	•	•	•	•	•	•	•	•
2.3	Information processing systems	•	•	•	•	•	•	•	•
2.4	Real time processing		•	•		•		•	•
2.5	Interactive computing	•	•	•	•	•	•	•	•
2.6	Batch processing			•		•		•	•
2.7	Multiprogramming and multitasking			•		•		•	•
3	**Data capture**								
3.1	Introduction	•	•	•	•	•	•	•	•
3.2	Design of data capture forms	•	•	•		•	•	•	•
3.3	Questionnaires					•		•	•
3.4	User interfaces	•	•	•	•	•	•	•	•
4	**Input methods**								
4.1	Input from keyboards	•	•	•	•	•	•	•	•
4.2	OMR, OCR and MICR		•	•		•		•	•
4.3	Bars and stripes		•	•	•	•	•	•	•
4.4	Point and touch methods	•	•	•	•	•	•	•	•
4.5	Input of pictures			•		•	•	•	•
4.6	Input of sound							•	•
5	**Output of data**								
5.1	Output on screens	•	•	•	•	•	•	•	•
5.2	Printers	•	•	•	•	•	•	•	•
5.3	Graphics and plotters			•				•	•
5.4	Other output methods							•	•
5.5	Choice of output method	•	•	•	•	•	•	•	•
6	**Storage**								
6.1	Introduction to storage	•	•	•	•	•	•	•	•
6.2	Main store	•	•	•	•	•	•	•	•
6.3	Backing stores	•	•	•	•	•	•	•	•
6.4	Magnetic discs	•	•	•	•	•	•	•	•
6.5	Compact discs	•	•	•	•	•	•	•	•
6.6	Magnetic tape			•		•		•	•
7	**Data files**								
7.1	Facts about files	•	•	•	•	•	•	•	•
7.2	Storage of files	•	•	•	•	•	•	•	•
7.3	Types of file			•		•		•	•
7.4	Updating files	•	•	•	•	•	•	•	•
7.5	Other operations on files	•	•	•	•	•	•	•	•
7.6	An application of files – stock control	•		•	•	•	•	•	•
8	**Security and integrity of data**								
8.1	Security problems	•	•	•	•	•	•	•	•
8.2	Making copies of files	•	•	•	•	•	•	•	•
8.3	Other ways of looking after data	•	•	•	•	•	•	•	•
8.4	Integrity of input data	•	•	•	•	•	•	•	•
8.5	Methods of avoiding input errors				•			•	•
8.6	Methods of detecting input errors	•	•	•	•	•	•	•	•
9	**Software**								
9.1	Programs	•					•	•	•
9.2	Software		•	•	•	•	•	•	•
9.3	Operating systems		•			•		•	•
9.4	Evaluation of applications software	•	•	•	•	•	•	•	•
9.5	Types of application package	•	•	•	•	•	•	•	•
9.6	General purpose application packages	•	•	•	•	•	•	•	•
9.7	Choosing the right package	•	•	•	•	•	•	•	•

Syllabus analysis

Unit	Topic	C&G	LONDON	MEG	NDTEF	NEAB	RSA	SEG	WJEC
10	**Presenting your work: word processing ...**								
10.1	Word processing	•	•	•	•	•	•	•	•
10.2	Entering, editing and improving text	•	•	•	•	•	•	•	•
10.3	Spelling	•	•	•	•	•	•	•	•
10.4	Tabs, margins and indents	•	•	•	•	•	•	•	•
10.5	Working with blocks of text	•	•	•	•	•	•	•	•
10.6	Further word processing techniques	•	•	•	•	•	•	•	•
10.7	Desktop publishing	•	•	•	•	•	•	•	•
11	**Handling information: database programs**								
11.1	Database programs	•	•	•	•	•	•	•	•
11.2	Planning – how to design a database	•	•	•	•	•	•	•	•
11.3	Creating a database file	•	•	•	•	•	•	•	•
11.4	Searches and queries	•	•	•	•	•	•	•	•
11.5	Statistics and sorts	•	•	•		•	•	•	•
11.6	More about databases	•	•	•		•	•	•	•
12	**Models of situations**								
12.1	What is a model?	•	•	•	•	•	•	•	•
12.2	Simulations	•	•	•	•	•	•	•	•
12.3	Other computer models	•		•		•	•	•	•
13	**Creating models: spreadsheets**								
13.1	Introduction to spreadsheets	•	•	•	•	•	•	•	•
13.2	Improving the look of a spreadsheet	•	•	•	•	•	•	•	•
13.3	Formulae	•	•	•	•	•	•	•	•
13.4	Copying cells	•	•	•	•	•	•	•	•
13.5	A spreadsheet as a model	•	•	•	•	•	•	•	•
14	**Presenting your work: graphics and charts**								
14.1	Graphics	•	•	•	•	•	•	•	
14.2	Paint packages	•		•		•	•	•	
14.3	CAD graphics	•		•		•			•
14.4	Graphs and charts	•	•		•	•	•	•	•
14.5	Types of chart	•	•		•	•	•	•	•
15	**Communications**								
15.1	Introduction to communications	•	•	•	•	•	•	•	•
15.2	Teletext	•		•	•			•	•
15.3	Networks	•	•	•	•	•	•	•	•
15.4	Local area networks	•	•	•	•	•	•	•	•
15.5	Wide area networks	•	•	•	•	•	•	•	•
15.6	Public viewdata networks	•		•		•	•	•	•
16	**Measurement and control**								
16.1	Control systems	•	•	•	•	•	•	•	•
16.2	Sensors and feedback	•	•	•	•	•		•	•
16.3	Process control			•				•	
16.4	Robots	•		•				•	
16.5	Data logging	•	•	•	•	•		•	
17	**Programming for control systems**								
17.1	Controlling a turtle with LOGO	•	•	•	•		•	•	•
17.2	Programming control systems	•	•	•	•		•	•	•
17.3	Solving control problems	•	•	•	•		•	•	•
18	**Solving problems using IT**								
18.1	Introduction to problem solving	•	•	•	•	•	•	•	•
18.2	The professional way – the system life cycle	•	•	•	•	•	•	•	•
18.3	A coursework project – what to do	•	•	•	•	•	•	•	•
19	**Documentation**								
19.1	Documentation and diagrams	•	•	•	•	•	•	•	•
19.2	System flowcharts		•	•	•	•		•	•
19.3	Representing algorithms – structure diagrams				•			•	
19.4	Program and algorithm flowcharts		•		•			•	
19.5	Example comparing a structure diagram and …				•			•	
19.6	User documentation	•	•	•	•	•	•	•	•
19.7	Technical documentation	•	•		•	•		•	•
20	**The implications of IT**								
20.1	Examinations and the implications of IT	•		•	•	•	•	•	•
20.2	The general effect of IT on our lives	•	•	•	•	•	•	•	•
20.3	Effect of IT on work and unemployment	•	•	•	•	•	•	•	•
20.4	The effect of IT on personal privacy	•	•	•	•	•	•	•	•

Examination Boards: addresses

C&G	**City and Guilds** 1 Giltspur Street London EC1A 9DD	Tel: 0171 294 2468
London	**Edexcel, London Examinations** Stewart House 32 Russell Square London WC1B 5DN	Tel: 0171 331 4000
MEG	**Midland Examining Group** 1 Hills Road Cambridge CB1 2EU	Tel: 01223 553311
NEAB	**Northern Examinations and Assessment Board** Devas Street Manchester M15 6EX	Tel: 0161 953 1180
NDTEF	**National Design and Technology Education Foundation** The Old Chapel House Pound Hill Alresford Hants SO24 9BW	Tel: 01962 735801
RSA	**Royal Society of Arts** RSA Examinations Board Progress House Westwood Way Coventry CV4 8HS	Tel: 01203 470033
SEG	**Southern Examining Group** Stag Hill House Guildford GU2 5XJ	Tel: 01483 506506
WJEC	**Welsh Joint Education Committee** 245 Western Avenue Cardiff CF5 2YX	Tel: 01222 265000

Revision and examinations

Written examinations

From the section on Syllabus analysis you can see that all of the courses analysed have written papers to be taken at the end of the course. The percentage of the total marks given to these papers is usually 40%.

This means that one or two short examination papers are about as important to your grade as is all your coursework. However, you should not worry too much about this. Be positive about it. These examination papers are your chance to show how hard you have worked and how well you understand what you have been doing. You will have nothing to worry about if you:
- prepare for them carefully;
- answer them calmly and methodically.

Preparation for examinations
Work steadily over a long period.

1. Take every opportunity throughout the course to work around the subject in your own time:
   - read notes you have been given;
   - use books – find the topic you are doing in class and write notes about it in your own words.
2. Start your revision programme as early as you can – months before the actual examination.

Planning your revision programme
Produce a revision timetable for yourself.
- Draw up a simple calendar from now to the date of the exam with realistic numbers of hours allowed for each day.
- Leave slots of about an hour each - or whatever length of time you know you can work for.
- In each slot list a topic or some material you intend to revise.

In doing this remember:
- be realistic – everything takes longer than you think it will;
- you do need some time for relaxation however determined you are;
- all topics need some time spent on them – with those you are not keen on needing most;
- time must be allocated for doing practice questions and self-testing.

Revision technique
Revision has to be active.
You cannot revise by just reading notes or a book. You will just start daydreaming or allowing yourself to be distracted.
- Write notes on what you read. Write down the important points of each section as you work through it. The notes you make will also be useful later for last minute revision.
- Test yourself. Close the book and ask yourself questions. Do the self-test questions from the book. Do some sample exam questions.

Learning is best done in short bursts.
Try half an hour of intensive study on one topic and then a short break and half an hour on another subject.

In the examination
Spend time understanding the questions.
It is very important to make sure that what you write answers the question set. The examiner who marks it will be looking for certain points. Marks are only given if you include these. You cannot be given any marks if you have written about the wrong thing – however well you have done it.

Starting points

- Read the questions thoroughly.
- As you read a question underline the important points.

Divide your time sensibly between the questions.
It is vital to do all the questions required.
- Usually in GCSE Information Technology you have to do all of the questions.
- If you do miscalculate and are running out of time you must still do all the questions – in quick note form if necessary.

Make each answer the right length.
Each answer should be neither too long nor too short. Some questions can be answered with a few words but others require carefully planned sentences. Remember that some answers will be checked for spelling, punctuation and grammar.

You can tell how long to make each answer and whether carefully written sentences are required by:
- the number of marks allocated to the question. A question with one mark can be answered very briefly; one with six marks will need a discussion or diagrams;
- the space provided for the answer. Most papers expect you to write answers on the question paper. They leave ample room for your answer;
- the words used in asking you for an answer, e.g.

  Ring, Tick: Do not write anything – just draw a ring round one of the answers or tick one of the boxes provided.

  Complete, Fill in: Just write one or two words in the space provided.

  Name, State, Identify, Give, Write down, Suggest, List

  Usually a question using one of these instructions requires only a word or a short phrase for each answer.

  Explain briefly, Describe briefly

  The use of 'briefly' is to tell you that sentences are required but not to spend too long on the question - there probably are not many marks for it.

  Explain, Describe: Answers require a paragraph. You need to quickly plan out what you are going to say before you start.

  Design, Produce: These are usually longer answers – often in the form of a diagram.

Avoid vague answers.
The good candidate provides factual detail in an answer.
- If you really do not know the answer to a question, then go on to something else.
- If you are not absolutely sure that an answer is correct then be brave – go for it. It is better to give a clear, bold answer than to be so vague that you do not get any marks anyway.
- Answer the question. It is a waste of time writing about something off the point because you know all about it. The examiner can only give marks for points on the mark scheme.

Draw simple, clear diagrams.
An answer to a question is often helped by drawing a diagram.
- It does not matter that you are not artistic as long as the diagram is clear.
- State what type of diagram it is and what it represents.
- If you draw a program flowchart, a structure diagram, or a system flowchart stick to the rules for that type of diagram (see Chapter 19).

General rules.
- Write legibly. There is no point in rushing so much that the examiner cannot read what you have written.
- Do not use liquid paper. Cross out a mistake clearly and simply by drawing one or two lines through it.

Read what you have written.
At the end of an examination paper it is difficult to make yourself read your answers through but you must do it.
- Read every word you have written. Add anything new which occurs to you.
- Think twice before you cross anything out – it is easy to have an impulse that an answer is wrong when it is not.
- Check for errors of spelling, punctuation and grammar.

Information technology topics

Chapter 1
Information and data

1.1 Introduction

KEY TERMS

Information *consists of facts and items of knowledge. It can be anything that has meaning to people.*

Usually information is expressed in words and numbers. However, it can be expressed in other forms, such as sounds, measurements or pictures.

EXAMPLES: *of information*
1. A list of names and addresses.
2. The contents of a letter.
3. What is said in a telephone conversation.
4. The words of a song.
5. A map.

KEY TERMS

Data *is information in a form in which it can be processed.*

Before information is processed by a computer it is coded into a form the computer can accept. This coded information is called data. So when you use a computer, what you see on the screen and what you type is information. What the computer works on internally is called data.

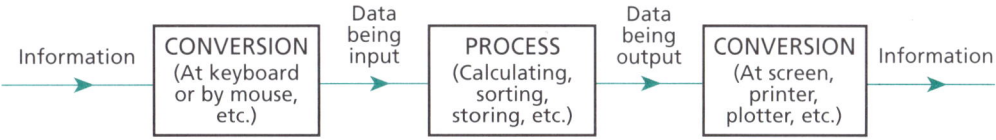

Fig. 1.1 Information and data

EXAMPLES: *of data*
1. A word-processed letter stored on a floppy disc. It is stored as a set of binary codes.
2. A telephone conversation converted to electrical signals to be sent down the wires.
3. A song written as sheet music so that it can be played.
4. A date encoded as a six-figure number – two digits each for the day, the month and the year.

Chapter 1 Information and data

1.2 Data types

KEY TERMS

Data type is the term to describe the kind of data used, e.g. whether it is a number or a letter.

For each item of data the type determines:
1. what sort of data it is and what it can be used for;
2. how it is processed;
3. how the computer will store it, e.g. because numbers have arithmetic operations done on them they are stored in a form which makes addition and subtraction easy.

Some commonly used data types are defined below.

KEY TERMS

A *character* is one of the symbols which are used to make up data. The term applies particularly to text but also to other data such as graphics.

Sometimes pictures and graphs are built up by printing carefully chosen characters of various shapes. These are called **graphics characters**.

Some devices can be controlled by sending them special characters called **control characters**. These are not displayed or printed but instead cause the device to carry out some special function.

A *string* is a group of characters treated as a unit.

Alphanumeric data is made up of letters and numbers. The term is also commonly used to include other keyboard characters such as £ $ and punctuation marks such as . , ; : "

Numeric data consists of numbers. It is usually seen by the user as a decimal and is made up of digits, with possibly a sign and/or a decimal point.

An *integer* is any whole number, either positive or negative.

EXAMPLES: *of characters*

A letter, a punctuation mark or one digit of a number.

of a graphics character

One of the blocks of colour which make up the borders on a teletext screen.

of control characters

1. The characters produced by the arrow keys and the 'Page Up' and 'Page Down' keys on a keyboard.
2. A character sent to a printer to cause it to move the paper to another page.

of strings

1. 'This is a string of letters'
2. 'THIS IS AN ALPHANUMERIC STRING OF LENGTH 55 WITH SPACES'

Note: For further data types see Unit 11.2 under 'Field Types'.

KEY TERMS

A *character set* is the complete set of all the different characters used by a given system.

EXAMPLE: *of character sets*

The character set for a computer terminal is all the characters on its keyboard or which it can print.

1.3 Data storage in computers

The main store

KEY TERMS

A *store* is a part of a computer system where data and instructions can be held, ready for later use.

The **main store** of a computer is the fast access store in the central processing unit. It is also called the **main memory**.

The main store of a computer is directly accessed by the processor. It contains the data and the program which the processor is currently using (see Unit 2.2 for central processing unit and processor).

KEY TERMS

The main store is divided up into small equally sized units called **locations**.

Each location can be accessed by the computer using a number called its **address**. Each location has a different address.

Bits and bytes

All data storage in modern digital computers is binary. Usually we write the two values used in computer storage as 1 and 0.

KEY TERMS A **binary digit** (or **bit**) is a 1 or 0 used to represent data. The term is also used for the smallest unit of storage, which just stores a 1 or a 0.
Each location may contain as few as 8 bits but often there are 16 or 32 or more.

KEY TERMS A **byte** is a small group of bits treated as a unit. It is usually the number of bits needed to store one character. Normally a byte consists of 8 bits.

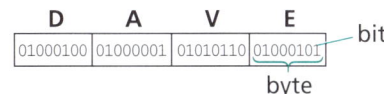

Fig. 1.2 A 32 bit location. Each group of 8 bits is a byte and stores the letter shown above it. The location stores the word 'DAVE'. The letters are stored in ASCII code

Contents of a storage location

Each storage location is full of 1s and 0s. You cannot tell by looking at them what these represent.

EXAMPLES: *of what a location can store*
1. A number.
2. A character or a string of characters.
3. Part of a picture.
4. A computer instruction.
5. The address of a location in store.

KEY TERMS
K is 1024 – short for **kilo**
1 **Kb** is one **kilobyte** – 1024 bytes
M is 1048576 – short for **mega**
1 **Mb** is one **megabyte** – 1048576 bytes

Notes: In most subjects kilo stands for 1000 (one thousand) and mega for 1 000 000 (one million). However, because of the way that computer data is stored this is not convenient. Instead we use the nearest power of 2 to these numbers.

1.4 Coding of information

Converting information to data – encoding and decoding

KEY TERMS To **encode** means to convert information or data into a form ready for processing.
To **decode** means to convert data back to a form in which it can be understood.

EXAMPLE: *of encoding*
Information about foods is encoded into bar codes which are then printed on food labels. This data can then be input via a laser scanner on a point-of-sale (POS) terminal at the checkout (see Unit 3.1).

EXAMPLES: *of decoding*
1. On a school data file, the names of the teachers are stored. For this two letters of each surname are used. Thus, Mr Smith is stored as SM, Miss Small as SL and Mr Sanders as SA.
   The computer has a reference file of these codes. To print out a name the computer uses the reference file to decode the two letters. It can then print out the full name.
2. An electronic circuit can be made to decode binary numbers into decimal numbers.

1.5 Using codes to simplify data

If large amounts of data are being processed, some items of data are often replaced by codes. This happens particularly to an item which has to be keyed many times. Usually the code is used by the person keying in the data and internally by the computer. However, when the item of data is displayed or printed it will often be written in full. This means that the people reading the output do not have to know the codes.

KEY TERMS

A *code* is a character or group of characters used to replace a particular item of data.

EXAMPLES: *of codes used to replace items of data*
1. In a personal record the person's gender may be written as M or F.
2. Postcodes – a few letters and digits are used to identify any address, e.g. SO9 identifies an area of Southampton; SO9 5NH is the University. If the postcode is written on the envelope by the sender, it is later keyed on to the envelope as a series of dots at the sorting office. The letter can then be sorted automatically.
3. Bank branch numbers – any bank cheque has a number on it which identifies the bank branch of the person who wrote the cheque, e.g. 60-18-46 is the Romsey branch of the National Westminster Bank.
4. Dates of birth – these are often written as three two-digit numbers, e.g. 03 07 38 would be 3 July 1938. In this case we are all sufficiently familiar with the code to understand it when it is displayed on a screen.

ADVANTAGES: *of replacing data with codes*
1. Codes make the data shorter so that it takes less time to key.
2. Encoded data takes up less storage space.
3. The code forms a standard. Every time the item is keyed in it will be the same.
4. It is easier for a computer to validate the data. There will only be a limited number of codes and the computer can be given a list of them to check through.

DISADVANTAGE: *of replacing data with codes*
The person keying the data has to be familiar with the codes or they will have to keep referring to a list of codes.

EXAMPLE: *of a code forming a standard for an item of data*
For a school pupil records system pupils are asked for their mode of transport. Of those who cycle they reply in different ways: 'cycle', 'cycling', 'bicycle', 'bike', etc. All of these are coded 'BI' so there is no confusion.

Note: The problem of the different versions of 'cycling' could be avoided by having a list of modes of transport printed on the data capture form. Each pupil would then choose the one which applied. (See Unit 3.1 for data capture forms.)

1.6 Processing information

KEY TERMS

Information processing is the organisation, manipulation and distribution of information.

EXAMPLES: *of information processing*
1. Sorting a list of names and addresses into alphabetical order.
2. Producing a letter with a word processor, saving it on floppy disc and then sending it by electronic mail.
3. Transmitting a conversation over the telephone system.

People can process information without using machines.

EXAMPLES: *of processing information without machines*
1. Listening to songs and deciding which ones are best.
2. Reading a map to get from one place to another.

The data processing cycle

KEY TERMS — *When data is collected and processed, whether by computer or by other means, a set of operations is carried out on it. The sequence of operations: data collection, input, process, output is called a **data processing cycle**.*

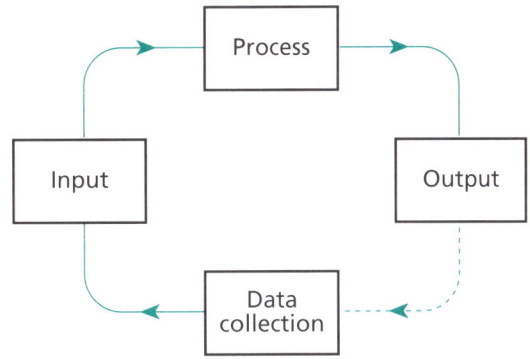

Fig. 1.3 The data processing cycle

Fig. 1.3 is a very general diagram of a processing cycle. Data which is output may be used as input, perhaps at a later date, thus completing the cycle. (In the diagram Output is linked to Data collection by a broken line to indicate that this only happens sometimes.)

Other operations during the data processing cycle

In particular cases other operations may occur between the four operations shown in Fig. 1.3 or as part of them:

- **STORAGE**
  Data may be held for various lengths of time on a suitable material (or **medium**) (see Chapter 6).

EXAMPLES: *of storage*
  1. As the last stage of data collection, data may be keyed on to a disc, where it is stored while awaiting input to a computer.
  2. During the processing stage, data may be stored in the immediate access store of a computer.

- **CHECKING**
  Data often has to be checked to see that it has been copied accurately and/or to see that it is reasonable.

EXAMPLES: *of checking data*
  1. Data which has been keyed on to a disc may be checked to see that it has been keyed correctly (see Unit 8.6 – verification).
  2. Data which has been collected and input to a computer may be checked by the computer to see that it is suitable for processing (see Unit 8.6 – validation).

Quick test

1. What do you call information when it has been converted for processing?

2. Data is prepared for each of 20 players in a cricket squad. State a suitable data type for each of the following:
   (a) name of player,

(b) number of runs scored,
(c) number of innings played,
(d) batting average.

3 The main store of a computer holds the data being used. What else does it store?

4 How many:
(a) bits in a byte?
(b) bytes in a kilobyte?
(c) kilobytes in a megabyte?

5 Give two reasons why data is often replaced by a code.

6 In storing exam results which of the following data could be replaced by a code:
(a) candidate's name
(b) subject
(c) Examining Board
(d) grade?

Summary

1 **Information** is any facts or items of knowledge. **Data** is information in a form in which it can be processed.

2 Each item of data has a **type** which determines what sort of data it is and how the computer will store it. Some of the data types commonly used are character, graphics character, control character, string, alphanumeric character, numeric, integer.

3 The **main store** of a computer is directly accessed by the **processor.**
It contains the data and the program which the processor is currently using.

4 Frequently used data is often coded to simplify it.
- Codes make the data shorter so that there is less to store and to key.
- The code forms a standard and makes the data easier to check.
- The disadvantage of codes is that they can only be used by someone familiar with them.

5 The data processing cycle is the sequence of operations: data collection, input, process, output.

Chapter 2
Information systems

2.1 Information technology

KEY TERMS *Information technology (IT) is all types of equipment and programs which are used in the processing of information.*

EXAMPLES: *of information technology*
1. A computer.
2. A computer program, such as a word processor or a database.
3. A calculator.
4. A compact disc – holding either music or computer data.
5. A fax machine.
6. A telephone.

Uses of information technology

The term 'information technology' is also used to refer to the uses of this technology. The main types of use involved are:

1. **Presentation of information**
   Setting out information for others to see using word processors, desktop publishers and graphics packages (see Chapters 10 and 14).
2. **Handling information**
   Searching data, sorting it into order and analysing it using databases and other packages (see Chapter 11).
3. **Producing models of real situations**
   Using spreadsheets, simulation programs and expert systems to form models. This allows a situation to be investigated by investigating the model (see Chapters 12 and 13).
4. **Data communication**
   Sending data from one place to another using telephone, radio and cables (see Chapter 15).
5. **Control and measurement**
   Using computers or electronic circuits to control machines and processes. This could include a microprocessor controlling a robot or a specially designed circuit controlling a camera. Linked to this control is automatic sensing and logging of measurements made (see Chapter 16).

Digital and analogue data

KEY TERMS *A device is **digital** if some quantity in it can be set to a number of different separate values or states. Data is then represented by combinations of these values. Usually the devices are binary and data is represented as a succession of 1s and 0s (see Unit 1.3).*

Chapter 2 Information systems

*An **analogue** device is one in which data is represented by some quantity which is continuously variable. The value of a data item at a given time is represented by the size of the quantity, measured on a fixed scale.*

EXAMPLES: *of analogue and digital systems*

1. An electronic calculator. The display is digital with the numbers in decimal. Each digit can have any of ten separate states (the numbers 0,1,2,3,4,5,6,7,8,9). The circuits inside are digital with binary digits represented by 0 volts or 5 volts.
2. Some watches have an analogue display, where hands move continuously round a dial. The time is represented by the positions of the hands on the dial.
    Other watches have a digital display – the time is represented by digits shown on a little display screen.

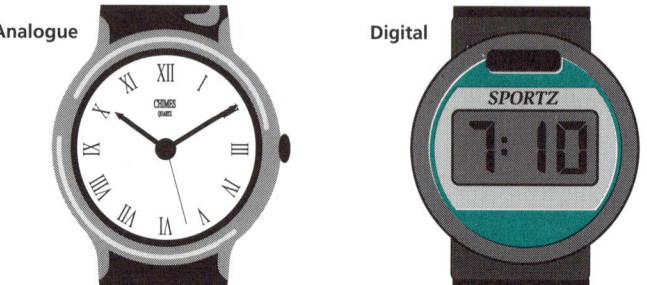

Fig. 2.1 Two watches – one with an analogue face, one digital

3. Conversations travel on old telephone circuits as an analogue signal. The size of the signal depends on the loudness of the speech. The words spoken show up as changes in the frequency of the signal.
    The new exchanges being installed by British Telecom are digital.

CHARACTERISTICS: *of analogue and digital devices*

Analogue
1. The quantity used to represent data gets bigger or smaller depending on the size of the data itself.
2. Any value can be represented because the quantity can take any value in the range used.

Digital
1. With digital devices the quantity used can only take a few different values – usually only two.
2. The data is held as a code.

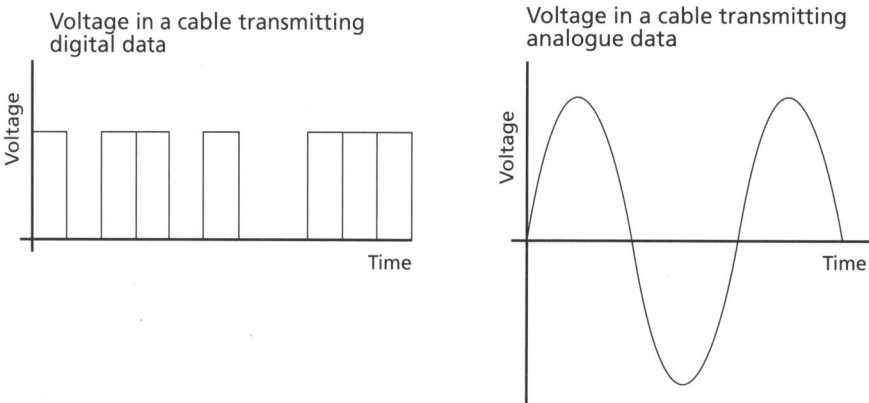

Fig. 2.2 Voltage in cables transmitting digital and analogue data

2.2 Computers

KEY TERMS

A **computer** is a machine which automatically inputs and processes data, and outputs the results. The actual process carried out is fixed beforehand, usually by a program stored in the machine.

Practically all modern computers:
1. are electronic;
2. are digital;
3. are binary;
4. have a stored program.

Note: All computers we normally see are digital. However, analogue computers are still sometimes used for special purposes. An analogue computer *is* electronic, but it is *not* digital, is *not* binary and it does *not* have a stored program.

Digital computers

KEY TERMS

A **microprocessor** is an integrated circuit which contains the processor of a computer all on one 'chip'.

A **microcomputer** is a computer in which the main processing is done by a microprocessor.

A **personal computer (PC)** is a microcomputer intended for interactive use by one person.

Small computers which are not microcomputers are usually called **minicomputers**. They are often used as host to a number of terminals in a situation where a microcomputer is not powerful enough but a mainframe is unnecessarily expensive.

Large powerful computers with a range of input, output and storage devices are called **mainframe computers**.

Fig. 2.3 A typical personal computer system

Note: The file server for a school network is usually a microcomputer. It is not a minicomputer or a mainframe.

The central processing unit

KEY TERMS

The **processor** is the area of circuitry in a digital computer which controls the running of the computer and carries out the instructions. In an ordinary PC the processor is all on one large integrated circuit (or 'chip').

The **central processing unit (CPU)** of a computer is the main part of the computer. It contains the processor, the main store and various circuits needed to communicate with devices outside it. In a PC the CPU is usually the contents of the main box of the computer.

The **peripherals** are all the input, output and storage devices outside the CPU but controlled by it.

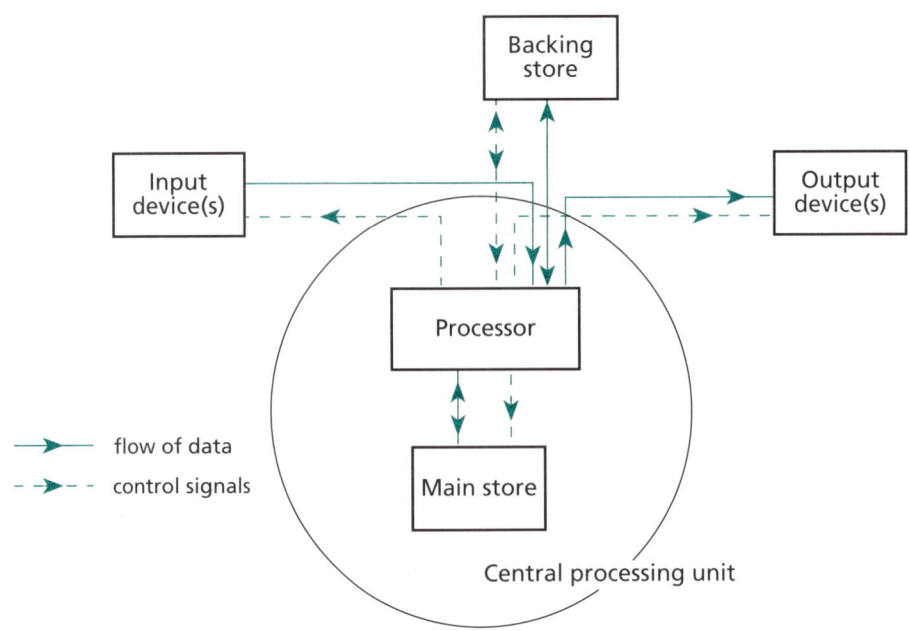

Fig. 2.4 Layout of a typical digital computer

Note:
The peripherals of a personal computer are usually:
- for input a mouse and a keyboard,
- for output a monitor and a printer,
- for backing storage a floppy disc unit, a hard disc unit and a CD-ROM drive.

2.3 Information processing systems

KEY TERMS   *A **system** is a set of components which works as a unit.*
*An **information processsing system** consists of everything required to carry out a particular processing task. This includes the equipment involved, the software, the people and the methods that they use when working.*

EXAMPLES: *of systems*
1. A camera system – the camera together with all its lenses, filters, flashguns, etc.
2. A central heating system – the boiler, pipes, radiators, thermostats, pumps and control box.

EXAMPLES: *of information processing systems*
1. The stock control system for a shop (see Unit 7.6). The system comprises:
   - the methods of checking on stock levels, of ordering new goods, of recording their delivery, and so on;
   - the means of communicating with suppliers;
   - the computer hardware and software if the system is computerised.
2. The working system in an office. This would include:
   - the methods of communication – whether by letter, by telephone or by electronic mail;
   - the methods of storage of information – whether on computer discs or in filing cabinets;
   - the methods of producing letters – perhaps they are dictated to a secretary who later produces them on a word processor;
   - the equipment – computers, fax machines, photocopiers, etc.

Hardware and software

KEY TERMS   *__Hardware__ is the term used to describe all the actual pieces of equipment in an information processing system.*
__Software__ is a general term for programs which are written to help computer users.

EXAMPLES: *of hardware*
1. Input devices such as a mouse, output devices such as a printer and storage devices such as a hard disc drive.
2. Input media such as floppy discs and output media such as printer paper.
3. The CPU of a computer.
4. A modem for connecting a computer to the telephone line (see Unit 15.3).

of software (see Chapter 9)
1. A spreadsheet program.
2. A payroll program.
3. The operating system of a computer – the program which controls the operation of the computer (see Unit 9.3).

Components of an information processing system

In general a computerised information processing system includes:
1. computers and other hardware;
2. computer software;
3. methods of:
   - collecting,
   - checking,
   - inputting data;
4. methods of communication:
   - for data transmission,
   - between people in the organisation;
5. data files – the data held and the methods of:
   - updating files,
   - keeping them secure;
6. processing operations carried out on data;
7. methods of outputting data.

2.4 Real time processing

We are all used to doing our information processing by interacting with a microcomputer. However, there are many different types of computer and many different ways of using them.

KEY TERMS A *real time* system is one which processes data without significant delay.

CHARACTERISTICS: *of real time systems*
1. The computer is always ready for data to be input. As soon as this data is received it is processed, and results are output straight away.
2. Because the output can be produced very quickly, it is often used to influence the system producing the input data. Real time systems can be used to control processes (see Unit 16.3).
3. The computer is often **dedicated** to the real time application. It is working on that application and on nothing else. It just runs the same program all the time.

APPLICATIONS: *of real time systems*
1. **A computer controlling a flight simulator**
   The situation
   The simulator is built to resemble a plane cockpit, with all the controls and instruments. The windows are replaced by screens which show simulated landscapes. A trainee pilot sits in the cockpit and reacts to values which appear on the instruments and to the pictures on the screens.
   What the computer does
   - The computer presents the pilot with a flying situation selected from a number of choices, e.g. landing.

- It is programmed to react to the pilot's handling of the engine controls and the joystick in a realistic way. It can change the readings on the instruments, the picture on the screen and can also tilt the whole simulator.

2 **A computer controlling an industrial process**
The situation
A food processing plant produces canned soups. The cans have to be sealed within a certain temperature range.
What the computer does
A temperature sensor at the point where the cans are sealed is connected to a computer. This can alter the temperature if it starts to move outside the set range.

3 **An interactive game**
The user has to react to what is happening on the computer screen by pressing keys quickly.

ADVANTAGES: *of real time processing*
1 Fast response.
2 Output from the computer may be used to adjust and improve the input.

DISADVANTAGE: *of real time processing*
A computer being used for a real time application often cannot be used for anything else.

2.5 Interactive computing

KEY TERMS An *interactive* system is one where use of the computer takes place as a conversation between the user and the computer.

An interactive system may be on its own or it may be connected to other computers.

EXAMPLES: *of interactive computing*
1 On-line conversational use of a terminal which is linked to a mainframe computer.
2 Using a personal computer via a keyboard and screen.

Standalone single-user systems

KEY TERMS A *standalone* computer is one which is not connected to any other computers.
A *single-user* system is a computer which can only be used by one person at a time.

EXAMPLE: *of a standalone single-user system*
A typical single-user system consists of a personal computer with a keyboard, a mouse, a screen, a disc unit and a printer. If this computer is not connected to a network, then it is also standalone.

APPLICATIONS: *of standalone single-user systems*
1 A 'home' computer
   A computer in the home can be used:
   - for entertainment – to play games;
   - to write letters using a word processor;
   - to work out the family budget;
   - as a source of reference information – particularly if it has a CD-ROM drive (see Unit 6.5).
2 In a newsagent's shop
   A small computer can be used:
   - to store details of which newspapers are required by the different customers;
   - to organise the newspaper rounds so that each person doing a round has a reasonable number of houses to deliver to;
   - to work out customers' accounts and print the bills.

ADVANTAGES: *of a standalone system*
1 It is not affected by the breakdown of other equipment.

2.5 Interactive computing

❷ It can be moved without having to worry about communications.

ADVANTAGES: *of a single-user system*

❶ Inexpensive – cheap enough to be used:
- as a home computer;
- by a small business;
- dedicated to one application, such as process control or word-processing.

❷ The user has better control over:
- the uses to which the computer is put;
- what changes are made to the system;
- maintenance.

❸ Mobile and small – a microcomputer can be:
- moved from place to place;
- attached to equipment in order to control it.

DISADVANTAGES: *of single-user systems*

In comparison with a minicomputer or a mainframe computer a single-user system often has:

❶ slower processing;
❷ less storage;
❸ fewer and slower peripherals.

These disadvantages can be partly overcome if the single-user system is connected to a network.

KEY TERMS   A computer **network** *is a system of computers and workstations which are linked.*

Notes:

❶ Networking allows computers to share storage, printing facilities and/or computer power.
❷ Networks are dealt with in detail in Unit 15.3.

On-line systems

KEY TERMS   *A computer **terminal** is a device used to communicate with a central computer. It is simply a means of sending data and receiving it. The central computer does all the processing work.*

Notes:

❶ Usually a terminal has a keyboard and screen but the word 'terminal' can be applied to other devices which send and receive computer data.
❷ Although a terminal does not need any processing power, a personal computer is often used for this purpose. This is done by running a program in the personal computer which makes it act as a terminal.

KEY TERMS   ***On-line*** *means directly connected to a computer and under its control.*
Off-line *means not under the control of a computer's central processing unit.*

EXAMPLES: *of on-line and off-line systems*

❶ When a computer terminal is connected to a computer it is on-line. When it is disconnected from the computer it is off-line.
❷ When a tape cartridge is stored in a box it is off-line. When it is placed in a tape drive it is on-line.

KEY TERMS   *A **multi-access** or **multi-user** system is one where a number of users with terminals work on-line to the same computer at the same time. The **response time** of a multi-access system is the average length of time the computer takes to react to an instruction from the user. Usually it is the time between pressing the 'ENTER' key and getting a reply.*

Note:

Each terminal user in a multi-access system is able to interact with the computer as if he or she were the only user. The computer is so fast compared with the terminals that it can do work for all of them and still give each user a fast response.

EXAMPLE: *of a slow response time*

A company has a mainframe computer supporting 100 terminals which have an average response time of half a second. When the number of terminals is increased to 200 the response time becomes about 4 seconds. This problem could be cured by buying a more powerful processor for the mainframe computer.

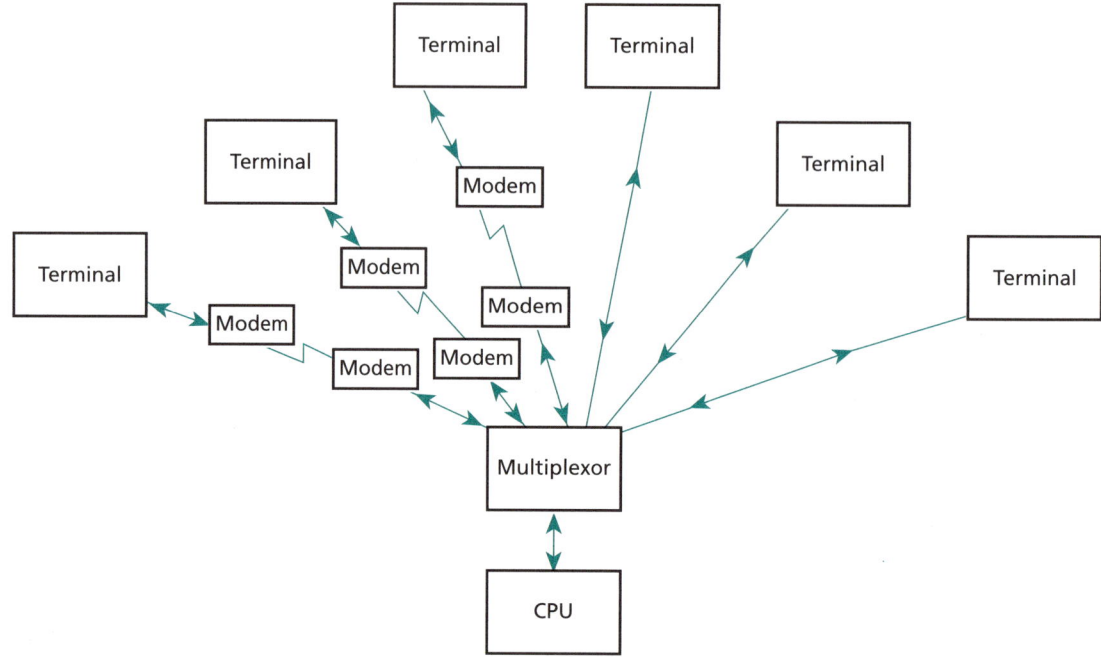

Fig. 2.5 A multi-access system The diagram shows a multi-access system with six terminals, of which three are connected directly, and three are connected using modems and telephone lines

APPLICATION: *of a multi-access system*

Airline bookings

The situation

A large airline operates planes throughout the world. These planes fly on routes and at times which are worked out a long time ahead. Passengers can book seats on these flights in advance and from almost anywhere in the world. Immediately a flight is fully booked any further requests for it have to be refused.

The system for bookings (see Fig. 2.6)

A customer can use one of several methods to book flights.

1. Each airline has visual display terminals at its booking offices. Customers can go to these offices or telephone them.
2. Customers can use a travel agent.
   - A small travel agent will then simply telephone the airline booking office.
   - For larger travel agents, each local office usually has its own terminal. This terminal is linked to a computer which can connect to the computer of any individual airline.

Safeguards

If a ticket is booked from a terminal, this will be put into effect immediately. If someone else then tries to book the same seat from another terminal, they will be told it is taken.

Notes:

1. The airline booking system is a multi-access system which is also a real-time system.
2. There is no need for the travel agent to have a computer - only a terminal which sends data to a central computer. This computer can then control the bookings from all the agents.

ADVANTAGES: *of multi-access systems*

1. Allow interactive use of a powerful computer.
2. Can be used at large distances from the computer (e.g. using modems and a telephone line).

2.6 Batch processing

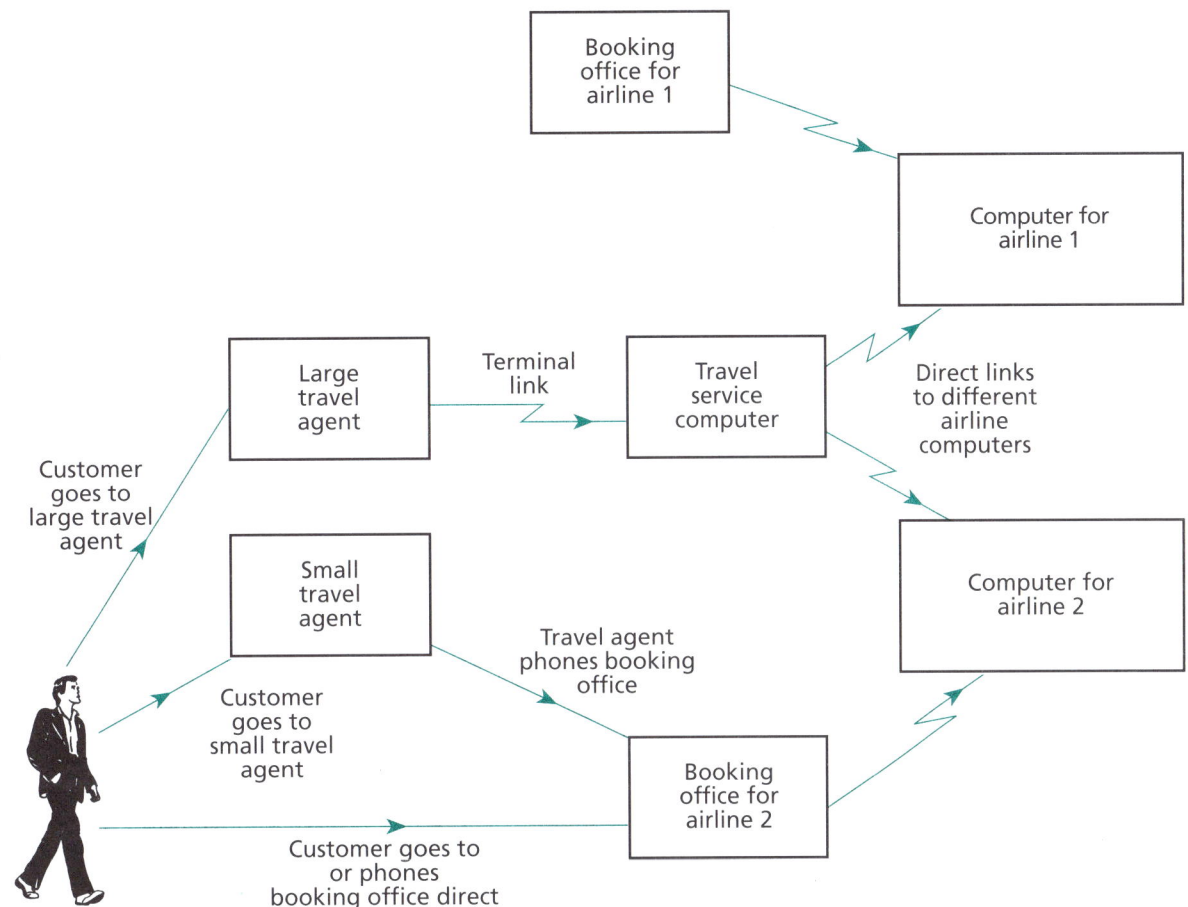

Fig. 2.6 Methods of connecting to the airline computers

DISADVANTAGES: *of multi-access systems*

1. Response time may be too slow for many real time operations.
2. It is often not practical to run jobs with large amounts of input or output data.

2.6 Batch processing

KEY TERMS *A **batch processing** system is one where programs and data are collected together in a batch before processing starts.*

*Each piece of work for a batch processing system is called a **job**. Often a job simply consists of a program to be run and the data for it.*

*A **job queue** is a number of jobs stored while they wait to be processed.*

CHARACTERISTICS: *of batch processing systems*

1. Jobs are stored in job queues until the computer is ready to deal with them.
2. There is no interaction between the user and the computer while the program is being run. Computers which do batch processing often operate all night so the user might be at home asleep.
3. Batch processing is often used where a large amount of data has to be processed on a regular basis. The program is not changed and it is so routine that there is no need for anyone to be present while the program is running.
4. Batch processing is normally done on large mainframe computers.

APPLICATION: *of batch processing*
Gas board bills
The situation
A batch processing run at a gas board produces bills for customers. The input data is a batch of meter reading slips completed in pencil by the meter reader and accompanied by a batch header.
What the computer does
The batch of slips is read by a document reader and stored on disc until the computer is ready to deal with them. Later the computer processes the data from each slip and produces a bill for that customer.

ADVANTAGES: *of batch processing*
1. There is no need for the user to be present when the job is run.
2. Preparing the work and operating the computer are done by trained people and not by the user.

DISADVANTAGES:
1. There is always a delay before work is processed and returned.
2. The user cannot take action if anything is wrong. The job has to be corrected and input again.
3. Batch processing usually involves an expensive computer and a large number of staff.

2.7 Multiprogramming and multitasking

KEY TERMS *Multiprogramming is a method of running several different programs in a computer apparently at the same time.*

The term is normally used to describe what happens when a mainframe computer with only one processor is handling work for a number of users.

In fact, the processor can only execute one instruction at a time. It switches between programs very quickly giving each in turn a short burst of activity. Because the computer executes millions of instructions a second, it appears to be running several programs at once.

KEY TERMS *Multitasking is a method of running several different tasks in a computer apparently at the same time.*

The reasons for multitasking are as follows.
1. The user wants to carry out several different operations at the same time and it is an unnecessary expense to use more than one computer.
2. The tasks depend on one another in some way so they have to be carried out at the same time.

Differences between multitasking and multiprogramming

Multiprogramming and multitasking are very similar. In both cases a computer which can only run one program at a time appears to do several things at once. The differences between multitasking and multiprogramming are as follows:
1. The term multitasking is usually applied to a small computer, such as a PC, which is carrying out several tasks for one person. Multiprogramming usually refers to a large computer which is running different programs for different people.
2. The 'tasks' carried out by a multitasking computer may be all running the same program.

Quick test

1. State whether each of the following systems is analogue or digital:
   (a) a voltmeter with a moving needle,
   (b) a voltmeter where the voltage appears as digits on a small screen,
   (c) a mercury thermometer,
   (d) a chip in a computer which produces synthesised speech.

For questions **2** to **4** give one term which names the part(s) of a computer system being described:

2. contains the processor and the main store,
3. the disc unit, printer, screen and mouse of a personal computer,
4. carries out the instructions in a computer program.

5. From the following list pick out those items which are (a) hardware or (b) software:
   - (i) floppy disc
   - (ii) printer
   - (iii) analogue
   - (iv) word processing package
   - (v) mouse
   - (vi) spreadsheet program
   - (vii) multitasking

For each of the applications in questions **6** to **8** state which would be the best method of dealing with it: batch, real time or interactive processing. In each case give a reason for your choice.

6. Checking a customer in a shop to see if they should be allowed credit.
7. Controlling a robot arm which is welding car doors.
8. A telephone company printing the bills at the end of a three-month period.

Summary

1. **Information technology (IT)** is all types of equipment and programs which are used in the processing of information.

2. - A device is **digital** if some quantity in it can be set to a number of different separate values or states.
   - An **analogue** device is one in which data is represented by the size of some quantity which is continuously variable and measured on a fixed scale.

3. A **computer** is a machine which automatically inputs and processes data, and outputs the results. The process is determined by a program stored in the machine.

4. - The **processor** controls the running of the computer and carries out the instructions.
   - The **peripherals** are all the input, output and storage devices outside the CPU but controlled by it.

5. - **Hardware** is the equipment in an information processing system.
   - **Software** is the programs which help computer users.

6. A **real time** system is one which processes data without significant delay.

7. - An **interactive** system is one where a conversation takes place between the user and the computer.
   - A **standalone** computer is not connected to any other computers.

- A **single-user** system can only be used by one person at a time.
- A system of linked computers is called a computer **network**.
- A computer **terminal** is a means of sending and receiving data.

8 A **multi-access** system allows a number of terminal users to interact with a computer at the same time.

9 A **batch processing** system is one where programs and data are collected together in a batch before processing starts.

Chapter 3
Data capture

3.1 Introduction

KEY TERMS — *Data capture* means obtaining data for a computer.

EXAMPLES: *of data capture*
1. Collecting documents which have been filled in, and preparing them for a keyboard operator.
2. Making measurements and keying them into a computer.
3. Asking people to fill in questionnaires.

APPLICATION: *of data capture*
Magazine subscriptions
Staff at a magazine obtain lists of possible customers. Application forms for subscriptions to the magazine are then sent out to people on the list. Those who do want the magazine fill in the forms and send them back. The forms are then checked by the staff and the details are typed into a computer via a keyboard.

KEY TERMS — *Automated data capture* means obtaining data directly by an input device.

There is no need for anyone to actively produce the data by using a keyboard or a mouse as it is read automatically.

EXAMPLES: *of automated data capture*
Many applications use automated data capture and these are dealt with in other chapters of the book. They include:
1. using document readers to read text from documents (see Unit 4.2);
2. scanning coded data such as bar codes and magnetic stripes (see Unit 4.3);
3. scanning pictures and text from documents (see Unit 4.5);
4. using sensors for data logging (see Unit 16.5).

APPLICATION: *of automated data capture*
Producing a receipt at a supermarket checkout
In some supermarkets each item has a bar code printed on the packet as part of the packet design. When the shopper gets to the checkout, the assistant uses a scanner to read the bar code on each item. The scanner is part of a **point-of-sale (POS) terminal**. This is connected to a computer in the store. The terminal sends the numbers which have been scanned from the bar codes to the computer which:
- sends back the name of the item and its price to be printed on the receipt;
- totals the bill and sends the total back to the terminal to be printed.

In some cases the computer also uses the bar codes to adjust stock levels. The stock files are changed to allow for the items sold. (See Unit 4.3 for other applications of bar codes.)

Note:
Even if a shop uses the POS terminals to check stock the amount of stock has to be checked by hand every so often as well. This is to allow for goods which are damaged or which are lost or stolen from the shelves.

ADVANTAGES: *of POS terminals using bar codes*

❶ For the customer:
- The time spent at the checkout is shorter.
- The customer's receipt lists all the items bought by name.
- Stock control is improved so stock is fresher.

❷ For the shop management:
- Improved stock control means no waste of money or space on excess stock.
- Faster throughput at the checkout means fewer staff need be employed.
- Fewer errors are made at the checkouts.

❸ For the employees:
- There is relatively little keying to do.

(See also Unit 4.3 for advantages and disadvantages of bar codes.)

ADVANTAGES: *of automated data capture*

❶ No data has to be keyed.
❷ There are very few errors or inaccuracies.

DISADVANTAGE: *of automated data capture*

Many automated data capture systems are expensive to set up.
For this reason a small shop may decide not to use them.

Capturing data on forms

When data capture is not automated then it usually involves data being written down. To do this it is best to produce a standard form which people fill in.

KEY TERMS   A *data capture form* is a form designed to have computer input data written on it.

EXAMPLES: *of data capture forms*

❶ A membership subscription form (see also Unit 11.2).
❷ A questionnaire.
❸ A turnaround document.

ADVANTAGES: *of capturing data using forms*

❶ Data is standardised – all records are set out in the same way.
❷ People collecting the data know exactly what data is required.

Turnaround documents

KEY TERMS   A *turnaround document* is a form which is produced by a computer, has more data added to it and is then input to the computer again for further processing.

When the computer first produces the document it prints information on it which can be used to recognise the document when it is input again. For example, on a membership renewal form for a video club, the computer would print the person's membership number on the form.

APPLICATION: *of a turnaround document*

Gas board meter reading

A gas board uses the following system for its customer accounts.

When the meters in an area are due to be read the computer prints out forms (see Fig. 3.1) for the meter reader. She is given a set of meter reading slips for a particular road within her area. The computer has already printed on each one the customer's address and account number and probable usage of gas. The meter reader then has to go to each house and fill in the slip carefully in pencil.

The batch of completed slips is returned by the meter reader and read by the computer. The customers' bills are then printed out by the computer and sent out by the staff.

The meter reading slips are turnaround documents because the computer reads both information it has printed previously and information the meter reader has added.

3.2 Design of data capture forms

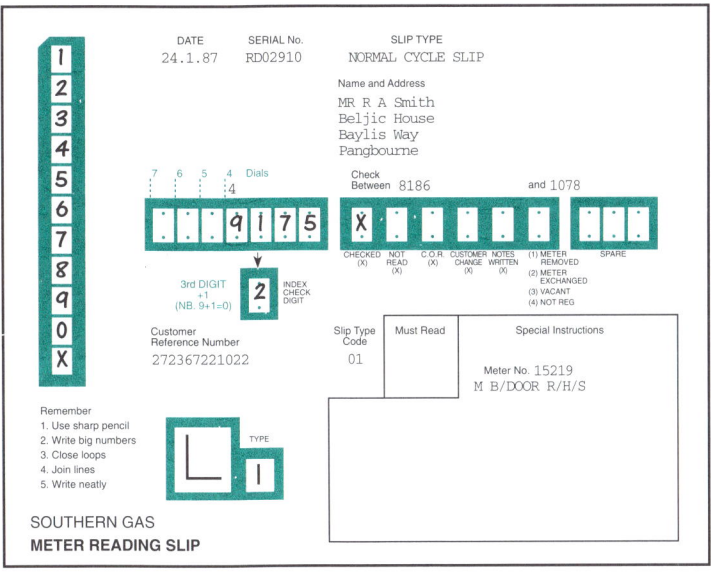

Fig. 3.1 A meter reading slip

ADVANTAGES: *of turnaround documents*
1. Data which is already known to the computer does not have to be written or keyed again.
2. The computer can recognise each individual document using information it has already printed on it.

3.2 Design of data capture forms

Data capture forms should be designed to be:
1. simple
   - Ask for the minimum of information. There is no need to ask for information already within the information system.
   - Keep printed text to a minimum.
2. clear
   - Give clear instructions. It should be obvious what to write.
   - Keep labels close to spaces for information. It should be clear where to write.
3. interesting
   - If a form is laid out in an attractive manner it is less effort to fill it in.

EXAMPLE: *of improving a data capture form*
The form shown (Fig. 3.2 on p. 42) is for renewal of a photographic magazine. The form is unsatisfactory because:
1. The layout is rather unattractive.
2. It is for renewal of the subscription so the name and address are already known to the system.
3. The message about block letters appears below the address. As most people work through a page from top to bottom and left to right they may not see this until it is too late.
4. It is not at all clear what to write to obtain a newsletter and to describe your method of payment.

Fig. 3.3 shows the following improvements.
1. It is simpler.
   - The person only has to fill in the name and address if it has changed.
   - The amount of text has been reduced.

Chapter 3 Data capture

2 It is clearer.
- The message about block capitals is in a better position.
- The subscriber has boxes to tick to make choices.

3 It is more interesting in the way it is laid out.
- Different fonts have been used.
- The layout has been improved.

Positive Photography Magazine

P.O.Box 38, Leechester, Hants, SO10 ZNW
    Telephone 0794 68888
Membership renewal for 1997

Kindly complete and return this form together with your remittance to ensure magazines until December 31st 1997

    NAME ....

    ADDRESS ....

    ....

    .... POSTCODE ....

PLEASE USE BLOCK LETTERS

Subscription Rates: Inland £15.00
                       Europe £17.00
                       Other Countries £19.00

Please state whether you want the Newsletter ....

Please state method of payment...

PLEASE MAKE CHEQUES PAYABLE TO: POSITIVE PHOTOGRAPHY

Fig. 3.2 Subscription form for *Positive Photography* magazine

---

POSITIVE PHOTOGRAPHY MAGAZINE
P.O.BOX 38, LEECHESTER, HANTS, SO10 ZNW
TELEPHONE 0794 68888

Membership renewal for Period 1/1/97 to 31/12/97

Please complete IN BLOCK CAPITALS and return together with your remittance.
PENELOPE COOKE
24, THE STREET
NEWTOWN
ESSEX
NT1 2PH
Please write correct address if different from the above.
NAME..
ADDRESS..
....
.... POSTCODE ....

Subscription Rates: I would like to pay by:
Inland   £15.00   ☐ Cheque
Europe   £17.00   ☐ Cash
Other Countries £19.00   ☐ Credit Card: Access/Visa/Amex

☐ I wish to receive   No. ☐☐☐☐☐☐☐☐☐☐☐☐
   the Newsletter (£2 extra)   Expiry date ☐☐☐☐

Amount paid £..........................

Please make cheques payable to: POSITIVE PHOTOGRAPHY

Fig. 3.3 Improved version of subscription form for *Positive Photography* magazine

3.3 Questionnaires

KEY TERMS *A **survey** is an operation to obtain information by observation or by asking questions.*
*A **questionnaire** is a set of questions used in a survey to collect information from people.*

Steps in conducting a survey using a questionnaire

A survey using a questionnaire needs to be carried out carefully so that:
1. the information collected does help to solve a problem;
2. the people being questioned are happy to co-operate;
3. the data collected can be analysed easily.

The steps to be carried out are as follows.
1. Define carefully the problem which makes the survey necessary.
2. Work out what the survey should find out.
3. Decide what information to collect and who to collect it from.
4. Work out the best way of analysing the results.
5. Design a questionnaire:
   - make the questions as few and as simple as possible;
   - make sure you include headings so that people know what the survey is;
   - decide where to put the questions on the page and in what order;
   - make sure enough space is left for written answers.
6. Produce copies of the questionnaire – perhaps on a word processor.
7. Test the questionnaire by trying it on a sample group of people. Change the questionnaire if necessary.
8. Decide how to conduct the survey.
9. Carry out the survey.
10. Analyse the results and present them in an organised way. The result would normally be a word processed report.

Designing questions

Questions can be of several different types.
1. Questions requiring YES/NO answers.
   These are easy to analyse but do not apply to many situations, e.g.

	YES	NO
Do you come to school by public transport? (Please tick)	☐	☐

2. Questions with several possible answers.
   These can be designed to give a simple choice, e.g.

	BUS	CAR	CYCLE	WALK	OTHER
What is your main method of transport to get to school? (Please tick one box)	☐	☐	☐	☐	☐

   If 'OTHER' please specify ....

This question could be redesigned:

> Is your main method of transport to school:
> 1. Bus   2. Car   3. Bicycle
> 4. Walking   5. Some other method   [.....]
> (Please answer 1,2,3,4 or 5)
> If some other method, please specify ....

This makes the answer a simple number which is easy to check, to record and to analyse.

❸ Questions where the answer is a number which measures a quantity, e.g.

> Roughly how many minutes does
> it take you to get to school?   [............]

Numbers can easily be analysed using a spreadsheet or a database and graphs can be produced from them.

❹ Open questions which allow the subjects to answer as they wish. These are difficult to analyse and take time to answer. However, they do allow the subjects freedom of expression, e.g.

> What is your opinion of your present method of school transport?
> ....
> ....
> ....

APPLICATIONS: *of surveys and questionnaires*

❶ School refectory improvements

A school is considering improvements to its refectory. A questionnaire is devised asking pupils what they like and dislike about it. It also asks them to number possible improvements in order of importance.

The results are put into a database set up to receive the survey data. The database is used to produce statistics showing the most common likes and dislikes.

It also produces totals in favour of each possible improvement giving a higher value to a first choice than to a second choice, etc.

❷ Village bypass

A small village has a main road passing along one edge of it. In recent years this road has had an increasing number of accidents along it. The Ministry of Transport has agreed in principle to a bypass and there are a number of proposed routes. Meetings are held to make clear the advantages and disadvantages of the different routes. Each householder is then sent a questionnaire. The villagers are asked which route they prefer. One of the options is to have no bypass. Those who take this option are then asked to choose the best of a number of alternatives for making the existing road safer.

The questionnaires are analysed and the results are considered along with the views of MPs and the councils of neighbouring parishes before a decision is made.

3.4 User interfaces

KEY TERMS A *user interface* is the method by which the user of a computer system interacts with it.

EXAMPLES: *of user interfaces*
1. The user of a batch processing system may have to precede each job by a set of commands to the operating system.
2. The user of a word processing package may have the choice between using the keyboard or using the mouse to select options from the menus.
3. Usually the user interface for a network includes a password system and for a standalone computer it does not.

KEY TERMS A *command line interface* means that the user has to communicate with the computer using typed commands.

A *prompt* is a character or group of characters which the computer displays to let the user know that a command can be input.

The conversation consists of the following sequence:
1. the computer displays a prompt;
2. the user types a command and presses the ENTER (or RETURN) key;
3. the computer carries out the command.

This is repeated until the user quits.

EXAMPLE: *of a command line interface*

The DOS prompt

On an IBM-compatible PC the user can communicate with the operating system using the language DOS interactively. The prompt used usually ends with >

Typical commands are:

    dir   list the directory
    copy copy a file
    del   delete a file

```
C:\ISBOOK> dir p*.wp

 Volume in drive C has no label
 Volume Serial Number is 0A14-11D4
 Directory of C:\ISBOOK

PHOTOS    WP        13044 02/02/95     20:17
PICTURES  WP        49021 05/02/95     14:12
       2 files(s)       62065 bytes
                     61640704 bytes free

C:\ISBOOK> copy pictures.wp a:
    1 file(s) copied

C:\ISBOOK> copy photos.wp a:
    1 file(s) copied

C:\ISBOOK> del p*.bak

C:\ISBOOK>
```

Fig. 3.4 Screen with a DOS conversation. Here the user is using the directory ISBOOK from the hard disc drive (drive C).
The user:
- lists the word processor (.wp) files whose names begin with 'p'
- copies the two files which are listed onto a floppy disc (drive A)
- deletes the backup (.bak) files for both of them as they are no longer needed

Chapter 3 Data capture

ADVANTAGES: *of a command line interface*
1. A user who knows a package well can issue commands with the keys very quickly.
2. Each command can usually be followed by different options so that a wide variety of choices can be made.

Menus

KEY TERMS A *menu* is a list of choices presented to the user by an interactive program. The user selects one of these options to say what the program should do next.

A *menu bar* is a set of menu titles displayed across the screen at the top or the bottom so that the user can pick a menu.

A *pull-down menu* is a menu which appears below the menu bar when it is selected.

Notes:
Usually a menu in a menu bar is selected either:
1. by moving the mouse pointer to it and clicking a button,

OR

2. by pressing a function key on the keyboard,

OR

3. by using a combination of other keys.

EXAMPLE: *of a menu bar and a pull-down menu*
Fig. 3.5 shows a menu bar with the File menu selected. It could have been chosen either by using the mouse OR by pressing the ALT and F keys together. The file menu is a pull-down menu.

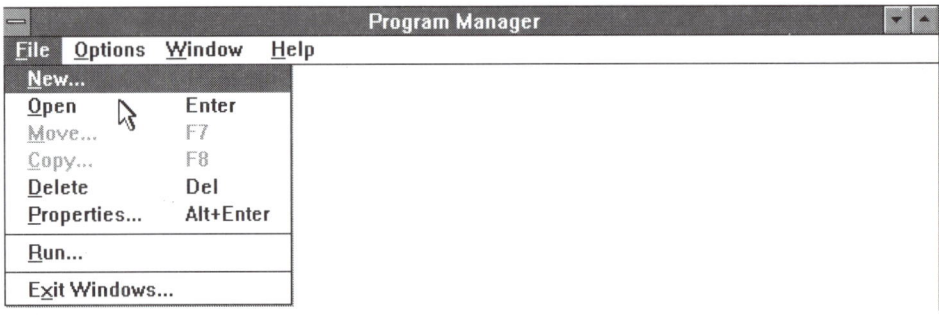

Fig. 3.5 Menu bar of Microsoft Windows with the File menu selected

ADVANTAGES: *of a menu over a command line interface*
1. It is not necessary to remember the possible commands, as they are all displayed.
2. If you do not know the package you can guess how to use it.

KEY TERMS A *full screen menu* is one which takes up all or most of the screen.

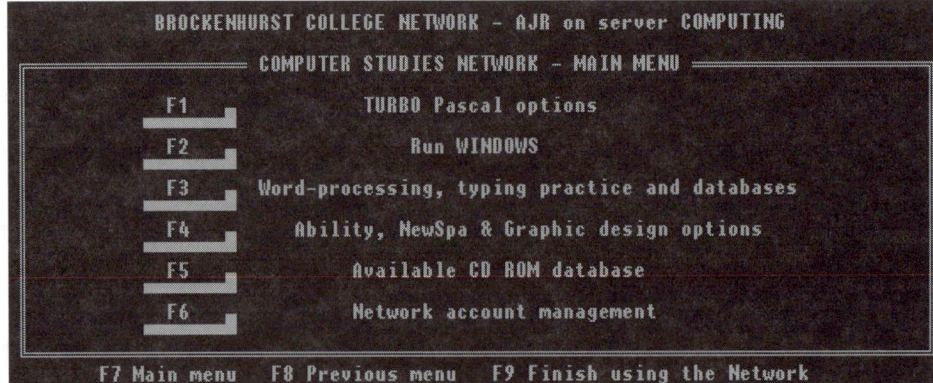

Fig. 3.6 A full screen menu

ADVANTAGE: *of a pull-down menu over a full screen menu*
The user can have the menu and their work both on the screen at the same time.

ADVANTAGE: *of a full screen menu over a pull-down menu*
More information can be given against each menu option.

3.4 User interfaces

Graphical user interfaces

KEY TERMS

A ***window*** is a rectangular area of the screen selected for a particular display. You can split the screen up into a number of windows each showing output for different programs or different parts of the same program.

Notes:
1. Usually the user can use a mouse to:
   - move the borders of a window to make it larger or smaller;
   - move the window itself around the screen.
2. Usually a window can be reduced to an icon for use later.

KEY TERMS

An ***icon*** is a small symbol on the screen which you can select from a menu instead of a word. The shape of the icon indicates the action being selected.

EXAMPLES: *of icons*

A drawing package has as icons a pen for drawing lines and a rubber to erase parts of the picture (see Fig. 3.7).

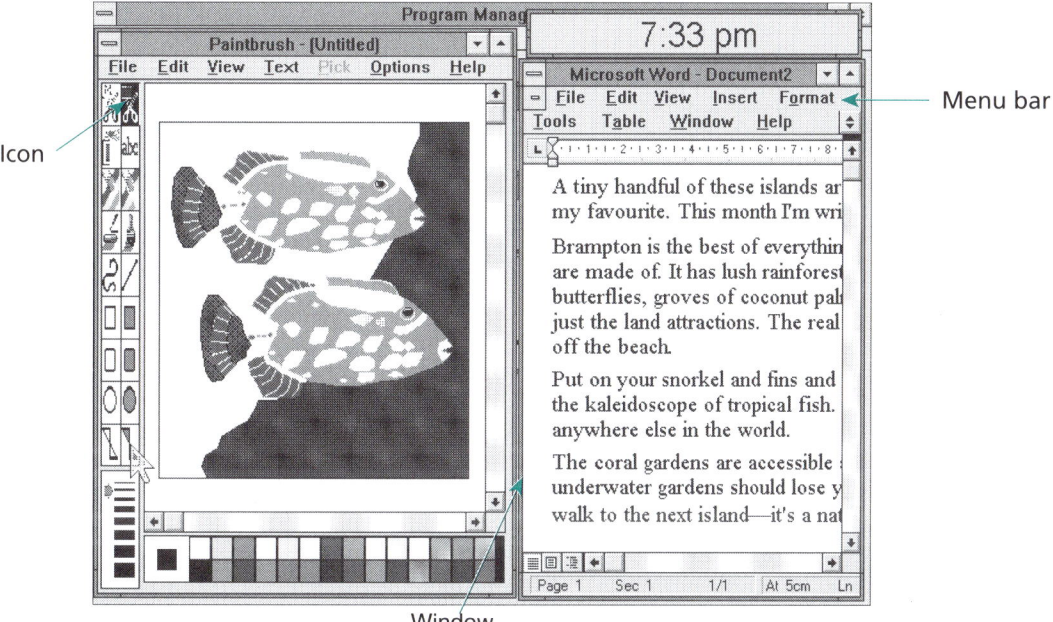

Fig. 3.7 A screen showing three windows. The windows contain a clock, a simple picture and a piece of text

KEY TERMS

GUI stands for ***Graphical User Interface***. The user interacts with what is shown on the screen, usually using some sort of pointing device.

WIMP stands for ***Windows Icon Mouse Pointer***. A WIMP environment makes use of windows, icons, a mouse and pull-down menus.

APPLICATIONS: *using a WIMP environment*

1. A data logging program
   In a data logging application temperatures are being monitored in a furnace.
   Different windows on a screen display:
   - a clock;
   - a graph of the temperatures for the last hour;
   - a table showing the values for the last minute.
2. Writing a book
   Using a word processor an author works on two different chapters of a book. Part of each chapter is displayed in two different windows on the same screen.

Note:
With most WIMP packages you can also select menu options from the keyboard. If you know them the keys may be quicker for some options than using the mouse. Also if your mouse stops working you should at least be able to save your work and quit.

ADVANTAGES: *of a GUI*

1. You can perform operations on windows, files and blocks of data which would be very complicated using the keyboard.
2. Many operations are intuitive so that you do not have to remember complicated commands.

User friendliness

One important aspect of a package is its user friendliness – how easy it is to use. A user friendly program should help you by:

1. having clear options:
   - using obvious names for operations in menus;
   - using icons whose meaning is obvious.
2. having a good system of help messages. Usually each menu has a help option.
3. having a clear manual. You may be able to work out how to use a package from the menus and the help messages. However, you will not find some of the more difficult functions without a good manual.

Quick test

1. Choose *two* examples of automated data capture from the following list:
   (a) scanning a picture;
   (b) drawing a picture with a CAD package;
   (c) reading bar codes at a checkout.

2. Choose *two* examples of a data capture form from the following list:
   (a) a questionnaire on favourite television programmes;
   (b) an examination paper asking for essays to be written on a separate sheet;
   (c) a multiple choice examination paper with spaces to make pencil marks.

3. Choose *two* examples of a turnaround document from the following list:
   (a) a gas board meter reading slip;
   (b) a cereal packet with a bar code printed on it;
   (c) an electricity bill which has to be sent back with the cheque.

4. For each of the following two questions say what is wrong with putting them on a questionnaire in this form:
   (a) Gender?
   (b) What type of TV program do you watch most?

5. Name *two* ways of making program choices which do not involve menus.

6. Give *three* ways a package can help you to understand how to carry out a particular operation.

Summary

1. - **Data capture** means obtaining data for a computer.
   - **Automated data capture** means obtaining data directly by an input device without using a keyboard.

2. **Data capture forms** are designed to have computer input data written on them. This is so that:

- data is standardised with all records set out in the same way;
- people collecting the data know what data is required.

3 A **turnaround document** is produced by a computer, has more data added to it, and is then input to the computer again.

4 Data capture forms should be designed to be **simple**, **clear** and **interesting**.

5 Questions on questionnaires can be of several different types:
- questions requiring YES/NO answers;
- questions with several possible answers giving a simple choice;
- questions where the answer is a number which measures a quantity;
- open questions which allow the subject to answer as they wish.

6 A **user interface** is the method by which the user of a computer system interacts with it. Interactive user interfaces may use:
- a command line,
- menus,
- icons.

7
- A **graphical user interface (GUI)** encourages the user to work intuitively.
- A **WIMP** environment is a type of GUI which makes use of windows, icons, a mouse and pull-down menus.

8 A user friendly program should help you by:
- making clear the options on the screen;
- having a good system of help messages;
- having a clear manual.

Chapter 4
Input methods

KEY TERMS *An **input device** is a peripheral which accepts data and sends it to the central processing unit.*

Data presented to an input device has to be in the right form for the device (e.g. a bar code reader will only read bar codes). The input device converts the data into a binary form which the central processor can accept.

EXAMPLES: *of input devices*
1. The keyboard of a microcomputer.
2. A light pen.
3. An electronic digital weighing scale interfaced to a computer.
4. A document reader.
5. A mouse.

(See Unit 16.2 for direct input from sensors and instruments.)

4.1 Input from keyboards

There are many different input devices, but most data for computers is still in the form of text and is typed on keyboards.

The usual keys supplied are:

1. **the alphabet**
   These keys normally produce **lower case** (small) letters. To produce **upper case** (large) letters you press the 'Shift' key while typing the letters. 'Shift Lock' or 'Caps Lock' can be pressed before typing to produce upper case letters all the time.
2. **the digits 0–9**
   These often appear twice:
   - along the top row for keying mixed alphanumeric data;
   - in a keypad at the right for completely numeric data.
3. **other text characters, e.g.**
   - punctuation (. , ; : etc.);
   - mathematical symbols (% & # etc.).
4. **cursor and other control characters**
   - arrow keys, the TAB key and keys such as PAGE UP and PAGE DOWN;
   - editing keys such as INSERT and DELETE;
   - control keys such as ENTER (or RETURN) and ESCAPE.
5. **keys which change the function of other keys**
   e.g. the keys marked SHIFT, CAPS LOCK, NUM LOCK, ALT and CTRL. Sometimes the changes these make depend on the software – particularly for the SHIFT, ALT and CTRL keys.
6. **function keys** – usually numbered F1, F2, etc.
   The function of these is set by the program which is running. Extra functions can usually be obtained by using the SHIFT, CTRL and ALT keys.

EXAMPLES: *of uses for function keys*
1. Select a choice from a menu.
2. Delete a line of text in a word processing package.
3. Draw a circle for a graphics package.

ADVANTAGES: *of keyboards*
1. Very reliable. Other methods of text input such as voice input and optical character recognition are prone to errors.
2. Every computer has a keyboard. No extra equipment needs to be bought.

4.2 OMR, OCR and MICR

There are a number of different methods of reading data from documents in the form of characters or marks. These methods are examples of automated data capture (see Unit 3.1).

Document readers

KEY TERMS *A document reader is a device which can read data straight from a form.*

EXAMPLES: *of document reading*
1. Optical Mark Reading (OMR).
2. Optical Character Recognition (OCR).
3. Magnetic Ink Character Recognition (MICR).

Optical Mark Reading (OMR)

KEY TERMS *OMR is a system of reading lines or 'marks' which have been made in exactly the right positions on a card or document.*

CHARACTERISTICS: *of OMR*
1. The documents to be read have empty boxes to take the marks. These have been preprinted on to the documents together with information telling the user what to do. The person preparing the data makes pencil or ink marks in the appropriate boxes.
2. The data to be input has to be simple because the user can only make marks and cannot write any information.
3. There has to be a large number of documents to justify designing and printing them.

APPLICATION: *of mark reading*
A multiple choice question paper
For each question several choices are given. Each choice has a small oval box beside it in which a mark can be put. The oval has a rectangle above it (see Fig. 4.1). The candidates are given clear instructions:
- to use a soft pencil to make the marks,
- to only mark firmly one oval box for each question,
- to make sure the mark does not go outside the oval,
- not to rub marks out; if a mark is wrong they are to mark the rectangle above it as well.

The answer sheets are sent to the examining board and are marked by a computer with an optical mark reader.

ADVANTAGES: *of using marks*
1. Fewer mistakes are made by machines reading marks than are made reading handwritten characters.
2. Data can be prepared without any special equipment.
3. Data can be prepared where it is collected, e.g. a market researcher can mark a questionnaire while asking people questions in the street.

Chapter 4 Input methods

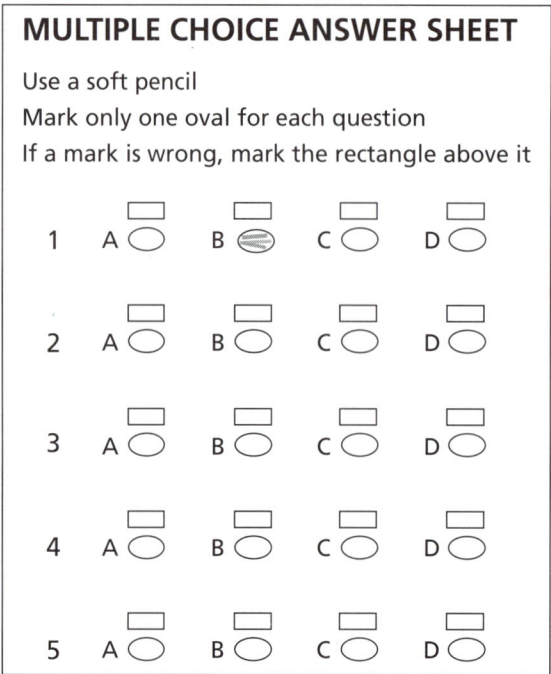

Fig. 4.1 A typical multiple choice question with boxes to fill in and one pencil mark made

DISADVANTAGES: *of using marks*

1. Documents for mark readers are complicated to design. If an item has several values, then the form has to have a different box to mark for each possible value.
2. Input of data to the computer is slow. For example, a marked card reader is far slower than a disc unit.
3. It is difficult for a computer to check marked data.
4. The person putting the marks on the document has to follow the instructions precisely.

Optical Character Recognition (OCR)

An optical character reader can recognise characters from their shape. As with OMR, light is reflected from the paper and from the ink. In OCR however the reader has to work out what the characters are.

Scanners (see Unit 4.5) were originally designed to scan pictures but they can also be used to read text. This system relies on sophisticated OCR software in the computer.

The following types of character can be recognised by scanners and OCR readers.

1. **Handwritten characters**

   The documents are usually preprinted with spaces provided. The characters have to be written carefully in the right places.

2. **Printed characters**
   - Characters on turnaround documents. These have previously been printed on to documents by the computer's printer (see Unit 3.1).
   - Characters in fonts specially designed for OCR readers. (A font is a character set of a particular size and style.) Practically all OCR document readers recognise at least one of two fonts, known as OCRA and OCRB.
   - Ordinary printing. As software improves OCR readers and scanners can recognise a greater range of fonts.

APPLICATION: *of OCR*

Charity fund donations

Names and addresses of prospective donors are preprinted on donation forms. The forms are sent to the donors. Each donor sends back a form with some money. The date and amount given are carefully hand printed on the form by an operator. An OCR reader reads the name, the date and the amount. The computer then uses the information to update the donor file and the accounts.

ADVANTAGES: *of OCR*

  over MICR (see the next section)
  1. Different printed fonts can be used (the MICR font is fixed).
  2. OCR usually accepts hand printing and normal type.

  over OMR (see the previous section)
  The documents do not have to be designed so precisely for OCR.

  over other media
  1. The data for OCR can be read and checked by people.
  2. Written data and printed data can be read at the same time.
  3. Documents can be read directly into a computer without any typing, e.g. documents received by fax, old books, etc.

DISADVANTAGE: *of OCR*

  OCR systems often fail to recognise characters – particularly if they are handwritten or in unusual fonts.

Magnetic Ink Character Recognition (MICR)

An **MICR** reader recognises characters formed from magnetic ink. As the document passes into the reader the ink is magnetised and the characters are recognised by the strength of the magnetism.

Fig. 4.2 A bank cheque showing characters in magnetic ink *(By kind permission of Lloyds Bank)*

APPLICATION: *of MICR*

  Bank cheques
  The major British banks all use MICR to encode along the bottom of cheques the following information:
  - the cheque number
  - the branch number of the bank
  - the customer's account number.

  This information is printed on the cheques before they are issued to the customer. The customer then writes a cheque and pays someone with it. This person pays it into a bank and it is sent to a clearing house. Here the amount of money is added to the bottom of the cheque in magnetic ink using an MICR encoder. The cheque can then be sorted automatically and sent back to the bank of the original customer. The money is then deducted from his or her account.

ADVANTAGES: *of MICR*
  1. MICR is difficult to forge.
  2. Documents can still be read when folded, written on, etc.

DISADVANTAGES: *of MICR*
  1. MICR readers and encoders are very expensive.
  2. The system can only accept a few different characters.

4.3 Bars and stripes

Increasingly in our lives we use tickets or cards or buy goods which have computer data already on them. These are being used everywhere – in shops, banks, libraries, even at school. These are further examples of automated data capture.

Two types in common use are the bar code and the magnetic stripe (or strip).

Bar codes

KEY TERMS   A **bar code** is a set of parallel printed lines of differing thicknesses (usually alternately black and white), which represent a number. Often the number represented by the bars is also printed above or below the bar code.

Fig. 4.3 A bar code

When bar codes are used on shop goods, the number coded identifies the product, usually giving a number code for:
1. country of origin;
2. manufacturer;
3. an item number for the product.

Notes:
1. The price is not included in the data on a bar code. This is because prices change so often. Instead the price is stored in the computer and when a price is needed it is retrieved from there.
2. The number on a bar code is printed out as an actual number as well. Thus if the scanner cannot read a bar code the number can be keyed in instead.

Bar codes may be read by:
1. a hand-held 'wand', which is passed over the code perpendicular to the bars, the wand is attached to a computer terminal or a recording device (see Fig. 4.4);
2. a stationary scanner using a laser beam, which scans the bar code as the product is passed across a window.

ADVANTAGES: *of bar codes*
1. Bar codes can be printed by normal printing methods.
2. Staff do not have to write down or key in the name of the item or its price.

DISADVANTAGES: *of bar codes*
1. Bar codes are not suitable for recording prices. Customers still have to be informed of prices (e.g. by labels or catalogues).
2. Bar codes have to be read by machine.
3. Only numbers can be coded in this way.

(See Unit 3.1 for advantages of POS terminals.)

APPLICATION: *of bar codes*
Recording loans of library books
In many local libraries every book has a bar code inside the front cover. This contains a number which uniquely identifies the book. Each user of the library is issued with a card which also has a bar code printed on it. The coded number uniquely identifies the user.

The library counter has on it a number of terminals. These are connected directly to the county library's central computer. Each terminal has a bar code reader in the form of a wand.

When a book is taken out, the librarian uses the wand to read the bar code on the book and then the bar code on the borrower's card. The central computer receives these numbers and records the book loan in a loans file.

When the book is returned, the librarian uses the wand to read the bar code in the book. This is automatically transmitted to the main computer which deletes the loan from the loans file.

Note:
This system makes it easier if a reader wishes to borrow an unusual book. The central computer holds a record of which library has the book and whether it is on loan. It can also stop the present borrower from renewing the book.

Fig. 4.4 A wand used to read bar codes in a public library

Magnetic stripes

KEY TERMS

*A **magnetic stripe** (or strip) is a short length of magnetic coating printed on to the surface of a ticket or card. The stripe usually contains information to identify the ticket or card or its user.*

*To **swipe** a card with a magnetic stripe means to move the card through a reader so that the stripe can be read.*

Notes:
1. Often, but not always, the stripe has information written on to it only once. After that it is read but data can no longer be written to it.
2. The magnetic stripe is often encased in a plastic film for protection.
3. A card with a magnetic stripe on the back is sometimes called a **swipe card**.

EXAMPLES: *of cards and tickets which often have magnetic stripes*
1. Tags attached to clothes in a shop.
2. Railway, bus and underground tickets.
3. Credit cards and bank cards.

APPLICATIONS: *of magnetic stripes*
1. **On credit cards**
   A shop or business with a terminal can have the card checked and authorise the payment. The terminal is linked to the shop's own bank. This in turn calls up the credit card company's own computer. This checks that the card is valid and has not been lost or stolen. This message is sent back to the retailer who can then go ahead with the transaction.

Note:
Some small shops will not accept credit cards. Credit card companies do make a percentage charge for their service. A shop may decide not to pay this so that they can keep their prices down.

Chapter 4 Input methods

Fig. 4.5 A bank card (*By kind permission of Lloyds Bank*)

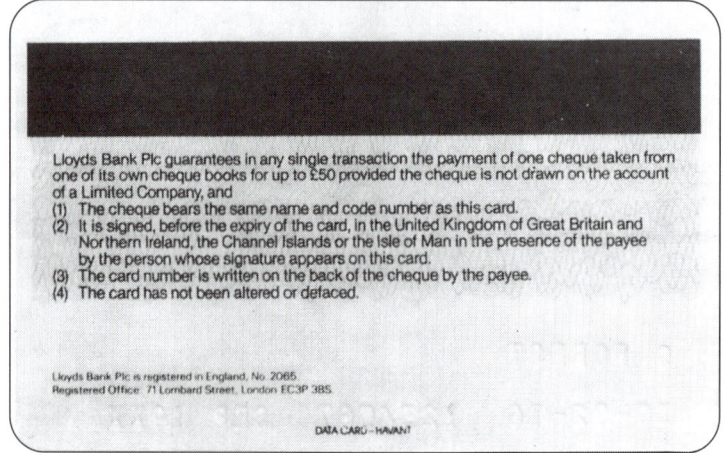

Fig. 4.6 The reverse of a bank card showing the magnetic stripe

❷ **On bank cards**

Banks issue plastic cards with a magnetic stripe for various purposes (see Figs 4.5 and 4.6).

Examples are:

- **self-service cards for cash issuing terminals**

  A **cash issuing terminal** is a machine, connected to a bank or a building society's main computer, which can issue money and carry out other tasks direct for the customer. A cash issuing terminal is also called an **automatic telling machine** or **ATM**. These terminals are situated on walls at banks, building societies and in public places such as supermarkets.

  A **self-service card** is the card which a customer needs to use a cash issuing terminal. The card has stored on it the person's account number and bank code, and its own expiry date. The customer inserts the card into the terminal to be checked. He or she then types in a **Personal Identification Number (PIN)** which is also checked. This PIN is a kind of password for that card and the customer has to memorise it. The customer keys in details of the service required and the amount of any money to be withdrawn. The terminal returns the card, the money and issues a receipt if necessary.

- **a Switch card**

  The Switch card allows money to be credited to a retailer's account directly. Many shops and garages have small Switch terminals. When a customer comes to pay by Switch the card is handed to the cashier who swipes the card through the terminal. The card details and the amount to be paid are stored in the terminal. Later they are transferred electronically to the retailer's bank. The amount of money is credited to the retailer's account. Details of the amount are also sent to the customer's bank to be deducted from that account.

③ On a phone card

Some telephones do not accept coins. Instead a card is used which has been bought previously at a Post Office or shop. The value of the card is recorded on a magnetic stripe. As a user makes a call the number of units stored on the card is reduced.

Some telephones also accept credit cards as a means of payment. The number of the credit card account is read from the card so that payment for the call can be charged to this account.

ADVANTAGES: *of cash issuing terminals (ATMs)*
1. The banks do not need to employ so many staff.
2. Customers can obtain money and other banking services at any time of the day or night.
3. Customers do not have to queue.

DISADVANTAGES: *of cash issuing terminals (ATMs)*
1. If there is a problem the customer often has no one to ask for help.
2. For bank employees there is the problem that fewer staff are needed.

ADVANTAGES: *of magnetic stripes*
1. They are simple to produce.
2. They are not easily damaged (except by magnetic fields).
3. Each stores a fairly large number of characters (usually about 72).
4. They cut down the amount of writing involved in a transaction.

DISADVANTAGES: *of magnetic stripes*
1. The data can be changed or erased by magnetic fields.
2. The stripe can be damaged by scratching.

New developments

New methods of storing data on cards have become available. They include:

1. **laser cards**
   Data is stored on these as small holes in a polished surface. The cards are read using reflected light. Some readers contain a laser but cheaper versions do not. One card can store over 2 million characters.
2. **smart cards**
   These have very thin memory chips sealed into them. Some of the data in them can be changed. One card can store about 8000 characters.

4.4 Point and touch methods

As well as a keyboard, a computer often has an extra device such as a mouse, a light pen or a joystick. This is to help the user:
1. to make selections from menus or to choose icons;
2. to position the cursor on the screen;
3. to produce graphics;
4. to move images and create windows on the screen.
   (See Unit 3.4 for menu, icon and window.)

Light pen

KEY TERMS *A **light pen** is a pen-shaped device, held in the hand, which can detect the presence or absence of light.*

The pen is used to select a point on a screen. The screen is 'refreshed' about every 1/50th of a second by a point of light travelling rapidly across it. The pen detects this point of light and the computer can work out by precise timing where the pen is.

Note: A bar code wand works on a similar principle (see Unit 4.3).

Chapter 4 Input methods

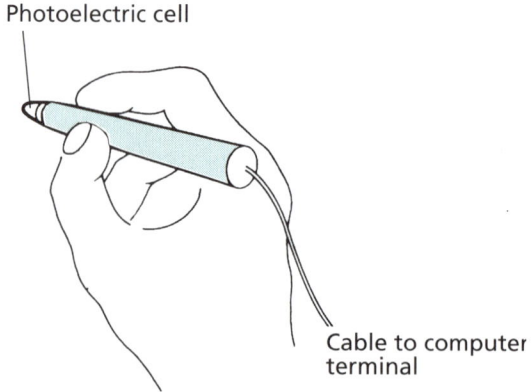

Fig. 4.7 A light pen

APPLICATIONS: *of using a light pen*
A Computer Aided Design (CAD) package
The pen is used to select options from a menu printed at the top of the screen, by pointing it at the options required. A drawing made up from selected shapes is produced on the screen. These shapes appear as icons at the right of the screen. The light pen is used to indicate which shape to draw, where it should be drawn and at what size.

ADVANTAGE: *of using a light pen*
It is more direct and precise than using a mouse.

DISADVANTAGES: *of using a light pen*
1. It can record only the presence or absence of light.
2. It requires software written specially for it.

Mouse

KEY TERMS A **mouse** is an input device designed to fit snugly under a hand while it is moved about over a table. Moving the mouse produces movements of a cursor or a pointer on the screen.

The mouse is also provided with one, two or three **buttons.** These are pressed to produce action when the user has moved the cursor to the right place.

EXAMPLES: *of uses for a mouse*
1. To select options from a menu or from a set of icons.
2. To position the cursor when editing text or using a design package.
3. To select an object in a drawing or a piece of text to be copied, moved or deleted.

ADVANTAGES: *of using a mouse*
1. It is easy and convenient to use.
2. It is inexpensive.
3. Most modern software includes an option to use it.
4. It selects a position on the screen more quickly than is possible with a keyboard.

DISADVANTAGES: *of using a mouse*
1. It cannot be used to input text easily – you still need a keyboard to do that.
2. It is relatively slow for selecting options from menus. A user who is familiar with the software can select options more quickly with the keys.
3. It is not very accurate for drawing purposes.
4. The mouse requires a flat surface to operate.

Note:
A **tracker ball** is like a mouse upside down. The device stays still while the user moves the ball.

ADVANTAGE: *of a tracker ball over a mouse*
A tracker ball does not require a large flat surface.

Joystick

KEY TERMS A *joystick* is a device which enables the user to control movement on the screen by manoeuvring a small lever.

The lever can be moved in any direction from its zero position. It can also be made to produce faster movements on the screen by pushing it further from the zero position. The joystick usually has buttons with which actions can be carried out once the cursor is in the right place. Some joysticks give more control on the screen by rotating the stick as well.

EXAMPLES: *of uses of a joystick*
1. Controlling objects in computer games.
2. Producing graphics.

ADVANTAGE: *of a joystick*
The joystick allows the fast interaction needed in games.

DISADVANTAGE: *of a joystick*
The joystick cannot be used to accurately select options from a screen.

Note:
Many systems specifically for games have an improvement on the joystick referred to as a **games paddle**.

Fig. 4.8 A joystick

Touch screens

KEY TERMS A *touch screen* is a screen through which data can be entered into a computer just by touching it with a finger. Items are selected just as they would be with a mouse pointer or a light pen.

ADVANTAGES: *of a touch screen*
1. No extra peripherals are needed except the monitor – although this of course has to be adapted to respond to touch.
2. The system is very effective in situations where a keyboard or a mouse would become wet or dirty. The screen can be positioned above and out of the way of the work area.
3. It is very useful to help a person whose job involves standing and moving about.

Chapter 4 Input methods

DISADVANTAGES: *of a touch screen*
1. It is not suitable for office use. It is tiring to keep reaching to touch the screen.
2. It is unsuitable for inputting large quantities of data. Data can only be input by selecting what is already on the screen.

APPLICATION: *of a touch screen*
Above the bar in a public house
Data capture
Two touch screens are positioned above the bar. They are out of the way of drink spillage but can easily be reached by the bartenders.
What the computer does
The touch screens are on-line to a microcomputer in an office behind the bar. This deals with:
- stock in the cellar;
- sales over the bar.

The screens can display a series of menus and other displays including a plan of the cellar.

When drinks are sold the bartender selects these on the screen and the computer adds up the bill. The customer is charged accordingly and the computer updates the accounts.

If a barrel or a bottle is running out the bartender can display part of the cellar and check that there is a replacement. If he has to go and get another one he touches the item on the display and the computer updates the cellar stock record.

4.5 Input of pictures

KEY TERMS To **digitise** *data means to convert it from an analogue form to a digital form (see Unit 2.1 for an explanation of digital and analogue).*

The term is used particularly to describe using a computer input device to capture a picture.

Pictures can be input to a computer by:
1. drawing them using a mouse or a graphics tablet with a Computer Aided Design (CAD) or drawing package. (This is dealt with in detail in Unit 14.3.);
2. using a graphics tablet to digitise an existing drawing one feature at a time;
3. using a scanner to digitise every point of a picture automatically.

Graphics tablet

KEY TERMS *A **graphics tablet** (or digitising tablet) is a board which can detect the position of a pointing device on its surface.*

The tablet can be used:
1. to hold a drawing while the user copies it on to the screen with the pointing device;
2. to hold a sheet of menus, icons and shapes to which the user can point to select options. This allows the user to:
   - have the whole screen free for drawing;
   - select from a very wide range of options.

KEY TERMS *A **stylus** (or **pen**) is a pointing device for a graphics tablet in the shape of a pen. The method which the stylus uses to report its position can be:*
EITHER
- *by signals along a cable attached to the tablet*
OR
- *by transmitting the data directly by radio signals without a cable.*

*A **puck** is a mouse-like input device for a graphics tablet which is moved over the surface of the tablet. The puck has:*
- *cross-hairs to enable the user to position it very accurately;*
- *a number of buttons which give the user a choice of actions.*

4.5 Input of pictures

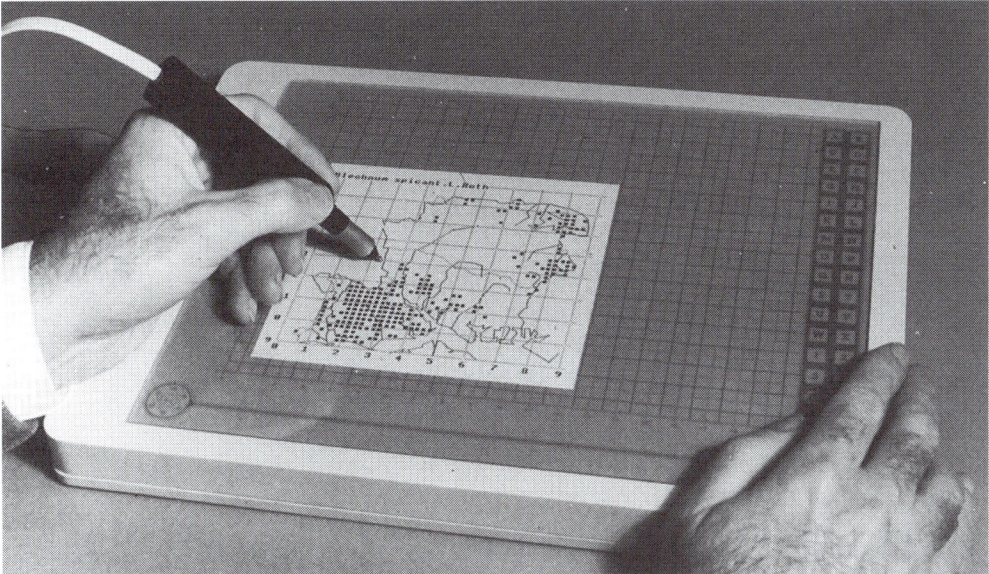

Fig. 4.9 A graphics tablet being used to digitise a map

ADVANTAGE: *of a stylus*
A stylus can be pointed to positions on the tablet very quickly.

ADVANTAGE: *of a stylus which does not need a cable*
The stylus can be carried in a pocket.

ADVANTAGES: *of a puck*
1. The cross-hairs make the puck very accurate.
2. The puck has a number of buttons which give the user a choice of actions to take.

ADVANTAGE: *of a graphics tablet*
It can be used to digitise drawings with great accuracy.

APPLICATIONS: *of graphics tablets*
1. **Digitising maps**
   The Ordnance Survey now stores many of its maps in digital form on magnetic tape cartridges and hard discs. To start with this required all the existing maps to be digitised using graphics tablets.
2. **Using a CAD package for engineering designs**
   The situation
   The design department of an engineering firm is gradually digitising the drawings for their designs. This has meant that many draughtsmen have had to retrain or have become redundant. One of the main advantages of digitised drawings is that new designs can be produced very quickly by making modifications to old designs (see Unit 14.3).
   Data capture
   The designers use graphics tablets in two ways:
   - to digitise an existing drawing:
     The drawing is put on to the board and its shape is traced out with a puck. The designer positions the puck over a feature on the drawing and clicks a button to send its coordinates.
   - to produce a new drawing:
     The designer places a template on the graphics tablet. This has marked on it all the different options available on the CAD package used. The designer does the drawing by pointing to shapes and options on the template.

KEY TERMS *A **scanner** is a device used to examine methodically pictures, text or other information and represent them as computer data.*
*To **scan** an object is to use a scanner to produce data.*

Scanners are of two main types:

1. a hand-held device which is moved across the picture being scanned;
2. a flat-bed scanner. The picture is laid flat on this and the scanner remains stationary on a table while the picture is scanned.

Notes on scanners:

1. As well as digitising pictures scanners can also be used for capturing text from documents (see Unit 4.2 for OCR).
2. Some of the devices used for capturing bar codes are also called scanners (see Unit 4.3).

ADVANTAGE: *of a hand-held scanner*
It is cheap and portable.

ADVANTAGE: *of a flat-bed scanner*
It is very accurate, giving a high resolution image.

DISADVANTAGE: *of scanned pictures*
Scanned pictures take up far more storage space than pictures which have been digitised with a graphics tablet. This is because every dot on the picture has to be stored.

APPLICATIONS: *of scanners*

1. **A school logo**
   The situation
   A school has a competition to produce a logo for the school. This is a design which will then be printed on to the school's official letters, information booklets and the school magazine.
   What the computer does
   The winning design is scanned into a computer. It is then converted to a form which can be used in the school's word processor and desktop publishing packages.

2. **Restoring old photographs**
   The situation
   Some very old photographs were taken on glass negatives. These are often cracked and faded or very badly stained. It is not possible to clean or repair them because the emulsion on the surface is too delicate.
   What the computer does
   The images are scanned into a computer. It is then possible to use an image manipulation program to:
   - improve the brightness and contrast of the image;
   - get rid of cracks and blemishes. This is done by copying small areas of undamaged parts of the image into the damaged parts. The process is very time-consuming but very effective.

4.6 Input of sound

Speech recognition

Using a microphone (or a telephone handset) human speech is coded into a sequence of electrical signals. The computer being used searches a set of stored patterns for the sound which has been input.

APPLICATIONS: *of speech recognition*

1. **Fighter pilot**
   Voice recognition is useful where only a few different commands are required and the hands are busy. On some advanced fighters the pilot has a small display of some of the instruments. This display can be changed by using one of a number of simple pre-stored voice commands.

2. **Telephoning the bank**
   A certain Japanese bank allows customers to telephone the bank's computer. The

computer can recognise a caller from a spoken code and tell him or her the state of a requested account by synthesised voice. It can also accept simple commands such as 'repeat'.

ADVANTAGES: *of speech recognition*
1. No typing or data preparation is necessary.
2. The system can be used remotely by telephone, or by those who are handicapped or who have their hands occupied.

DISADVANTAGES: *of speech recognition*
1. At present the method does not give good results. Relatively few words can be recognised and the error rate is high.
2. Recognition of words is slow.
3. The system is not suitable for use in noisy places without a shielded mouthpiece.

Quick test

1. What is the most-used device for encoding large amounts of data for input to computers?

For each of questions **2** to **6** state which of the following would be the best system to use for the application given:
(a) bar codes
(b) magnetic stripes
(c) OCR
(d) MICR

2. checking train tickets,
3. checking goods at the checkout in a food shop,
4. storing information on bank cheques,
5. storing identification information on a credit card,
6. reading data from a printed document.

7. Name *four* methods of input which could be classed as automated data capture.

For each of questions **8** and **9** state what method of input is being described.

8. The characters are rather odd shapes. They also use a special ink so they are difficult to forge.
9. The number is represented by a small block of black and white lines with the number printed above them.
10. What would be the best way to input commands to a computer system:
    (a) in a situation where you could not use your hands,
    (b) in a dirty and noisy environment?

Summary

1. - An **input device** is a peripheral which accepts data and sends it to the CPU.
   - Most data for computers is still typed on keyboards.
2. **OCR (Optical Character Recognition)**, **OMR (Optical Mark Reading)** and **MICR (Magnetic Ink Character Recognition)** are examples of automated data capture.

3 A **bar code** is a set of parallel printed lines of differing thicknesses which represent a number.
- Often the number is also printed above or below the bar code.
- When bar codes are used on shop goods, the number coded identifies the product but not its price.

4 A **magnetic stripe** is a short length of magnetic coating on the surface of a ticket or card. The stripe usually contains information to identify the ticket or card or its user.

5 A **light pen** is a pen-shaped device, held in the hand, which can detect the presence or absence of light.

6 A **mouse** is an input device which fits under a hand while it is moved about over a table. Moving the mouse produces movements of a pointer on the screen.

7 A **joystick** is a device which enables the user to control movement on the screen by manoeuvring a small lever.

8 A **touch screen** is a screen through which data can be entered into a computer just by touching it with a finger.

Chapter 5
Output of data

KEY TERMS An **output device** is a peripheral which receives data in the form of electrical pulses from the CPU. It then converts this data into information or into further data.

Notes:
1. If the data is output as information then people can read, look at, listen to or otherwise experience it.
2. If the output device converts the data into other data this may be so that it can be: stored, or sent somewhere, or used to control other devices.

EXAMPLES: *of output devices*
1. A PC screen.
2. A printer.
3. A 'turtle' (see Unit 17.1).

(See Unit 16.1 for direct output to control other devices.)

5.1 Output on screens

Display screens (or monitors) are being increasingly used for computer output.

Terms used for screens

KEY TERMS A **pixel** is the smallest area of the screen which the computer can change.

The **resolution** of a screen is a measure of how fine the detail is on it. Screens are usually classed as **low resolution**, **medium resolution** or **high resolution**.

The **screen mode** is the way a computer uses the screen for graphics and text. Usually users have a choice of modes – they can choose between:
- modes with high resolution or low resolution;
- modes with more colours or fewer colours.

A **monochrome** screen is one on which data is presented in just one foreground colour on just one background colour, e.g. white on black OR light blue on dark blue.

Notes:
1. Any display on the screen is made up by making the pixels light or dark (or by giving them the appropriate colour).
2. High resolution displays use more pixels than low resolution.

APPLICATIONS: *of screens with high and low resolution*
1. **Computer Aided Design (CAD)**
   CAD enables the user to produce accurate and detailed drawings (see Unit 14.3). It requires a high resolution monitor to make sure that curves and straight lines are accurately represented.
2. **Teletext**
   Teletext pictures are received as part of the signals sent out by BBC and ITV television channels (see Unit 15.2). Teletext uses letters which are large and are

Chapter 5 Output of data

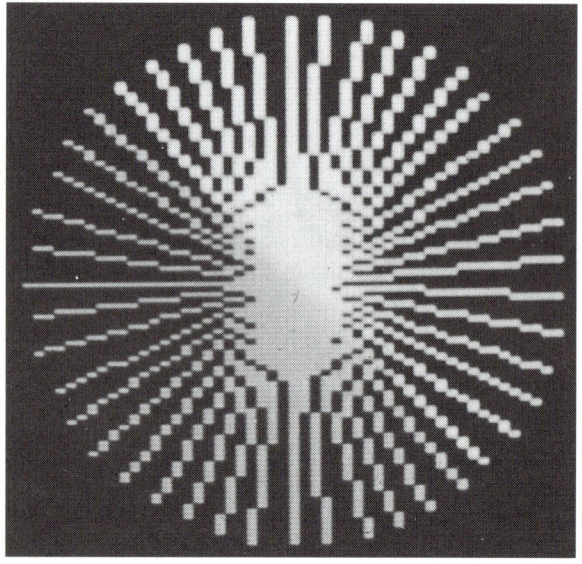

Fig. 5.1 A spoked pattern in monochrome on a low resolution screen

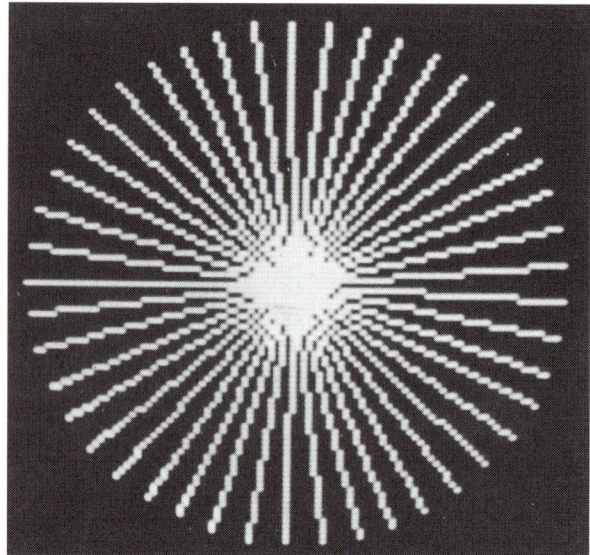

Fig. 5.2 The same pattern on a high resolution screen

made up from simple shapes. The graphics are made up from rectangular blocks of colour. A low resolution screen is suitable for Teletext and in fact a standard television screen is used for it.

ADVANTAGES: *of high resolution over low resolution*
1. Drawings can be produced more accurately and appear detailed.
2. Text can be read easily without eye strain.

DISADVANTAGES: *of high resolution*
1. A high resolution display uses more pixels and this uses more storage.
2. High resolution pictures take longer to process, e.g. it takes a very fast processor to animate a high resolution picture smoothly.
3. High resolution pictures need to be viewed on an expensive display screen or the extra detail is wasted.

ADVANTAGES: *of using colour*
1. Colour makes screens more attractive.
2. Colour can be used to highlight error messages and menu options, etc.
3. Colour is more restful on the eye than black and white.

DISADVANTAGES: *of using colour*
Screens with a lot of colours:
1. take up more storage;
2. take longer to process.

KEY TERMS *A **cursor** is a marker on the screen which shows the current position for printing or for entering data.*

Notes:
1. Often the cursor is in the shape of an arrow or a small rectangle.
2. With many programs the cursor flashes on and off so that it can be seen more easily.

Different types of screen

1. **Standard television set**
   An ordinary home television can be used for computer output. The pictures are not steady and have low resolution but they are adequate for Teletext output.
2. **Standard computer monitors**
   These have screens smaller than most television sets but of better resolution. Larger

monitors of better resolution are used for specialised applications such as CAD, desktop publishing and map making.

③ Liquid crystal displays (LCDs)
These are screens made up from two glass plates with liquid in between.

CHARACTERISTICS: *of LCDs*
① They are more limited in colours and resolution than standard computer monitors (although this is improving).
② They can be made small and very thin.
③ They can only be viewed from a very narrow angle.

APPLICATIONS: *of LCDs*
① As screens for small portable microcomputers.
② As displays for electronic calculators and watches.
③ On top of a camera to give information about the number of pictures taken, the speed of the film and the camera settings.

ADVANTAGES: *of screen output*
① High speed change of display.
② Display can include text, graphics and colours.
③ No noise.
④ No waste of paper.

DISADVANTAGE: *of screen output*
Needs a separate device to produce hard copy.

5.2 Printers

There are many different types of printer used for computer output.

Terms used for printers

KEY TERMS A **character printer** *prints one character at a time as the print head moves across the page.*
A **line printer** *prints a line at a time.*
A **page printer** *organises and prints a whole page at a time.*

KEY TERMS *The following two terms are used on ink jet and dot matrix printers.*
Draft quality *is a setting at which the printer produces output at a high speed but not at its best quality.*
Letter quality *is a setting at which printing is slower but the best quality the printer can produce. (On dot matrix printers this is usually referred to as NLQ – Near Letter Quality.)*
An **impact printer** *is one in which letters are formed by forcing the paper and the printing head together to print the characters.*

Notes on impact printers:
① Either
  - the printing head is pressed on to the paper,
  Or
  - a hammer hits the paper on to the character shape.
② An impact printer requires an inked ribbon next to the paper.

EXAMPLES: *of impact and non-impact printers*
① A dot matrix printer is an impact printer because the head strikes the ribbon on to the paper.
② Bubble jet and laser printers are non-impact printers.

Dot matrix printer

A **dot matrix printer** is an impact printer which has a vertical row of small pins in its print head. As the head moves across the paper the correct pins are pushed forward to form the shape of the letter required. (See Fig. 5.3.)

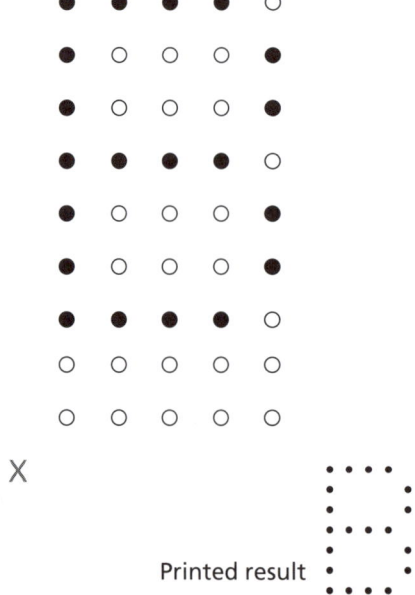

Fig. 5.3 9-pin dot pattern for the letter capital B

ADVANTAGES: *of dot matrix printers*
1. 9-pin models are cheap to buy and cheap to run.
2. 24-pin models give good quality.

DISADVANTAGES: *of dot matrix printers*
1. They are noisy, as they are impact printers.
2. The quality of printing is not as good as ink jet and laser printers.

Ink jet printer

An **ink jet printer** is a non-impact character printer. Very fine ink jets are directed at the paper. A version of the ink jet printer has become very popular as a printer for PCs and this is considered below.

ADVANTAGES: *of ink jet printers*
1. They are quiet.
2. Good quality output is produced.
3. There is little extra cost for colour printing.

DISADVANTAGES: *of ink jet printers*
1. A good quality paper is needed or the ink spreads.
2. The ink can be smudged.

Laser printer

A **laser printer** is a non-impact page printer. In the laser printer output is produced on a light-sensitive drum. The laser is a very narrow beam of light. It is directed very rapidly over the drum, being switched repeatedly on and off. Ink particles are then fused on to the paper wherever the laser beam hit the drum.

ADVANTAGES: *of laser printers*
1. Excellent print quality is produced.
2. They are quiet.

DISADVANTAGES: *of laser printers*
1. Expensive models are very fast but cheaper models are slow. The printer takes time to organise each page – repeats of the same page are produced quite quickly.
2. They are expensive to buy and run.

APPLICATIONS: *using a mixture of printers*

A school network

A school has two interconnected networks of microcomputers. One is in the business studies department. It is used mainly for word processing. The other is in the Information Technology Centre. The following printers were chosen.

The IT Centre has:
- Two ink jet printers. These are mainly used in draft mode at 200 characters a second although they can be switched to letter quality when students are handing in projects. These printers can also be switched to colour mode by special request.

The Business Studies department has:
- A laser printer for producing high quality typing. It produces about 6 pages a minute.
- An ink jet printer of the same type as the IT Centre but this is normally kept in letter quality mode. It does not have a colour option but instead it has a wider carriage so that it can take sheets of paper in landscape format (i.e. sideways).

5.3 Graphics and plotters

More and more computer output includes graphs, designs, maps, drawings and other graphical output. Increasingly high quality graphics can be produced on printers.

EXAMPLES: *of graphical output on printers*
1. Good quality maps can be produced on a fairly inexpensive printer.
2. More expensive printers can produce output of photographic quality.

Plotters are still required for high quality work.

KEY TERMS A **plotter (or graph plotter)** *is a device for producing graphical output on paper, particularly line drawings.*

Note:
On most plotters, characters can be produced but they have to be drawn by tracing out their shapes.

Types of plotter

Plotters may be classified as follows.
1. As **pen plotters** or as **penless plotters**.
   Penless plotters use various different technologies. At the moment high quality work for publication is done on electrostatic plotters.
2. Pen plotters are either **flat-bed plotters** (see Fig. 5.4) or **drum plotters** (see Fig. 5.5).

Flat-bed plotter

The paper is held stationary on a flat surface. For large plotters (sometimes they are several metres in length and width) the paper may be held in place by suction from underneath.

The pen is held above the paper and can move:
- up or down – when down it contacts the paper and draws lines;
- across the width in either direction;
- along the length in either direction.

By combining these movements lines can be drawn, broken or continuous, curved or straight, anywhere on the paper.

Drum plotter

The paper, usually a roll, is held on a drum which can be rotated backwards and forwards. The pen is held above the paper and can move:
- up (to move without drawing) or down (to draw);
- left and right across the paper.

Lines can be drawn anywhere on the paper by combining drum movements with pen movements.

Chapter 5 Output of data

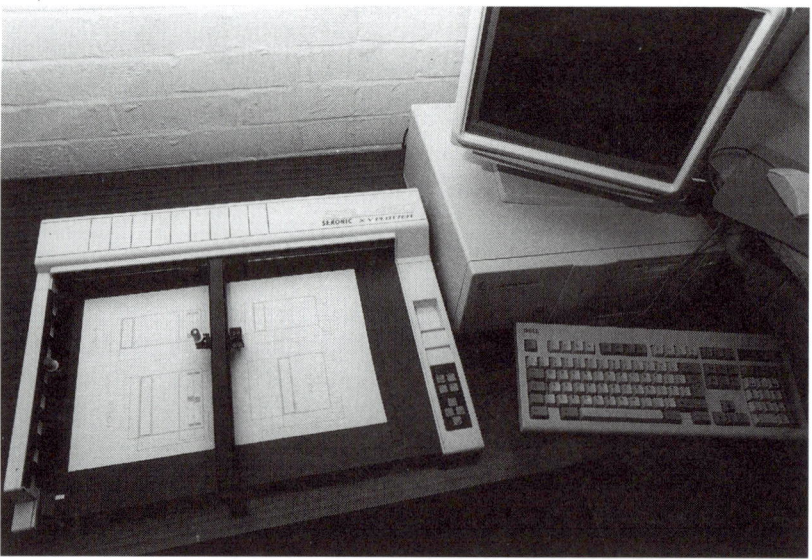

Fig. 5.4 A flat-bed plotter in use, driven by a microcomputer

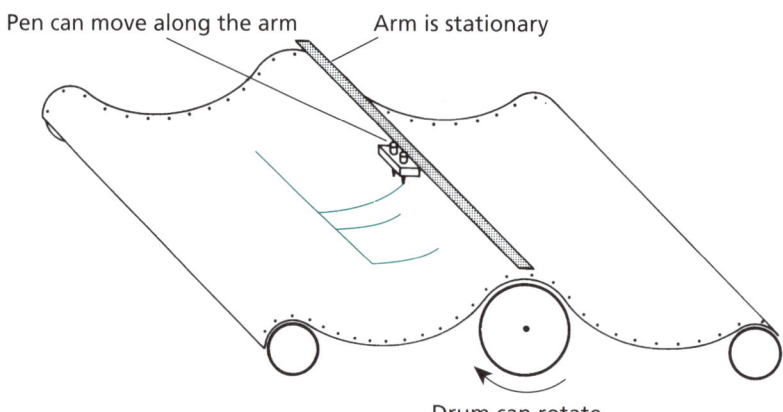

Fig. 5.5 A drum plotter

5.4 Other output methods

Output on to storage media

Media used include magnetic tape cartridges and discs. Data is output on to them:
1. to input it to a computer again at a later date;
2. to drive a piece of equipment off-line from the computer.

APPLICATION: *of computer output off-line*
An off-line plotter
Design engineers for a company produce new designs and store them on both hard discs and tape cartridges.
   The plotter used to produce the drawings has its own processor and tape unit.
   When a drawing is required, the appropriate cartridge is taken from a tape library and put into the plotter unit. The plotter's processor finds the drawing on the tape and plots it.

Computer output on microfiche or microfilm (COM)

KEY TERMS

COM stands for **Computer Output on Microfilm** which is much reduced output produced on high quality film.
   Microfiche is a rectangular sheet of microfilm large enough to contain a number of pages (or frames) of data – typically 30 to 300. It allows a large amount of data to be stored in a small space.

Voice synthesis

Voice output from computers is generally easier and more successful than voice recognition as a means of input. Voices can be successfully synthesised by storing word patterns as bit strings. When the computer wants to 'say' something the appropriate codes are sent to a 'voice response unit' which produces the sounds.

APPLICATIONS: *of voice synthesis*

1. **Communication without a terminal**
   Voice synthesis can be used to produce a response from a computer by telephone without the need for a modem or a terminal. Codes can be sent by pressing combinations of the buttons on the telephone and the computer replies with synthesised speech.
2. **Hand-held devices**
   A number of small hand-held devices are available which produce synthesised speech. They include:
   - A learning aid for small children which makes arithmetic problems more interesting. The device speaks the numbers which are pressed and makes encouraging suggestions.
   - A language translator. This can fit in a pocket and can translate several foreign languages.

ADVANTAGES: *of voice synthesis*

1. It can be accessed by telephone.
2. No reading ability is required by the user.

DISADVANTAGES: *of voice synthesis*

1. It is not suitable for noisy environments, or for quiet environments where other people are working.
2. There is no permanence – words not understood have to be repeated by the computer.
3. If words are repeated, the sounds are exactly the same. If you do not understand the message the first time you may well not understand it the second.

5.5 Choice of output method

When deciding on which output devices to obtain, an organisation has to consider:

1. whether the devices purchased will cope with the needs of users for:
   - speed of output;
   - quality of output;
   - range of different types of output;
   - noise level and environmental suitability.
2. the cost of:
   - the equipment;
   - running the device – e.g. printers need paper and ink cartridges;
   - maintenance – some devices are less robust than others.
3. adaptability – whether the equipment can be adapted to fit in with future needs.

A user will often decide on a combination of output devices.

APPLICATIONS: *using a combination of output devices*

1. A **designer** has:
   - a monitor of a graphical display unit to develop the design;
   - a laser printer for initial hard copies;
   - a large flat-bed plotter to produce the finished designs.
2. A **gas board** might have for its customer accounts:
   - monitors or VDUs (Visual Display Units) to check individual accounts;
   - an ink jet printer to print letters for customers and summaries for the management;
   - a line printer to produce the bills on preprinted fan-fold paper;
   - microfiche equipment for records of accounts which are more than two years old.

Quick test

1. What is the disadvantage of high resolution colour graphics?

2. Choose from the list *two* items which output data and do not input it:
   light pen   touch screen   flat-bed plotter   disc unit   liquid crystal display

3. Choose the output device or medium which would be most suitable for outputting data for long term storage:
   line printer   dot matrix printer   monitor   COM   flat-bed plotter   touch screen

4. Choose the output device or medium which would be most suitable for viewing designs before printing them:
   line printer   dot matrix printer   monitor   COM   flat-bed plotter   touch screen

5. Why is Teletext quite readable on an ordinary television screen?

6. Name a printer which would be suitable for each of the following tasks (the answers should all be different):
   (a) producing neat copies of a letter with no danger of smudging,
   (b) producing draft copies of a letter cheaply,
   (c) printing program listings quickly in a main computer room.

7. What is the disadvantage of voice output?

Summary

1. An **output device** receives data from the CPU and converts it into information or into further data.

2. Display screens are being increasingly used for computer output. Their advantages are:
   - high speed change of display;
   - display can include text, graphics and colours;
   - no noise;
   - no waste of paper.

3. Printer types include:
   - character printers;
   - line printers;
   - page printers.

4. The main types of printer for general work are:
   - dot matrix;
   - ink jet;
   - laser.

5.
   - The dot matrix is the cheapest printer to buy and run but gives the lowest quality.
   - The laser gives the best quality but is most expensive to buy and run.

6. Increasingly good quality graphics can be produced on printers but plotters are still needed for high quality work.

Chapter 6
Storage

6.1 Introduction to storage

Storage of data and programs is one of the most important features of an information processing system. This is done:
1. temporarily while a program is running;
2. long-term to preserve programs and data while not in use.

KEY TERMS To **write** data means to move it or copy it from the main store to backing store.
To **read** data means to move it or copy it from backing store to the main store.

Types of storage

Stores differ in:
- the speed with which they can be accessed;
- whether they can store data when the computer is not running;
- whether data on them can be changed;
- how data is stored.

The two main categories of storage are:
1. main store (see Unit 1.3 for a definition);
2. backing store.

KEY TERMS *Backing store is storage outside the CPU.*

It is necessary to have at least two types of store because:
1. the main store is needed:
    - to store the program currently being executed;
    - to hold data produced as the program is run;
    - to hold other data such as the contents of the screen.
2. the backing store is needed:
    - for long-term storage of data and programs;
    - for data and programs when there is not enough room in the main store.

6.2 Main store

CHARACTERISTICS: *of the main store*
1. The store is in the CPU.
2. Data can be written and read at very high speeds.
3. Data is transferred without any mechanical movement.
4. It is divided into locations. The computer can access any location directly using a unique number known as its **address**.
5. Main store usually contains two different types of memory:
    - **Read Only Memory (ROM)**;
    - **Random Access Memory (RAM)**.

Chapter 6 Storage

KEY TERMS — *Memory is another term for storage. It is usually used to describe the type of storage chips used in the main store.*
Read Only Memory (ROM) is memory which can be read from but not written to.
Random Access Memory (RAM) is memory which can be read from or written to.
*A **volatile store** is one which loses its data when the power is switched off.*

CHARACTERISTICS: *of ROM and RAM*

ROM is permanent:
- data and programs on it cannot be changed;
- it is not volatile. If ROM was volatile it would lose its data and it would not be possible to write it back.

RAM is temporary:
- its contents can be changed;
- it is usually volatile although some microcomputers have RAM which is maintained by batteries.

APPLICATIONS: *of RAM*

1. As the working store of the computer – as a temporary store for the program which is running and the data it is using.
2. To store data being transferred to and from peripherals.
3. To store the contents of the screen.

of ROM

To store frequently used programs essential to the normal running of the computer. These usually include a small program which runs when the computer is switched on to get it started.

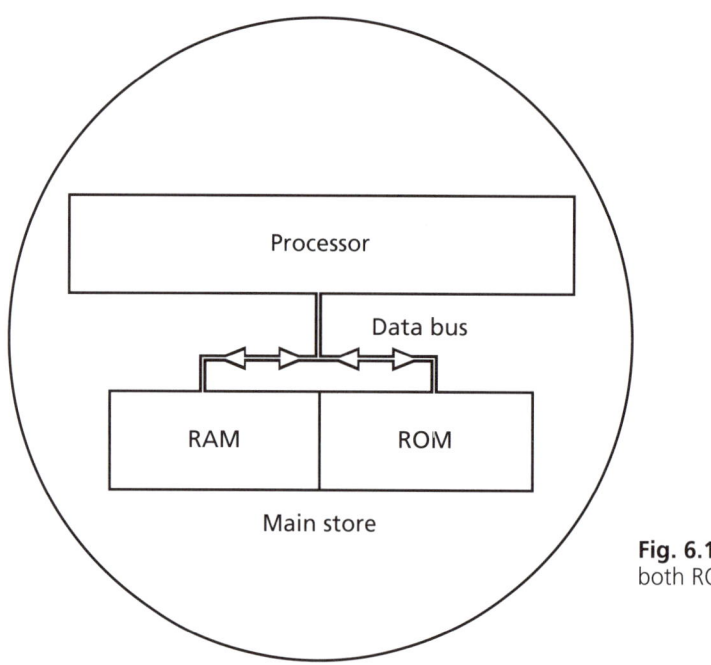

Fig. 6.1 The CPU containing both ROM and RAM

of ROM and RAM outside the CPU

In a computer printer

A printer often contains:
1. some RAM to store the next set of data to be printed;
2. some ROM to store:
   - programs to direct it how to print the data;
   - the shapes of the different printing fonts.

APPLICATIONS: *using ROM and RAM*

A programmable washing machine

Like many other machines these days, a modern washing machine contains a processor which controls the wash. The processor needs ROM to permanently store the control program and RAM to store temporary data created by the program.

6.3 Backing stores

KEY TERMS A storage **medium** is the material on which the data is stored, e.g. magnetic tape, floppy disc, CD-ROM.

A storage **drive** is the piece of equipment which rotates the storage medium and accesses the data on it.

A storage medium is **exchangeable** if it can be removed from the drive and replaced by another one of the same type, e.g. floppy disc, CD-ROM, tape cartridge.

CHARACTERISTICS: *of backing stores*
1. Data is usually accessed using read/write heads. These transfer the data while the medium rotates in the drive.
2. Access to backing store is slower than to main store.
3. They are non-volatile. The data is stored on the medium until it is deleted.

Backing stores are either **serial access** or **direct access**.

KEY TERMS In **direct access store** any data item can be accessed without reading other data first, e.g. magnetic discs.

In **serial access store** all data before the required item has to be read first before the data can be accessed, e.g. magnetic tape.

The main types of direct access backing stores used on PC systems are:
1. hard discs;
2. floppy discs;
3. CD-ROMs.

6.4 Magnetic discs

KEY TERMS A **hard disc** is a rigid magnetic disc.
A **floppy disc** is a light, flexible magnetic disc held in a protective jacket.

Magnetic discs

CHARACTERISTICS: *of magnetic discs*
1. A typical magnetic disc has two surfaces or sides (although sometimes disc packs on mainframe computers are made up of a number of discs).
2. Data can be written to or read from the disc.
3. Each surface holds data in circular tracks. Each track is divided into equal sections called sectors. (See Fig. 6.2.)
4. The discs are direct access. The track number and sector number are used as an address to find where data is on the disc.

CHARACTERISTICS: *of hard discs*
1. The discs are usually fixed in the drive. Each is built into a sealed unit to prevent contamination by dust and moisture.
2. Access to data is far faster than access to floppy discs.
3. Hard discs store far more data than floppy discs. The capacity of one disc is often several hundred megabytes.
4. They are more reliable than floppy discs – there is better protection against dirt.

APPLICATIONS: *of hard discs*
1. Storage of the operating system, applications software and users' files for a PC.
2. Storage of the operating system, software and files for a local area network.
3. Storage of work waiting to be printed on a network printer.

Chapter 6 Storage

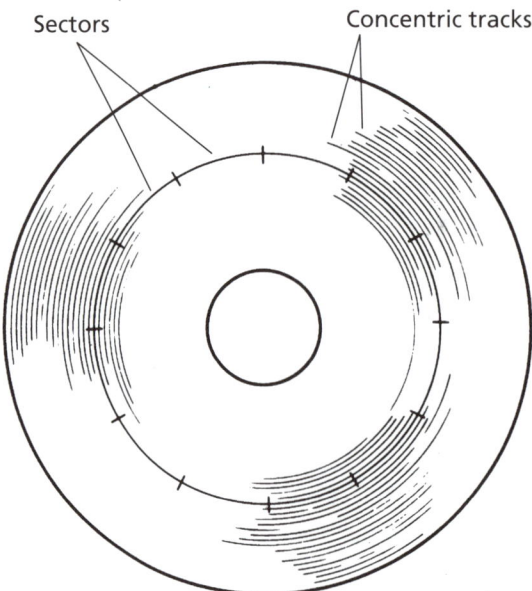

Fig. 6.2 How data is stored on the surface of a magnetic disc

CHARACTERISTICS: *of floppy discs*
1. Diameters vary but 3½ inches is the most common.
2. The amount of data stored varies but 1.44 megabytes is common.
3. Access to data is much slower than for hard discs.
4. The discs are exchangeable and easy to transport.
5. The disc is protected by a stiff plastic cover. This has a hole for the read/write heads which is protected by a sprung metal cover.
6. The data on the disc can be protected by sliding a small write protect tab which prevents the contents of the disc from being changed.

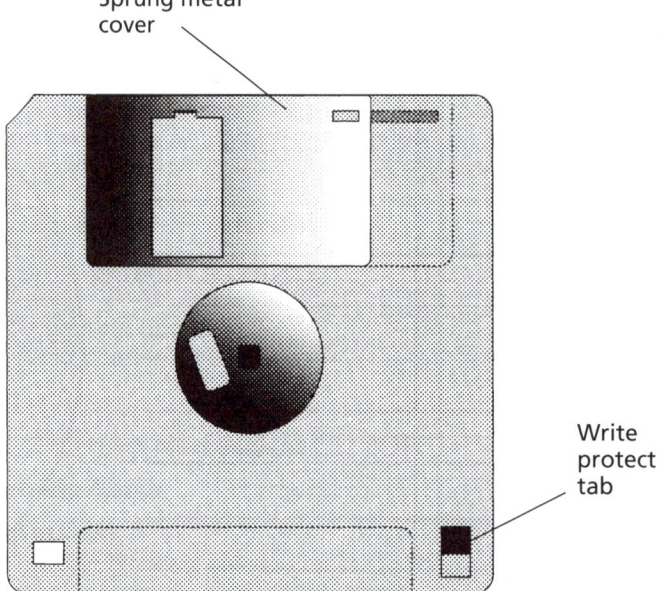

Fig. 6.3 A floppy disc showing the write protect tab and sprung metal cover

APPLICATIONS: *of floppy discs*
1. Storage of the operating system, applications software and users' files for a PC with no hard disc.
2. Back-up storage for a PC with a hard disc.

Note:
A computer with a hard disc has to have a floppy disc or a CD-ROM drive as well or it is difficult to load software into it. You also need floppy discs to carry data from one place to another.

76

ADVANTAGE: *of floppy discs*
They are light and portable.

ADVANTAGES: *of magnetic discs*
over tape
There is direct access – data can be accessed from anywhere on a disc equally quickly. This makes it suitable for information retrieval. Tapes are not suitable for this.
over compact discs
Data can be written to magnetic discs.

6.5 Compact discs

All types of compact disc (CD) can be read by a computer if you have the right player, interfaces and software. These include:
1. music CDs – standard music discs;
2. photo CDs – discs containing photographs;
3. CD-ROMs – compact discs designed for use as computer storage.

KEY TERMS *CD-ROM (Compact Disc Read Only Memory) is a form of compact disc used for the storage of computer data.*

CHARACTERISTICS: *of CD-ROMs*
1. A CD-ROM is a compact disc normally of about 12 cm in diameter. CD-ROMs of other sizes are available, e.g. electronic books which are 8 cm in diameter.
2. Data is written to the disc using a powerful laser beam to burn patterns in the surface. Data is read back using a relatively low-power laser to detect the patterns in the surface.
3. The discs are exchangeable and easy to transport.
4. Access to data is faster than access to floppy discs but slower than hard discs.
5. CD-ROMs store far more data than floppy discs. The capacity of one disc is usually about 550 megabytes but may be more.
6. Usually data is written on to the disc before it is sold. After that data can be read from the disc but not written to it.

Note:
New types of CD are being produced which can be written to by the user. These include the **WORM** disc (**Write Once Read Many**). This can be written to but each part of it can only have data written to it once.

APPLICATIONS: *of CDs in computers*
1. **Music CDs**
If you are not using the CD-ROM drive on your computer for anything else you can insert a music CD into the drive and listen to music while you are working on the computer.
This only works if you have the right software. This is a program which:
- converts data from a music CD into sound;
- will multitask with the other programs you are running (see Unit 2.7 for multitasking).
2. **Photo CDs**
Many shops run a service to put up to 100 photographs on to a CD for you. If you have the right type of CD player you can then view the pictures through a television. If you have the right software for your computer you can put the photo CD into your CD-ROM drive and look at the photos on your computer screen. This has the advantage that the screen is of a good quality. You can also use the computer to make changes to the photographs.

KEY TERMS *Multi-media means presentation on a computer of information combining animated and still graphics, sound and text.*

APPLICATIONS: *of CD-ROMs*

CD-ROMs can store about 550 megabytes of data. Because they store so much data, CD-ROMs are very good for multi-media presentations. They can be used to store:
- text – up to about 50 million words;
- sound – up to 72 minutes of sounds or music;
- still pictures – between 100 and 10 000, depending on how detailed they are;
- sequences of pictures – animations or video sequences.

CD-ROMs usually come supplied with software to help search through the data on them.

① Books

These range from:
- Just the text of a large number of famous books, e.g. *Greatest Books Collection* by World Library which contains the works of Shakespeare, Dickens, Conan-Doyle, Mark Twain and others.

  Obviously if you wanted to read any of these books you would not sit at a computer to do it – you would obtain the actual book from the library. However, the computer does give you a way of searching quickly through them. You can search for quotations you know or have been given, for the names of people or you can browse.
- Sets of books with illustrations, e.g. *Illustrated Bible*, *Illustrated Shakespeare* and *Illustrated Sherlock Holmes* all by Animated Pixels and *Jane Austen* by Nimbus/Harper Collins.

② Information sources
- Newspapers, e.g. about 250 000 articles from *The Times* stretching over 150 years are stored on one disc.
- Encyclopaedias and dictionaries – many of the encyclopaedias available are multi-media. Not only can you read about famous people but you can see pictures of them and listen to speeches they made or music they wrote.
- Databases, e.g. there are CD-ROMs with facts about all the monarchs of Europe, all the countries of the world, or jobs and education opportunities for school leavers.

③ Graphics
- Works of art – some discs contain hundreds of paintings as well as information about the artists.
- Clip-Art – these discs give you a library of pictures you can choose from to load into a drawing or painting package.
- Film clips, e.g. there are discs of animals in motion and birds in flight.

ADVANTAGES: *of CD-ROMs*

over hard discs

CDs can be carried easily and without damage.

over floppy discs

① A computer can read a CD-ROM faster than it can read a floppy disc.
② CD-ROMs store far more data than floppy discs.

DISADVANTAGE: *of CD-ROMs*

At the moment data cannot be written on to CD-ROMs without very expensive equipment.

6.6 Magnetic tape

Magnetic tape is the main type of serial access store.

Increasingly tape is being used in the form of a **cartridge** about the size of a music cassette.

CHARACTERISTICS: *of magnetic tape*

① Magnetic tape has serial access – an item can only be accessed by working through all the items before it.

❷ Tapes store a large amount of data for their size.
❸ The tapes are light and compact, easy to store for long periods and are easy to carry.

APPLICATION: *of magnetic tape*

Tape streamer on a file server

A school has a network of PCs controlled by a file server with a hard disc drive. The pupils all have their own accounts on the file server and store all their work on it.

Attached to the file server is a small magnetic tape unit called a tape streamer. This accepts tape cartridges which each store up to 160 megabytes of data.

Every week the technician in charge of the network backs up pupils' and teachers' work on to a tape cartridge. To do this she runs an 'archive' program which copies important files. She has four tapes and always uses the oldest.

If a file is corrupted or deleted accidentally it can be recovered even if it was lost up to four weeks ago.

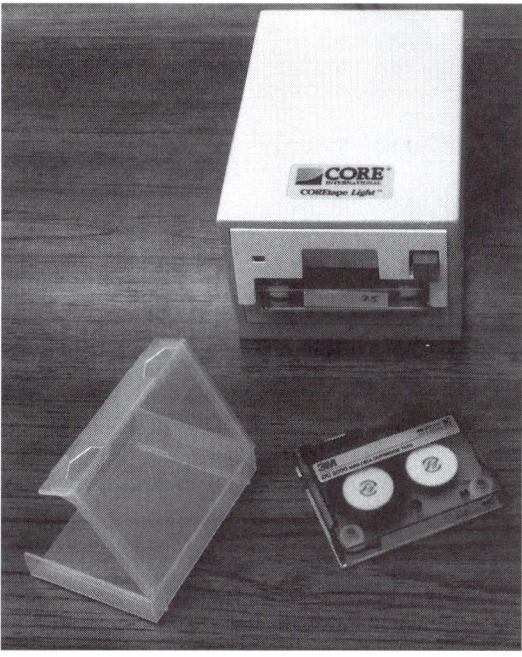

Fig. 6.4 Tape cartridge and tape streamer

Note:
At first the school used floppy discs for this backup. However, this used up a lot of discs and the technician had to be there all the time to change the discs over.

ADVANTAGE: *of magnetic tape*
Tape is light and compact and easy to carry and yet it stores far more data than floppy discs.

Quick test

1 Which *two* of the following can be used for backing store?

   ROM   magnetic tape   RAM   hard disc

2 If a computer only has one type of backing store which of the following would be best?

   magnetic tape   CD-ROM   floppy disc   hard disc

3 If you have an important piece of software on a floppy disc how can you make sure you do not overwrite it?

Chapter 6 Storage

4 If you wanted to buy a large dictionary in computerised form what type of storage medium would you expect it to be on? Why?

5 Name *two* types of store which are normally read only – one inside the CPU and one outside.

6 Which is the best storage medium for multi-media applications?

7 Why are CD-ROMs usually bought with data already on them?

Summary

1 Any system needs to store both programs and data and requires:
   - a main store for fast access storage;
   - at least one type of backing store for long term storage.

2 Main store usually contains two different types of memory:
   - **Read Only Memory** (ROM), which is permanent and its contents cannot be changed;
   - **Random Access Memory** (RAM) which is a temporary store used to store the current program and data and other items such as the screen contents.

3 Backing store:
   - is usually accessed using read/write heads;
   - does not allow such fast access as main store;
   - stores its data until it is deleted.

4 The main types of direct access backing stores are:
   - hard discs;
   - floppy discs;
   - CD-ROMs.

5
   - Hard discs are usually fixed in the drive in a sealed unit.
   - They are far faster than floppy discs and store more data.

6
   - Floppy discs are exchangeable and easy to transport.
   - 3½-inch discs are protected by a stiff plastic cover and data on the disc can be protected by a write protect tab.

7
   - CD-ROMs are exchangeable and easy to transport.
   - Access to data is faster than to floppy discs but slower than to hard discs.
   - CD-ROMs store far more data than floppy discs.
   - CD-ROMs are mainly Read Only. The data is written before the disc is sold.

8 Magnetic tape is the main type of serial access store.

Chapter 7
Data files

7.1 Facts about files

KEY TERMS The term **file** is used to describe any data or program stored on a backing store such as a disc or a tape.

EXAMPLES: *of files*
When they have been saved any of the following can be regarded as a file.
1. A computer program.
2. A piece of text stored by a word processor.
3. A spreadsheet.
4. A computer drawing.

KEY TERMS A **data file** is an organised collection of data. It usually consists of a number of separate parts called records.

A **record** is a sub-division of a file. It consists of a set of items of data which together can be treated as a unit. These items all relate to one person or object. Each record in the file is similar to the others in the way it is set out.

EXAMPLES: *of data files and records*
School records
A school administration computer stores a number of data files including:
1. A pupil file. Each record in this file holds the data on one pupil.
2. A teacher file. Each record in this file contains all the data about one teacher.

KEY TERMS A **field** is an area of a record reserved for one particular type of data item. Each field contains one data item.

An **item** of data here means the smallest piece of data that would be dealt with separately – a single name or a single number, etc.

EXAMPLE: *of records, fields and items*
Each **record** of a file of student records has the following **fields**:
Surname   Forenames   Birth Date   Address
One of the records in this file is:
WALTERS   DAVID ANDREW   21/02/75   3, BURNS RD, BISHOPSWICK
The Birth Date **field** contains the **item** 21/02/75.

EXAMPLE: *A file stored on the Police National Computer*
The file contains data on stolen cars. One **record** would be all the data on one car. The **items** in one record would include the car's:
- registration number;
- legal owner;
- make;
- colour.

The **fields** containing these items are called REGIST, OWNER, MAKE and COLOUR.

ADVANTAGES: *of using files on backing store*
1. Files are permanent and readily accessible.
2. Files can be very large and the main store may be too small for the amount of data being processed.

Fixed and variable length records

KEY TERMS A *fixed length* record is one which contains a set number of character positions.

A *variable length* record is one for which the number of characters in it is not determined beforehand.

In the same way it is possible to have **fixed length fields** or **variable length fields**. With variable length fields or records it is necessary to have a special character at the end of the data. This is called a **separator** and is used by the computer to detect the end of the field or record.

ADVANTAGES: *of variable over fixed length fields or records*

1. There is less waste of storage space. Although a variable length field has a separator as an extra character, fixed length fields have a lot of wasted space when the item is shorter than the field.
2. A variable length field can store an item however long it is.

ADVANTAGES: *of fixed over variable length fields or records*

1. Computer operations such as searching can be carried out quickly.
2. Allocation of storage space is more straightforward.
3. Updating of files is simpler – if one record is changed it still takes up the same amount of space, so other records do not have to be moved to make room for it.

Key field

KEY TERMS Usually one particular field of each record of a file contains an item which is used to identify the record. This field is called the **key field**, and the item in it is called the **key** to that record.

The value in the key field must be **unique** to that record. This means that the keys must all be different from one another, so that there is no confusion over which record is which.

EXAMPLES: *of field lengths and keys*

1. A stock file for the sales department of a garden centre. The fields are fixed length and are as follows:

Field name	Number of characters	Use
CATNO	6	catalogue number
PLANTNAME	20	name of plant
MIN	2	minimum height (metres)
MAX	2	maximum height (metres)
PRICE	5	price (pence)
STOCK	3	number in stock

    The key field is CATNO and the records are stored in order of these keys. Four of the records are as follows:

    ```
    002103ABIES GEORGEI        2  3  250  23
    002104ABIES GEORGEI        3  4  350  14
    002113ABIES GRANDIS        2  3  250   3
    002114ABIES LASIOCARPA     3  4  420   6
    ```

2. A program written in the language BASIC is stored on a floppy disc. Three lines of this program are as follows:

    80 FOR *I* = 1 TO 20
    90 PRINT *N*$
    100 NEXT *I*

    This program is a file with variable length records. Each line of the program is a record. It has two variable length fields – the line number and the BASIC statement.

    The key item is the line number and is used by the computer to search for a line when editing or running the program.

7.2 Storage of files

KEY TERMS

To *create a file* means to organise data into a file, e.g. when fields are set up in a database file and records are keyed into it.

To *save* a file means to copy all the records of the file from the main store on to a backing store.
To *load* a file means to read all the records of the file from backing store into the main store.
To *open* a file means to prepare it so that data can be read from it or written to it.
To *close* a file is the procedure which is necessary when the user has finished using a file.

Notes:

1. The terms 'load' and 'open' are used loosely as if they mean the same thing. Strictly a file can be open even if none of its records have been loaded into the main store.
2. As well as 'save' and 'open' many applications programs also allow you to import data from other software and export data for other software (see Unit 9.6).
3. Choose file names carefully:
   - make sure you obey the rules for file names – usually you cannot use spaces, commas etc. in a file name;
   - use a name which helps you remember what the file is, e.g. TVSURVEY is a better name than DATA2.

Directories

KEY TERMS

A *directory* is a small file on a disc which is used by the operating system to locate the other files on the disc.

The directory contains a list of names of files and the information needed to access those files on the disc. The information given in a directory can include:
- the size of the file in bytes,
- the time and date the file was written.

Note:

The word **directory** is also used in other ways.

1. The area of a disc where files are stored is called a directory. The main directory on a disc is called the **root** directory. A **sub-directory** is a part of the root directory which can be accessed separately.
2. A list of all the files in an area with information about them is also called a directory. A simple list of files without any information is usually called a **catalogue**.

```
C:\AJR\CH1TO9> dir

 Volume in drive C is RACKHAMS C
 Volume Serial Number is 0A14-11D4
 Directory of C:\AJR\CH1TO9

IS3        WP        61305  14/01/95   18:03
IS2        WP        91014  14/01/95   23:02
IS7        WP        77695  14/01/95   15:40
IS1        WP        49593  11/01/95   17:14
IS4        WP        71580  14/01/95   23:04
IS6        WP        43748  14/01/95   11:53
IS9        WP        71747  14/01/95   15:20
IS8        WP        48430  14/01/95   16:01
IS5        WP        57343  14/01/95   15:12
       9 file(s)         572455 bytes
                       61566976 bytes free
```

Fig. 7.1 A screen showing a directory

Disc formats

KEY TERMS

To *format* a disc means to add control information to it so that it is ready for storing files.

The operating system locates files on a disc using a numbering system for the tracks and

sectors. Usually a disc is formatted by running a 'format' program which:
- writes track and sector numbers on the disc;
- creates an empty directory.

Notes:
① You cannot use a new disc until it has been formatted.
② Only blank or unwanted discs should be formatted as the operation will effectively erase any data already on them.
③ Different operating systems use different disc formats. A disc formatted on one computer will not necessarily be read by another operating system. However, sometimes a program can be run to accept the other disc format.

Using the operating system to handle files

A computer's operating system (see Unit 9.3) usually allows users to operate on their files interactively. Options usually include:
① create and access sub-directories;
② obtain a list of a given directory;
③ save, load, delete, rename and copy files.

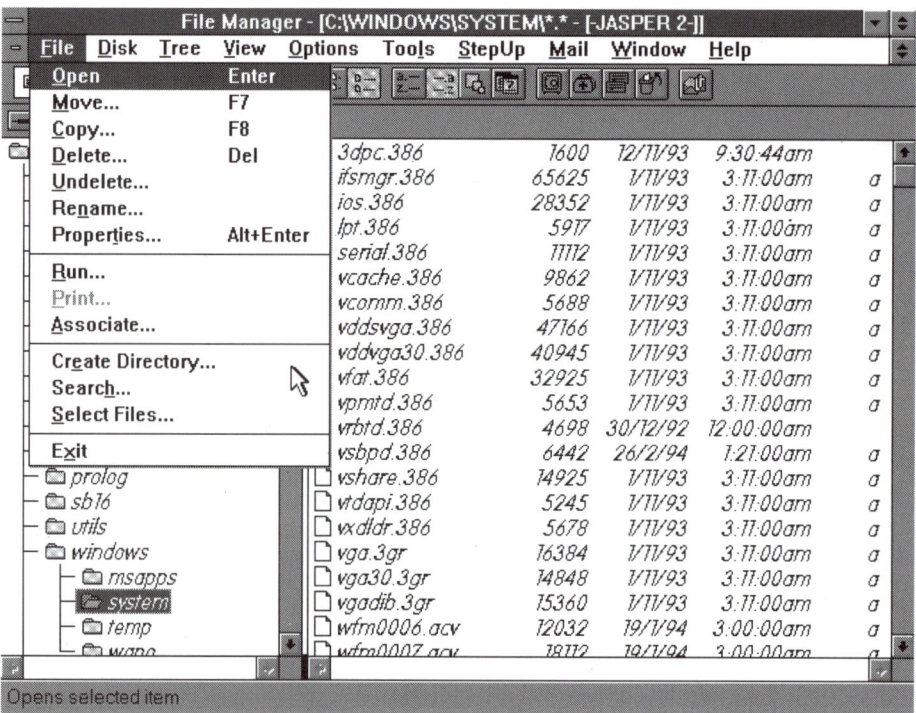

Fig. 7.2 A file menu showing options

Notes:
① When a user deletes a file it can no longer be used. Usually the file is not actually erased from the disc. The reference to it is erased from the directory and the space on the disc is made available for other data.
② When a user renames a file, the name of it is changed in the directory. The file itself is not altered.
③ When a file is copied, it is read into the main store, in sections if necessary, and a copy of it is written onto a new disc or another part of the same disc. After the operation there are two identical files, although the user may choose to give the new file a different name.

Reasons for using the different file operations

Sub-directories are usually created:
① to keep files on different topics separate from one another;
② when there are so many files in a directory that you cannot see them all on the screen at once.

Copying a file is usually done:
- ❶ to make a second copy of a file in case the original file is corrupted or accidentally deleted (see Unit 8.2), e.g. you might copy a file from your school network on to a floppy disc;
- ❷ to help move a file from one directory to another. Some systems do not have a 'move' instruction. It is necessary to make a copy of the file and then delete the original version.

Deleting is usually done:
- ❶ as part of a file moving process after a file has been copied;
- ❷ as part of tidying up, particularly if there is a shortage of storage space, e.g. a student is only allocated say 2 megabytes of storage on the network hard disc. He or she could delete old letters and assignments, backup files, temporary files, etc.

Files are renamed:
- ❶ if the present name of a file does not help you to remember what it is;
- ❷ if a file is to be changed but a copy of the old version is still needed.

7.3 Types of file

KEY TERMS

*The method of **organisation** of a file refers to:*
- ❶ *the way in which the records are arranged within the file;*
- ❷ *the method of working out where each record is stored in the file.*

*The method of **access** to a file refers to the way in which a program reads data from a file or writes data to it.*

Different methods of access to files

KEY TERMS

*A **serial access** file has data stored on it in the order in which it was written. Each new record goes at the end of the file. To read a record from the file it is necessary to read through all the preceding records first.*

*A **sequential access** file has data stored on it in the order of the data in a key field.*

KEY TERMS

*A **direct access** file is one where any record can be accessed without having to access other records first. This is also known as **random access**.*

Notes:
- ❶ Files stored on a tape cartridge are always serial or sequential access. A direct access file would involve too much movement of the tape backwards and forwards.
  Direct access files can only be stored on a direct access medium (such as magnetic disc).
- ❷ The term 'sequential' is sometimes loosely applied to ordinary serial files.

ADVANTAGES: *of direct access over sequential*
- ❶ Selected records can be accessed far more quickly from direct access files.
- ❷ Records can be accessed in any chosen order.
- ❸ Records do not have to be put into any particular order before the file is created.

ADVANTAGES: *of sequential access over direct*
- ❶ Sequential files can be stored on magnetic tape as well as on discs.
- ❷ It is usually easier to write programs to handle sequential files.

ADVANTAGE: *of sequential access over serial*
Often operations are carried out involving two files both with the same key field. This is made relatively easy with sequential files because both are in the same order, e.g. using a transaction file to update a master file (see Unit 7.4).

Reasons for choosing different methods of access

The choice of method may depend on:

❶ the number of records to be accessed

If not many records are to be accessed, direct access should be used. Sequential files would be inefficient for a small number of records but better if most of the records are involved.

❷ the size of the file
- For a large file sequential searches take a long time and direct access is better.
- For a small file the time delay is not important and a sequential file is acceptable.

❸ whether or not the application is interactive
- Sequential access is often suitable for batch applications.
- On-line applications such as information retrieval usually need direct access.

❹ the type of storage medium being used

On magnetic tape files have to be serial or sequential – direct access to tape files is not practical.

APPLICATION: *of both direct and sequential access to a file*
Service records for a lift repair firm

The situation

Engineers from a lift repair firm service the lifts in buildings and keep records of what they do.

Files

The firm has a computer system and the service records are stored on an index sequential file. The data is stored in the order of the dates on which the services take place. An index is held in the computer's main store which shows where each record is stored.

EXAMPLE: A typical record includes the date, building, name of customer, address and type of contract (3 or 6 months):

11/04/95 SABRE HOTEL   MORLEY FOODS   BRYANT SQUARE, MOSSTOWN   6

What the computer does

- **Searching**

  If the computer is given a date it searches the index to find whereabouts the records are for that day and retrieves them using direct access. Searches for any other data, such as a firm's name or an address are done using sequential access.

- **List of calls for a particular day (direct access)**

  When working out a day's work for the engineers a list is produced of all the lifts which should be serviced on that day. The lifts are on either 6-month or 3-month contracts. The computer checks only the two dates, 6 months and 3 months before that day. It then prints out a list of all the 6-month contracts on the first date and all the 3-month contracts on the second date.

- **Records of calls to a particular building (sequential access)**

  To list all the repair and service calls made to a particular building, sequential access is used. The computer reads the whole file, a record at a time. It checks the second field in each record for the building in question. Each time the right name appears that record is printed out.

12/7/95 **Williams Lift Services** CR/1

Call Record for SABRE HOTEL, Bryant Square, Mosstown
Between 30/6/94 and 30/6/95

Date	Type of Call	Engineer
13/10/94	6 month	Brewer
29/12/94	Emergency	Wilkins
25/02/95	24 hour	Brewer
11/04/95	6 month	Brewer

Fig. 7.3 List of calls to Sabre Hotel

7.4 Updating files

KEY TERMS

To **update** a file means to alter it with new information.
Updating can involve:
1. **insertion** – adding new records to a file;
2. **deletion** – removing existing records from the file;
3. **amendment** – changing the items within existing records.

A file can be updated:
1. **interactively** – the file is updated on-line one record at a time. This is done by a keyboard operator using a file updating program;
2. **by batch processing** – another file is prepared off-line of all the changes to be made to the main file. An updating run in batch mode then compares the two files and makes the changes.

KEY TERMS

A **master file** is a file used as a reference for a particular computer application. It may be updated when necessary.

A **transaction file** is a file of temporary data which has been prepared in order to update a master file. It contains details of all records which are to be added, deleted or changed.

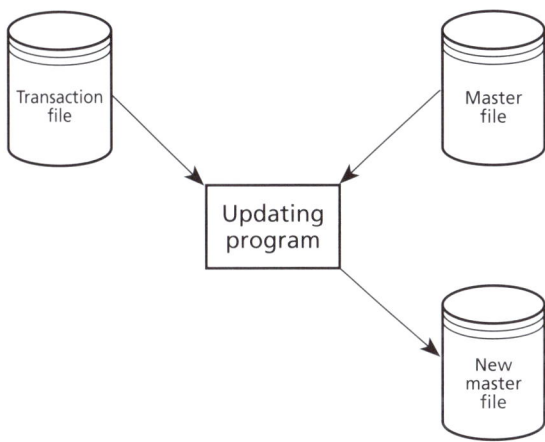

Fig. 7.4 Using a transaction file to update a master file

ADVANTAGE: *of interactive updating*
Changes are made quickly and simply.

ADVANTAGE: *of updating using a transaction file*
The transaction file is a record of the changes which have been made. It is less likely that errors will be made. If they are made it is easier to check up on them and put them right.

Steps in updating a sequential file using a transaction file

1. The transaction file is prepared containing all the updating information.
2. The records on this file are sorted into the same order as the records on the master file. This is done by having both files arranged with their keys in ascending order.
3. An updating program is run which:
   - reads the master file and the transaction file one record at a time;
   - writes the new records to an updated master file. The old master file is not changed.

Notes:
1. The old master file is not changed because:
   - it is not practical to try to insert, change or delete records on an existing sequential file, particularly on tape;
   - the old master file can still be useful. If there is an error in the transaction file then it can be corrected. The update run can then be repeated with the old master file.
2. The files are arranged with their keys in the same order to save time. If they were in a different order then every time a record was read from the transaction file, the computer would have to search right through the master file for it.

Chapter 7 Data files

APPLICATION: *master and transaction files*
Updating prices in shops
A file holds details of the goods stored by a chain of food shops. Each record consists of: product code, name of goods, price, minimum number to be held in stock. This file is the master file. Another file is prepared containing the product code and new price for some of the goods on the master file. This is the transaction file and it is used to update the prices on the master file.

APPLICATION: *updating sequential access files*
A payroll application
Files
For a particular payroll application the main file of employee details is stored on magnetic tape. Each record contains the details of one employee including an employee number which can be used as a key.
What the computer does
The main operations to be done are:
1. weekly pay run – the computer goes through the employees in sequence working out their pay;
2. update run – a file of changes is produced in employee number order and the computer goes through this file and the main file in sequence, making changes to the main file.

Note:
It does not matter for these operations that individual records cannot be accessed quickly. In the weekly pay run every record in the file is processed anyway.

7.5 Other operations on files

Searches

KEY TERMS
To **search** a file means to scan it methodically looking for a given item.
A **linear search** is a search in which each record is read in turn and checked for the item. If the end of the file is reached without finding the required item then the search has failed (see also Unit 11.4 for examples and definitions of query and match).

EXAMPLES:
1. Word processor and editor programs allow the user to search for a word in a passage of text, and to replace it with another word if necessary (see Unit 10.6).
2. File enquiry or 'database' packages are available which allow the user to search a file for selected items (see Unit 11.4).

Sorts

KEY TERMS
The computing word **sort** means to rearrange data into order. The user decides:
- which fields are used for sorting and
- what rules are used to determine the new order.

A **numeric** sort is one where the records are sorted according to the value in a number field.
An **alphabetic** sort is one where the sort field contains words or names.
A file can be sorted into **ascending** or **descending** order.
Ascending order means the list starts with the lowest and works up to the highest.
Descending order means the list starts with the highest and works down to the lowest.

Files may be sorted for the following reasons:
1. File operations on two or more files are simpler if the files are in the same order (see Unit 7.4).
2. An operation on a serial file may be easier if the keys are in order (e.g. searching for a record if the key is known).
3. People reading files printed out on paper find them easier to use if they are in order.

KEY TERMS
To **merge** two files is to interleave their records to form one file.

If two sequential files, with their records in key order, are merged then the resulting file will still have its records in key order.

APPLICATION: *of file merging*

The parts department of a garage

A firm selling car parts has a master file of all the stock. Each record contains details of one part. The key item in each record is the part number and the file is stored sequentially in order of the part numbers.

When a new car model is introduced, a file is supplied to the firm detailing all the new parts. This file is then merged with the existing master file to produce a new file which includes parts for the new car.

EXAMPLE: *sorting and merging of files*

For the two files A and B, the first item of each record is an account number which is to be taken as the key by which they are sequenced. The other fields are Name and Balance of account. The files are:

File A
256023	A.F.SMITH	234.56
403214	J.P.JONES	156.25
207888	L.C.JACKSON	2478.00
365142	P.JONES	89.50

File B
864512	P.R.TAYLOR	105.23
956421	A.FREEMAN	325.20
125642	A.MAHMOUD	1025.60
320147	P.R.WEBER	68.25
403215	M.MACGAUTREY	512.00

1. File A when sorted in order of the keys is:

207888	L.C.JACKSON	2478.00
256023	A.F.SMITH	234.56
365142	P.JONES	89.50
403214	J.P.JONES	156.25

File B when sorted is:

125642	A.MAHMOUD	1025.60
320147	P.R.WEBER	68.25
403215	M.MACGAUTREY	512.00
864512	P.R.TAYLOR	105.23
956421	A.FREEMAN	325.20

2. The two files when merged give:

125642	A.MAHMOUD	1025.60
207888	L.C.JACKSON	2478.00
256023	A.F.SMITH	234.56
320147	P.R.WEBER	68.25
365142	P.JONES	89.50
403214	J.P.JONES	156.25
403215	M.MACGAUTREY	512.00
864512	P.R.TAYLOR	105.23
956421	A.FREEMAN	325.2

7.6 An application of files – stock control

KEY TERMS *The **stock** of a shop or firm means all the goods it has for sale. **Stock control** means managing sensibly the amount of goods in stock.*

The aims of stock control are to:
1. keep enough of each item in stock so that it does not run out;
2. avoid having too much of any item.

Chapter 7 Data files

The main jobs of a stock control system are:

① to keep a check on exactly what goods are in stock;

② to work out what goods are selling and to fix maximum and minimum stock levels for each item;

③ to reorder goods to replace the items which are sold so that stocks are kept between the maximum and minimum levels.

EXAMPLE: *stock control in a chain of photographic shops*

The situation

The shops deal mainly in cameras and photographic materials such as films. They also sell specialised items used for photography such as tripods and camera bags. The company has a computer at its head office, which has a warehouse adjoining it. There is a POS terminal in each shop and a terminal in the warehouse.

The computer controls the stock in the shops and in the warehouse (Fig. 7.5). The shops are supplied by a delivery twice weekly from the warehouse. The company orders goods to stock the warehouse from a number of different suppliers.

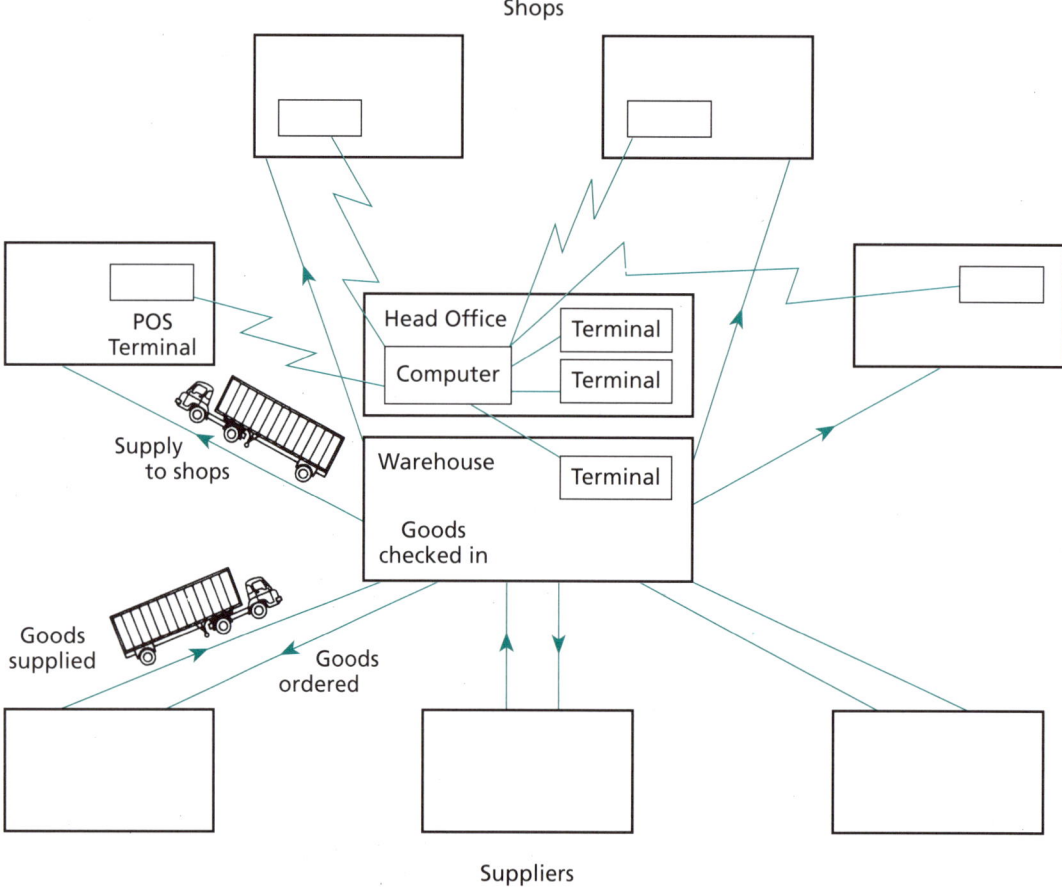

Fig. 7.5 The supply of goods for a chain of photographic shops

Data capture in the shops

As each item is sold, the sales assistant types in a code for it at the terminal. The terminal contains a microprocessor and some storage. This is used:

① To store details of all the day's transactions. These are stored during the day and sent to the main computer in the evening. The terminal is left connected to a telephone line overnight. The main computer telephones each terminal in turn automatically for its information. The computer uses the information to keep its file of the stock levels in each shop up to date. In this way the computer has a record of what items should still be on the shelves in the shop.

② To store a list of the names and the prices of most goods in the shop. The terminal has a small printer to produce a receipt for the customer.

Data capture at the warehouse

Entries have to be made of goods leaving or arriving:

1. when items are delivered from the suppliers to the warehouse;
2. when items are sent from the warehouse to the shops.

Files

1. The **stock master file**. This contains data on the stock in the warehouse. It has details of all the items which are stocked on a regular basis. Each of these is given an item number. The file is a sequential file and is in order of the item numbers. Each record refers to one item and contains:

Item number	– this is a key field for the record
Description of item	– the name and details such as size, etc.
Present stock level	– the number of items in the warehouse
Reorder level	– the item is reordered when stock falls below this
Maximum stock level	– used to decide how many to order
Minimum reorder number	– this is the smallest number which can be ordered from the supplier
Previous date	– date of previous order for this item
Supplier code	– this is a code indicating which supplier the item can be reordered from
Reorder situation	– this is a code indicating whether the goods are discontinued or to be reordered, etc.

2. The **suppliers' master file**. This contains data on all the suppliers which the company uses. Each record consists of:

Supplier code	– as stored on the master stock file
Supplier details	– name and address of the supplier
Status	– status of orders from that supplier

3. There is also a stock file kept for each shop. These stock files are similar to the master file for the warehouse.

What the computer does

The computer carries out many tasks including:

1. checking stock levels in each shop and working out what goods are to be sent to the shop;
2. checking stock levels in the warehouse and working out what goods are to be ordered from the suppliers (this is done by comparing Present Stock Level with Reorder Level);
3. storing orders so that goods from each supplier are together;
4. producing orders to send to the suppliers using the suppliers' master file;
5. adjusting stock levels in the files for the warehouse and the shops when a delivery is made from the warehouse to the shop. The computer produces a list of the items to be sent. The storekeeper indicates on the terminal when the items have been sent.
6. adjusting stock levels in the files for the warehouse when a delivery is made to the warehouse from the suppliers.

Output

1. Lists of goods to be ordered from each supplier.
2. Lists of goods to be sent to each shop.
3. Records of sales and forecasts for management so that decisions can be made about discounting products and introducing new ones.

Quick test

1. How does a computer know where a variable length field ends?
2. Why is Surname not a satisfactory choice for a key field in a pupil record file?
3. Why should you close any open files before leaving a program?
4. Why can you not use a new disc until it has been formatted?
5. What form of access is best for large files when you are only going to access one or two records at a time?

6 Why are direct access files not kept on magnetic tape?

7 When updating a master file with a transaction file why is it necessary to sort the transaction file?

8 What are the three different operations that can be carried out during updating?

9 For a stock control situation explain how the stock master file would be used to produce a list of all items which need to be reordered.

Summary

1 A **file** is an organised collection of data, usually on backing store.

2 A data file usually consists of parts called **records**. The data in a record consists of **items**, each stored in a different **field**.

3 Fields and records can be **variable** or **fixed** in length.
   - Variable length records waste less space but need separators.
   - A variable length field can store an item however long it is.

4 The value in a **key field** is **unique** to that record. This means that the keys must all be different from one another.

5 - You cannot use a new disc until it has been formatted.
   - Only blank or unwanted discs should be formatted.

6 The operating system allows users to:
   - create and access sub-directories;
   - obtain a list of a given directory;
   - save, load, delete, rename and copy files.

7 - A **serial access** file has data stored in the order it was written. Records are read by reading through all preceding records first.
   - A **sequential access** file is similar but records are in order of the key field.
   - Any record of a **direct (or random) access** file can be accessed without having to access the other records first.

8 Updating can involve:
   - **insertion** – adding new records to a file;
   - **deletion** – removing existing records from the file;
   - **amendment** – changing the items within existing records.

9 - A **master file** is used as a reference file and is updated when necessary.
   - A **transaction file** is temporary and is prepared in order to update a master file.

Chapter 8
Security and integrity of data

8.1 Security problems

KEY TERMS *The **security of data** means the protection of data.*

The term refers to all methods of protecting data and software from being:
1. lost;
2. destroyed;
3. corrupted;
4. incorrectly modified;
5. disclosed to someone who should not have access to it.

KEY TERMS *Data is said to be **corrupt** if errors are introduced into it. Usually the errors have been introduced by faulty equipment.*

Danger to files

Files may be in danger of accidentally or intentionally being:
1. lost, e.g.
   - by losing discs or tapes;
   - because the file is on the system but badly named.
2. destroyed, e.g.
   - by fire or flood;
   - by deletion.
3. corrupted, e.g.
   - by scratches on a disc or faulty disc drives;
   - by interference during a communication.
4. modified, e.g.
   - by being unintentionally written over;
   - for malicious reasons such as fraud;
   - by being updated with incorrect data.
5. accessed by unauthorised people.

Hacking

KEY TERMS *Hacking means obtaining access to a computer system without authority.*

Notes:
1. Many examples of hacking for fraud are by programmers within the company concerned.

2. Hackers from outside often use a modem from their own home computer to connect to the computer being hacked.

EXAMPLES: *of hacking incidents*
1. A hacker caused a Cancer Research centre's computer to close down for a day by overloading it. He caused it to run programs which made thousands of telephone calls and cost a lot of money.
2. Other hackers have gained access to the electronic mailboxes of famous people.

Protection against hacking

There are various ways to make hacking less likely:
1. By the use of passwords for users and for individual files.
   Great care should be taken in choosing and in securing passwords (see Unit 8.3).
2. By encrypting files (see Unit 8.3).
3. By arranging for a network system to be unfriendly to strangers, e.g. to disconnect a user after three unsuccessful attempts to key a password.

Hacking is definitely a criminal offence – with very severe penalties. The Computer Misuse Act of 1990 creates three main types of offence:
1. operating a computer to gain unauthorised access to programs or data;
2. impairing the operation of a computer by altering programs or data;
3. gaining access to a computer in order to commit a crime such as fraud.

Viruses

KEY TERMS *A computer **virus** is a program which copies itself without the user intending it to.*

Notes:
1. Often a virus attaches itself to other programs which are then saved with the virus added to them. Most viruses do not affect data files.
2. The virus usually does more than just copy itself. It may erase files or corrupt the data on the screen.

EXAMPLES:
1. **The Michelangelo virus**
   This infects files until 6 March, which was Michelangelo's birthday. On that day, if not stopped, it deletes the files on the hard disc of any infected computer.
2. **The cascade virus**
   This also has particular dates when it becomes active, causing all characters on the screen to fall in a jumbled mass to the bottom of the screen.

Protection against viruses

Viruses cost commercial firms a great deal of money. Even if their computers are not infected, they have to spend money making sure viruses are not introduced. Steps they can take are:
1. Make sure everyone in the organisation knows of the danger.
2. Use a commercial program which detects any viruses. Many of these can say which viruses are present and get rid of them.
3. Avoid the use of any programs of doubtful origin, such as 'free' software.
4. Back up files on a regular basis. This may not get rid of the virus, but if it deletes files, at least they can be recovered.
5. Make standard software write protected, so that a virus cannot change it.

Note: A virus program which does nothing dangerous is more likely to spread because people do not notice it.

8.2 Making copies of files

Data can be protected from destruction or modification by keeping copies, although care has to be taken that this does not make unauthorised access easier.

8.3 Other ways of looking after data

KEY TERMS

A *backup* file is a copy of a file which is kept in case anything happens to the original file.
An *archive* is a file or set of files which is being kept in long term storage in case it is required.

A backup file may be created by the user or may be produced automatically by the system.

EXAMPLES: *of backup files*

1. A particular word processor has two automatic backup facilities.
   (a) **Backup on saving**
   This is to ensure that when the user saves a file the old version is not lost. The old version of the file is automatically renamed before saving the new one. The old one is given a name ending in BAK so that the user can easily recognise what it is, e.g. LETTER.BAK is the old version of LETTER.DOC.
   (b) **Timed backup**
   This option is useful if there is a power failure. The word processor automatically saves the document in use every 15 minutes.
2. A pupil uses the school network. Every time she saves a file on the network she also saves it on her own floppy disc as well.

APPLICATION: *of backup and archive files*

Storage of maps

The Ordnance Survey has all its large scale maps digitised. This is part of the Superplan system which allows the customer to specify exactly the map required, e.g. if the customer's house is at the edge of an existing map, a new map which has the house in the middle of it can be produced from the data.

Currently about 230 000 maps are stored which take up about 36 gigabytes of storage (1 gigabyte is more than 1 thousand million bytes). The maps in each region of the country are stored on discs by local agents who sell the maps in the region. Each agent has over 20 000 maps stored on hard discs on their own computer system. With so much data, security is vital. The main computer system in Southampton has an archive and retrieval system which contains all the data on hard discs. As a backup to the two methods of storage there is also a security and recovery system which has all the maps stored on tape cartridges.

As new data is produced it has to be communicated to the relevant agents and to the archive and the security systems.

The archive and the security systems are in different buildings for extra safety in case of fire or flood.

Saving space when archiving or backing-up

Backup files and archives use a large amount of storage. Methods are devised of storing the data in a smaller space.

EXAMPLE: *of saving storage space*

Compression

A program is run which changes the individual bit patterns of the characters as they are being stored so that the data takes up less storage space.

The disadvantage of this system is that it takes time to decompress the data again if it is to be used.

8.3 Other ways of looking after data

Physical safeguards

1. **Locking files away**
   - To protect against fire, flood or theft, backup files and software are often kept in another building in a fireproof and waterproof safe.
   - Important data stored on floppy discs should be kept in a safe place.
2. **Protecting files against being overwritten**
   - Large magnetic tapes usually have to be fitted with a write permit ring before

data can be written on them.
- Tape cartridges have a small tab on the edge which can be snapped off to prevent anyone writing data on the tape.
- The data on floppy discs can be protected by sliding a small write protect tab (see Fig. 6.3).

3 Keeping people out
Only authorised personnel are allowed into certain areas of many computer installations.

Software safeguards

A large computer system or a network may have many users and many terminals or work stations. Use has to be restricted.

KEY TERMS *A **user identity** (or **ID**) is a name or number by which the system knows that user. Each user is given an area of backing store in which to store files. Often the user can decide which other users can access these files.*

*A **password** is a set of characters which a computer associates with a particular user identity. The password is known only to the user and usually he or she selects it. A password is usually kept secret and the computer does not display it on the screen as it is typed in.*

Users of a system with user identities and passwords have to **log in** and **log out** every time they use it.

KEY TERMS *To **log in** means to gain access to a system by giving the correct instructions and responses.*
*To **log out** means to exit from a system by giving the correct instructions.*

EXAMPLE: *of a log in and log out sequence*
A school has several small networks connected together.

1 Logging in
When you first come to a station a menu asks you which file server you require. You select one using the mouse. A screen appears with spaces for user identity and password. You type these in. The user identity appears as you type it but the password does not. A main menu then appears for you to select the software you wish to use.

2 Logging out
When you have finished using a software package you exit from it. You then return to the main menu. This has an option 'Exit from the network' which you can select to log out.

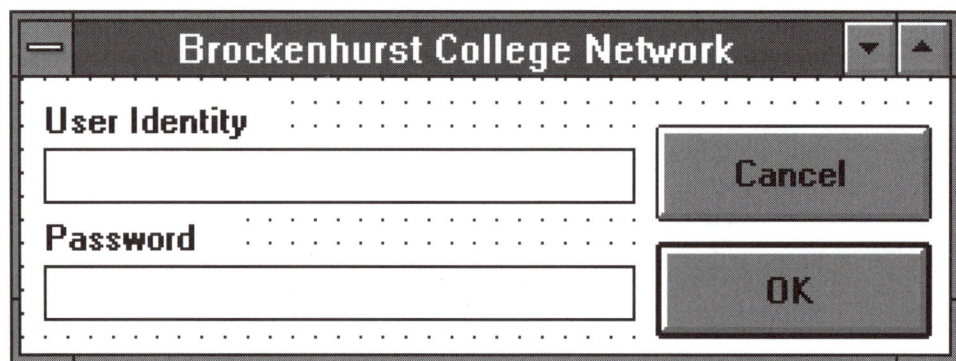

Fig. 8.1 Screen showing requests for identity and password

Advice about passwords

Many hacking problems arise from people finding out passwords or guessing them. Your files are much more secure if you stick to the following rules.

1 Choose a sequence containing no fewer than six characters. The more characters you have the harder it is for others to guess the password or to look over a shoulder and see what is typed.

2 Pick something you can remember but no-one else would think of, even if they

know you. Your boy or girlfriend's name is not safe. The name backwards of your aunt's dog which died 5 years ago is a better choice.
3. Never tell anyone what it is.
4. Never write it down.
5. Be careful who is looking over your shoulder.
6. Change it every week or so.

Note:
When a password or PIN is changed the system usually asks the user to key the new password twice. This is to ensure that it has been keyed correctly. Otherwise, if there was an error, the user would not know what the new password is.

Other software safeguards

1. Some files may only be accessible to certain passwords.
2. On some systems users may be able to give files an access code. For example, a file may be made 'read only'.
3. Individual files may be given passwords.
4. **Data encryption**.

KEY TERMS

To **encrypt** data is to encode it in such a way that it is unreadable to anyone who does not know how to decode it.

APPLICATION: *of encryption*

A company has a research facility distant from the company's headquarters. Documents about the research are sent to the head office by electronic mail. To avoid industrial espionage all the data is 'scrambled' by an encryption program before it is sent. The recipient at the head office runs a decryption program to decode it. The encryption and decryption programs need to be fed a **key** set of characters before they are run. The keys are changed regularly by agreement beforehand.

8.4 Integrity of input data

KEY TERMS

The **integrity** of data means its accuracy and completeness. Data has integrity if it has not been corrupted in any way.

In business and industry a great deal of time and effort is devoted to making sure that data is accurate and that it is not corrupted.

Causes of inaccuracies in input data

The following are common causes of errors in input data.
1. Mistakes or inaccuracies in capturing the data.
2. Failure to organise the data in the way required by the program.
3. **Transmission errors**.
4. **Read errors** – failure by an input device to read the data correctly.
5. **Transcription errors**.

KEY TERMS

A **transmission error** occurs when data sent from one device to another is changed owing to a hardware failure.
A **transcription error** is an error made while keying in data.

EXAMPLE: *of faulty data capture*

A computer is used to control the temperature at which a chemical process takes place. A digital thermometer connected to the computer is faulty and as a result the computer sets the temperature to the wrong value.

EXAMPLE: *of failure to organise the data for the program*

A program expects names to be entered as 'Christian name' (ENTER) 'Surname' (ENTER). The names 'JOHN SMITH', 'BARRY JONES' are entered. In each case the full name is entered before pressing the ENTER key. The computer takes JOHN

SMITH to be the Christian name and BARRY JONES to be the surname of the same person.

EXAMPLE: *of a transmission error*
The letter C is transmitted in ASCII code using a modem and a telephone line. One bit is changed and the character is read as the letter A. (In ASCII letter C = 1000011, letter A = 1000001.)

EXAMPLES: *of transcription errors*
1. A **transposition error**
   A keyboard operator keys two digits in the wrong order and types 3256 instead of 3526.
2. A keyboard operator misreads a 2 and keys a Z.

Note:
Often the Z is crossed, i.e. Ƶ, to distinguish it from 2. Similarly 0 (zero) is often crossed, i.e. Ø, to distinguish it from O (the letter). The letter I is given a bar at the top and the bottom to distinguish it from 1.

8.5 Methods of avoiding input errors

Organised methods of data capture

If a large amount of data is to be collected for a system, then data integrity can be improved by organising the data capture.

EXAMPLES: *of organised data capture*
1. **Preprinted forms**
   Forms are printed with spaces provided for the data to be filled in.
2. **Preprinted data**
   The data itself can be preprinted, e.g. in bar codes.

Check digits

KEY TERMS — A *digit* is one character of a number, e.g. 3 is the first digit of 38 762 and 2 is the last digit.
A **check digit** is an extra digit added to a number to ensure that, if the number is changed by mistake, the error will be detected.

Check digits are most commonly added to numbers which it is very important to get right, such as customer's account numbers.
 A calculation is done on the number which produces a value to add on to it. Then if the data is transmitted or typed the check digit can be checked by doing the same calculation again. If the value is different, then the data itself must have been corrupted in some way.

Notes:
1. Sometimes two digits are added to the number rather than one.
2. Occasionally letters are used as check digits as well as numbers.

EXAMPLE: *of a check digit calculation*
Five-figure account numbers have a digit added to them according to the following rules.
(1) Starting from the right, multiply the first digit by 1, the second by 2, the third by 3, etc.
(2) Add the results together.
(3) Use the last digit of the result as a check digit to add to the end of the number.
   (a) For the account number 56037, rules (1) and (2) give:
   $5 \times 5 + 6 \times 4 + 0 \times 3 + 3 \times 2 + 7 \times 1$ = 62
   From rule (3), the check digit = 2
   New version of the number = 560372
   (b) For the account number 50637, rules (1) and (2) give:
   $5 \times 5 + 0 \times 4 + 6 \times 3 + 3 \times 2 + 7 \times 1$ = 56
   From rule (3), the check digit = 6
   New version of the number = 506376

8.6 Methods of detecting input errors

Note:
The only difference between the two numbers 56037 and 50637 is that the digits 6 and 0 have been transposed. This check digit method seems complicated but at least it shows up transposition errors, which are very common.

APPLICATIONS: *of check digits*
International book numbers
Any recent book has been given an International Standard Book Number (ISBN). Many books have this printed in bar code form on the back cover. This often has the Book Number printed in two forms, above and below the bar code.

In each case the last digit of the number is a check digit. Often the two check digits are different, for example the number of a book could be printed as ISBN 1-85758-303-5 and as 9 781857 583038 (see Fig. 8.2). The two versions of the number are the same except that in the second version, ISBN has been replaced by 978. For bar codes, 978 indicates a book. The two check digits are different because in the second case the 978 has been included in calculating the check digit.

Fig. 8.2 Bar code and numbers

8.6 Methods of detecting input errors

Verification of data

KEY TERMS *Verification is the checking of data which has been copied from one place to another to see that it still represents the original data.*

EXAMPLE: *of verification of data*
Key to disc encoding – double entry
In a computer bureau, data is being encoded on to disc. A keyboard operator reads the data from a source document and keys it at a keystation, the data being recorded on disc.

This data is then verified by a second operator, who rekeys it all. The computer controlling the keystation checks the data stored against the data now being typed and reports differences, so that any errors can be corrected.

Validation of data

KEY TERMS *Validation is the checking of data before processing to see that it is acceptable for the process.*

Note:
Validation may be carried out by the program which is to process the data or by a separate program.

Validation of data may include:

1. a check to see it is in the right format;
2. a **type check** – that it is of the right type, e.g. a number;
3. a **length check** – that it has the right number of characters;
4. a **range check** – that it is within the range of possible values;
5. a **presence check** – that some data has in fact been keyed;
6. a **table look-up** – checking through a set of possible values to see if the data is one of them.

Chapter 8 Security and integrity of data

EXAMPLES: *of validation checks*

1 A type check
A set of numbers to be totalled is checked to make sure that:
- each character is either a decimal digit or a decimal point;
- there is at most one decimal point per number.

2 A range check
Dates of birth are being input to a pupil record program. Before accepting a date the program checks:
- the day is between 1 and 31 inclusive;
- the month is between 1 and 12 inclusive;
- the year is in the correct range for pupils at the school.

Note:
These dates of birth could also be checked to see:
1 that all parts of the date are numbers (a type check);
2 that February has 29 days in a leap year and only 28 days in other years.

Quick test

1 Which of the following are ways of protecting important data:
   (a) merging files,
   (b) locking discs in a safe,
   (c) using a data bank,
   (d) a password system?

2 Why do hackers and viruses cost money even for firms which do not suffer from them?

3 Which *two* of the following list are verification checks:
   (a) checking names to see if the characters are all letters,
   (b) keying data a second time so that the computer can check to see if it was keyed correctly the first time,
   (c) checking data sent by modem to see if it has been sent without errors,
   (d) making a backup file,
   (e) checking pupils' heights to see if they are all less than 2.5 m?

4 Which *two* of the list in question 3 are validation checks?

5 A date is to be input with the month as a number.
   (a) Give one type of validation check which could be used.
   (b) What is the name for this kind of check?

6 State which of the following ensure the integrity of input data:
   (a) passwords,
   (b) a range check,
   (c) the write tab on a floppy disc,
   (d) verification,
   (e) a check digit.

7 State which of the list in question **6** ensure the security of data.

8 Say whether each of the following is a type check, a length check or a range check:
   (a) seeing whether an input item is a number,
   (b) checking whether a name has less than 20 letters,
   (c) checking whether a name contains any digits,
   (d) checking whether a number is positive.

In questions **9** to **13** say what is being described:

9. a digit added on to the end of an account number as a check,
10. a program which adds itself to other programs,
11. a check on whether or not a disc file has been copied successfully,
12. a set of characters which is not displayed when you key them in at the start of a session on a network station,
13. a person who gains illegal entry to a computer system.

Summary

1. The **security of data** means the protection of data. Security involves protecting data and software from being lost, destroyed, corrupted, modified or disclosed.

2. **Hacking** means obtaining access to a computer system without authority. It is now illegal.

3. A computer **virus** is a program which copies itself without the user intending it to.

4. - A **backup** file is a copy of a file which is kept in case anything happens to the original file.
   - **Archive** files are kept in long term storage in case they are required.

5. Physical safeguards for data include:
   - fireproof safes;
   - devices on discs and tapes to protect files against being overwritten;
   - keeping unauthorised people from entering secure areas.

6. Software safeguards include giving users a user identity and a password.

7. Other safeguards include **data encryption** which involves encoding data in such a way that it is unreadable to anyone who does not know how to decode it.

8. The **integrity** of data means its accuracy and completeness. Data has integrity if it has not been corrupted in any way.

9. A **check digit** is an extra digit added to a number so that, if the number is changed, the error will be detected.

10. - **Verification** is checking data which has been copied from one place to another to see that it is still the same.
    - Verification of keyed data may involve rekeying it.

11. - **Validation** is checking data before processing to see that it is acceptable for the process.
    - Validation methods include format checks, type checks, length checks and range checks.

Chapter 9
Software

9.1 Programs

A computer cannot do anything without a program of instructions. A program is based on algorithms.

KEY TERMS   *A **program** is an ordered set of instructions which a computer carries out.*
*An **algorithm** is a sequence of steps or calculations for the solution of a problem.*

EXAMPLES: *of programs*
1. A word processor (see Chapter 10).
2. A set of LOGO instructions to drive a turtle (see Unit 17.1).
3. The operating system of a computer (see Unit 9.3).

EXAMPLES: *of algorithms*
1. A computer program.
2. A set of instructions in a kit telling you how to put the kit together.
3. A knitting pattern.
4. A cooking recipe.
5. A macro command on a word processor.
6. A key of the type used in science to identify a specimen.

Notes:
1. A program is an algorithm (example 1) but we tend to use the term to describe the method on which the program is based. This would probably be worked out using a flowchart or a structure diagram before the program itself was written (see Unit 19.3 and Unit 19.4).
2. A large program would be based on a number of different algorithms.

KEY TERMS   *A **macro instruction** (or **macro command**) is an instruction written by the user to carry out several basic instructions.*

A macro is written by the user to carry out a sequence of instructions which he or she frequently uses. Macros can often be used in:
- a low level language;
- the command language for an operating system;
- word processors, spreadsheets and databases.

Note:
Compare this idea with a procedure in a language such as LOGO (see Unit 17.1). Macros and procedures are very similar.

APPLICATION: *of a macro*
Switching two letters round in a word processor
A keyboard operator using a word processor keeps making the mistake of keying letters in the wrong order, e.g. she keys 'hte' instead of 'the'. She uses the word processor's macro facility to program the key combination ALT/S to carry out the following sequence to switch the letters back. The sequence starts with the cursor under the first of the two characters to be switched:

```
MARK BLOCK     ⎫
RIGHT ARROW    ⎬  pick up the first character
CUT            ⎭
RIGHT ARROW       move to the second position
PASTE             paste first character in second positon
```

Computer languages

KEY TERMS

Machine code refers to the basic set of instructions which the processor has built in to it. The processor can execute these without any translation.

A **computer language** is a set of words and symbols which a programmer uses to write a program. The computer has to translate a program from this language to machine code before it can be run.

EXAMPLES: *of computer languages*

❶ **BASIC (Beginners' All-purpose Symbolic Instruction Code)**
BASIC was originally a teaching language for interactive work. It has since been extended.

CHARACTERISTICS: *of BASIC*

❶ Every line has to be numbered.
❷ It is easy for beginners to learn.
❸ It is difficult to write programs which are easily understood.
❹ There are many different versions of the language.

❷ **LOGO**
This is an educational language to encourage logical thinking.

CHARACTERISTICS: *of LOGO*

❶ It enables the programmer to make a 'turtle' perform planned tasks. Originally a 'turtle' was a device to run around on the floor, but now it may be just a pointer on a screen.
❷ New instructions can be invented and defined. They can then be used in the program.
❸ It has facilities to process lists of data.

9.2 Software

The programs we use are referred to as software.

KEY TERMS

Software is a general term for programs which are written to help computer users.
A **software package** is a program or set of programs together with a full set of documentation.

EXAMPLES: *of software*

❶ A spreadsheet program.
❷ A program to back up files on to a tape streamer.

EXAMPLES: *of a software package*

❶ A spreadsheet program and the documentation which comes with it.
❷ A word processor program plus its manual.

Note:
The programs on a floppy disc or CD-ROM are software. The disc itself is hardware.

Systems software and applications software

A computer system requires two types of software:

❶ systems programs which make sure the computer works efficiently;
❷ applications programs which help users to solve problems.

KEY TERMS — *An **applications program** is a specialised program which allows a computer to be used for a specific application.*

EXAMPLES: *of applications programs*
1. A payroll program. As this is a common requirement for companies, there are many different payroll programs to choose from.
2. A desktop publishing (DTP) package (see Unit 10.7).
3. A program to produce graphs of experimental results for a research biologist. This is more a specialised type of program and may have to be specially written.

KEY TERMS — *A **systems program** controls the performance of the computer system or provides commonly used facilities.*

Notes:
1. A systems program improves the way the computer works. It is not directed to any particular application of the computer.
2. Systems software is often supplied by the computer manufacturer.

EXAMPLES: *of systems programs*
1. A compiler. This translates a high level program into machine code.
2. The operating system of a computer (see Unit 9.3).
3. A backup program which archives network files on to a tape cartridge (see Unit 6.6).

Note:
The backup program is an example of a utility.

KEY TERMS — *A **utility program** is a systems program which performs one, usually simple, task.*

EXAMPLES: *of utility programs*
1. A program to transfer the contents of a VDU screen to a printer (often called a **screendump**).
2. A program to sort a database file so that the key fields are in numerical order.
3. A program to merge two files into one large file.

9.3 Operating systems

The most important piece of system software in a computer system is the operating system which controls it.

KEY TERMS — *An **operating system** is software which controls the general operation of a computer. It consists of a set of programs and routines and for large computers is very complex.*

EXAMPLE: *of a microcomputer operating system*
On a particular microcomputer the operating system deals with:
1. instructions from the user to save, load, delete, rename and copy files;
2. instructions from the user to run and list programs;
3. displaying an error message if a device which the user requires is not ready for use.

Functions of the operating system

For computers generally
1. Creating a working environment in which the user can run programs.
2. Controlling the use of peripherals such as disc units and printers.
3. Controlling the loading and running of programs.
4. Organising the use of the main store – this has to be shared between the operating system and the user's program(s).
5. Dealing with execution errors and keeping the computer running when they happen.
6. Communicating directly with users and/or operators:

- displaying messages about errors and problems with peripherals – such as a printer out of paper;
- dealing with user commands to organise files and run programs.

For larger computers and networks

1. Producing a log, i.e. a record of the programs as they are run.
2. Maintaining security:
   - seeing that users give the right identification and password to use the system;
   - checking that users trying to access files have authority to use them.
3. Organising the use of storage. On a mainframe computer this means keeping several users' programs running at the same time. The storage has to be shared between them.
4. Working out the resources used by each program. If the user is paying for the service, then the computer works out the cost of running the program and charges the appropriate account.

Different operating systems

Computers have different operating systems:

1. because they have different types of processing system, e.g. a real time operating system would be quite different from a batch processing operating system (see Chapter 2 for different types of processing system);
2. when they have similar methods of processing but different processors.

EXAMPLE: *of different operating systems for similar computers*

Apple computers, Archimedes computers and IBM compatibles are all similar computers used for similar purposes. However, they have different processors and different operating systems.

9.4 Evaluation of applications software

KEY TERMS

Evaluation of software means checking to see if it is:
1. *of a good standard;*
2. *suitable for a particular application.*

Note:
GCSE candidates often need to evaluate software as part of their coursework.

In evaluating whether a package is suitable to solve a given problem or not you should:

1. begin an evaluation report (normally on a word processor). Each stage of the evaluation should then be described in this report.
2. read the documentation to see whether:
   - the program can be used to solve this type of problem;
   - the package is easy to use. Does it tell you clearly what to do? Is it easy to look up things which you want to know? Are there good examples?
3. run the program with test data. Think of some suitable test data. The data should be chosen to investigate all aspects of the program.
4. make sure the program is user friendly.
   - Are the messages clear?
   - When data has to be entered, is it easy to understand what is required?
   - Does it sometimes make you wait an unreasonably long time or without explanation?
   - Does it make you do more keying than is necessary?
   - Can you get the program to do what you want?
5. check that the methods of input and output suit your problem.
   If the program is interactive, is the type of user interface suitable? (See Unit 3.4.)
6. see that the program is versatile and adaptable. Can it cope with a variety of different situations? If your problem changes will the software be able to cope?
7. check the program is **reliable**. Does it carry out all the tasks required as it says in the manual?

8. check that the program is **robust**. Try to make the program go wrong. Enter incorrect data for each response. A good program will validate all data before processing it. If the data is not sensible, it should find this out and ask you to re-type it.

KEY TERMS *A program is **robust** if it can cope with errors in data while it is running.*
*A program is **reliable** if it does what the manual says it does.*

9.5 Types of application package

If there is a problem to solve the user has several options for the software.

1. A **custom designed program**
   A program could be designed and written just to solve this problem:
   - by a **software house** – a company which specialises in writing software;
   - **in-house** – by someone within the company.
2. An **application specific package**
   Many problems are the same for many companies so software houses produce programs to suit a particular type of application. It is possible to buy a ready-made package 'off the shelf'.
3. A **general purpose application** program
   Many programs are not written for any specific application but can be used in a wide variety of applications. Often such programs are described as **content free**.

EXAMPLE: *of a program which had to be custom designed*
Program to calculate wire lengths
A firm produces reels of various types of wire and cable. It needs to calculate the length of cable of a given thickness which will fill a reel of a certain width and diameter. As not many firms are doing this, it is necessary to have a program specifically written to solve the problem.

ADVANTAGE: *of a custom designed program*
The program is designed to fit the user's problem exactly.

EXAMPLES: *of application specific packages*
Programs to:
1. handle a stock control system;
2. organise the payroll;
3. automatically register pupils at a school;
4. design kitchens.

ADVANTAGES: *of application specific packages*
1. Because the package applies to other users, it is well tried and tested.
2. It will usually be cheaper than a custom designed program to do the same thing.

EXAMPLES: *of general purpose application programs*
1. A spreadsheet program.
2. A database.
3. A word processor.

ADVANTAGES: *of general purpose application programs*
1. Each package is well tested and well documented.
2. A package is not expensive. Often a set of general purpose applications are 'bundled', i.e. they are included with the computer.
3. Each program applies to a wide variety of applications.
4. There is a wide user base, providing:
   - plenty of other users with whom to discuss problems,
   - opportunities for training in the use of the package.
5. Other software can be linked to it – and use the same data.

DISADVANTAGE: *of general purpose application programs*
It is not usually possible to produce menus and screens which deal with a particular application. An employee familiar with the problem being solved but not with the package will not find it easy to use.

9.6 General purpose application packages

Many problems can be solved using general purpose applications packages. Details of the different packages are given in Chapters 10, 11, 13 and 14.

This section contains a summary of the commonly used packages and notes on which to use in a given situation.

Communication between packages

KEY TERMS
To **export data** *is to output data to a file from one software package in such a form that it can be read by a different software package.*

To **import data** *into a software package is to read data from a file which was produced by another software package.*

With a GUI (graphical user interface) data can be moved from one package to another using an area of memory instead of a file. This temporary storage area is known as a **clipboard** or a **notepad**.

KEY TERMS
To **cut** *data means to move data from a package into the clipboard, deleting the data from the package.*

To **copy** *data means to move data from a package into the clipboard without deleting the data from the package.*

To **paste** *data means to copy it from the clipboard into a package.*

The sequence for cutting and pasting is usually as follows:
1. create the data to be transferred and select it with a mouse;
2. copy or cut the data into the clipboard;
3. open the other package or switch to it;
4. paste the data from the clipboard into the second package.

Word processors

A **word processor** is a program for producing and editing text such as letters and reports.

CHARACTERISTICS: *of a word processor*
1. Simple entry and editing of text and correction of keying errors.
2. Improved appearance and style with features such as underlining, bold, italics.
3. Spell checking and even grammar checking.
4. Some control of layout – changing margins, page numbering, etc.
5. Some choice of fonts.
6. Facilities for printing and addressing a set of letters.

APPLICATIONS: *of a word processor*
1. Writing letters, reports, lists and other documents in an office.
2. Producing the text of books and articles. Although a book or magazine may be produced with another package such as a desktop publisher, the text is often written on a word processor first.
3. Personalising letters – producing a set of similar letters to be posted to a number of people.

Desktop publishing (DTP)

A **desktop publisher** is a program which makes it possible to produce text and pictures and to organise them into pages. It will produce work of sufficient standard for publication.

Fig. 9.1 DTP screen with a party invitation on it – with pictures and different fonts

CHARACTERISTICS: *of a desktop publisher*

1. The document is divided into pages and the pages may be divided into columns.
2. Good word processing capability with good range of fonts.
3. Some drawing capability using standard shapes such as lines and circles.
4. Good facilities for importing word processor and drawing files.
5. Good facilities for arranging text and pictures together and changing their sizes.

Note:
Typically a desktop publisher is used on a system with a mouse, a scanner and a laser printer.

APPLICATIONS: *of a desktop publisher*

1. To produce newspapers, newsletters and magazines.
2. To produce posters.
3. To add pictures, logos, etc. to letters to make them more attractive.

Database

A **database** is a program for handling files and retrieving information from them (see Unit 11.1 for a fuller explanation of the term).

CHARACTERISTICS: *of a database program*

1. Data is stored in the form of records, e.g. if the database is about people then each record would contain all the information about one person.
2. The user defines a record structure choosing:
   - the number of fields and their names;
   - the size of each field and the type of data it will hold;
   - the way the records are displayed on the screen.
3. Facilities to sort the data into different orders.
4. Facilities for information retrieval:
   - producing lists of all records which meet certain conditions;
   - calculating statistics for groups of records.
5. The ability to combine results into a report.

APPLICATIONS: *of databases*
1. Maintaining personal lists such as:
   - details of customers' names, addresses and accounts;
   - pupil records for a school;
   - a list of suppliers for a stock control system.
2. Allowing access to large stores of information such as:
   - an encyclopaedia stored on CD-ROM;
   - details of books currently in print with their authors, publishers and summaries of their contents;
   - details of possible careers.

Spreadsheets

A **spreadsheet** is a package which displays information in the form of a table. This is divided into rows and columns of individual boxes called **cells**. The spreadsheet allows calculations to be done on cells or groups of cells.

CHARACTERISTICS: *of a spreadsheet*
1. The user can enter text, a number or a formula into any cell.
2. A formula allows calculations to be done on other cells.
3. Formulae and other data can be copied into groups of cells.
4. A variety of operations can be carried out on rows or columns.

APPLICATIONS: *of a spreadsheet*
1. Displaying and calculating accounts and other financial information.
2. Performing calculations on data collected in experiments and surveys.
3. Producing columns of data from which graphs can be drawn, e.g.
   - calculating the average temperature for a graph of weather data;
   - a graph to solve a mathematical equation.

Graphics packages

General purpose packages which produce graphics are of a number of types including:
1. graphs and charts – often called 'Business Graphics';
2. painting and drawing programs;
3. Computer Aided Design (CAD) packages.

CHARACTERISTICS: *of graph producing packages*
1. Ability to import sets of data from a spreadsheet or database.
2. Choice of graphs usually including:
   - pie chart;
   - bar charts and/or histograms of various types;
   - line graph;
   - x–y or scatter graphs.
3. Ability to label the graph, the axes and/or the data.

APPLICATIONS: *of graphs and charts*
1. Presenting statistics in an easily understood form, e.g.
   - showing how something is shared using a pie chart,
   - showing how a quantity has changed from year to year using a bar chart or a line graph.
2. Sketching a mathematical function. (See Fig. 9.2.)

CHARACTERISTICS: *of painting and drawing programs*
1. Good facilities for freehand drawing:
   - wide choice of pens, brushes and styles of drawing;
   - wide choice of colours and patterns.
2. A limited range of standard shapes to include in pictures.
3. Choices made mainly with a mouse and icons.
4. Ability to mark an area for deleting, copying, moving, etc.
5. A **zoom** facility to change individual pixels.

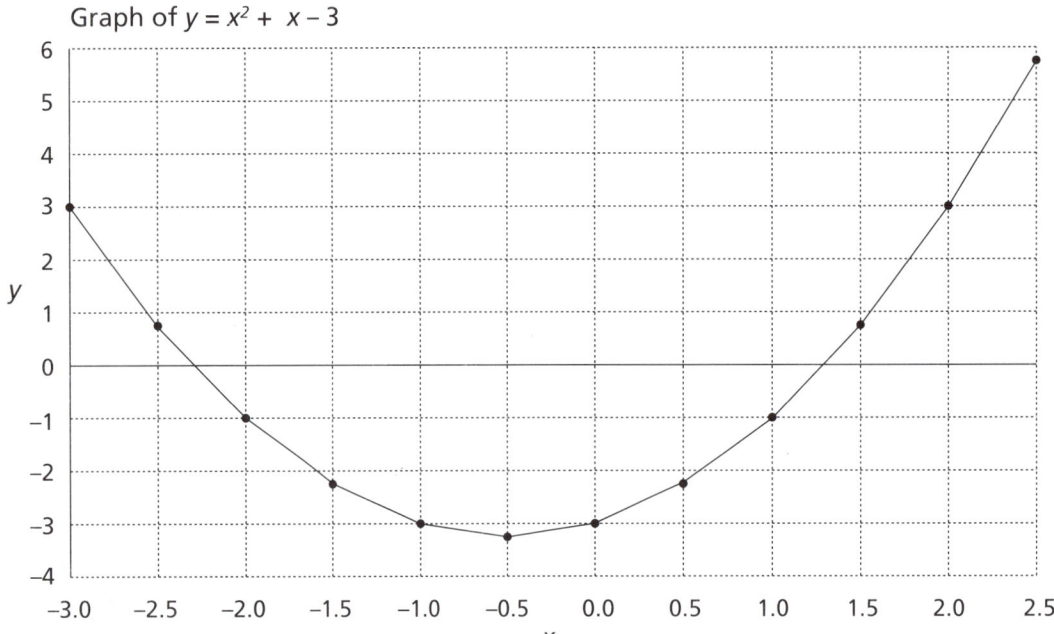

Data for the graph of $y = x^2 + x - 3$

x	y
−3.0	3.00
−2.5	0.75
−2.0	−1.00
−1.5	−2.25
−1.0	−3.00
−0.5	−3.25
0.0	−3.00
0.5	−2.25
1.0	−1.00
1.5	0.75
2.0	3.00
2.5	5.75

Fig. 9.2 Graph of $y = x^2 + x - 3$ and the figures which produced it

APPLICATIONS: *of painting and drawing programs*

1. A simple painting or drawing package allows you to draw pictures on the screen – a chance to be creative.
2. To produce simple illustrations – for instance the front cover of a school project.

CHARACTERISTICS: *of CAD packages*

1. Very accurate drawings which can be enlarged without losing accuracy.
2. Aids to accurate input such as a grid on the screen and a graphics tablet.
3. Far more standard shapes and functions than a simple drawing package.

A CAD package often has extra capabilities such as generating 3D pictures and costing the designs created.

APPLICATIONS: *of CAD packages*

1. In architecture for producing designs for building.
2. In engineering drawing.
3. Throughout industry where accurate drawings are required. For each application area it is usually possible to obtain a library of shapes for that application, e.g. electronic components for circuit diagrams.

Integrated packages

An **integrated package** consists of several general purpose applications programs which can use the same data.

CHARACTERISTICS: *of an integrated package*
1. It usually includes:
   - a word processor;
   - a database;
   - a spreadsheet;
   - a graphics program.

   It may also include a communication program to allow the computer to be used with a modem.
2. The programs come together in one package.
3. Data produced in one can be easily transferred for use in another.
4. Menus, icons and other features are similar for each program.
5. The individual programs may not be quite as powerful as separate programs to do the same thing.

APPLICATIONS: *of an integrated package*
1. To produce a report which consists of a well presented document which includes lists, facts and figures and graphs.
2. In situations where a spreadsheet, database and/or graphs are used but not often enough to justify the expense of buying the separate packages.

9.7 Choosing the right package

To decide which package to use to solve a particular problem it is necessary to first analyse the problem, working out:
- what form the input data will take;
- what processing operations are required on this data;
- what output is required.

You then consider how the characteristics of the various packages fit these requirements.

EXAMPLES: *of choosing a package*
1. **Writing a CV**
   A CV (curriculum vitae) is a document describing yourself and your achievements.
   - The **input** will be your own personal details.
   - The **processing** you will want to do will be to edit and rearrange the data. You will need to store the CV so that you can edit it and use it again at a future date.
   - The **output** should not be showy but needs to be clearly and neatly presented.

   The possible solutions are:
   - **a special program for writing CVs**. The advantage is that it has the headings and layout ready for you. The disadvantage is that the layout and headings may not suit you.
   - **a word processor**. With this you would have to do all the work but the CV would be set out just as you wanted it.

   A DTP package would not be appropriate as you want to use a simple format, a standard font and have no need for graphics. Most employers are not impressed by a showy CV.

2. **Producing a weather report**
   The situation
   A school weather station has produced sets of measurements for each month and for several years. The pupils involved wish to calculate averages, compare the months and the years for weather and produce a report with their conclusions.
   Data capture
   Some measurements are made each day but at the end of each month the pupils obtain readings for the month of:
   - maximum temperature;
   - minimum temperature;
   - rainfall.

What the computer will have to do
- Calculate average temperatures and rainfall.
- Produce lists of those months above and below certain temperatures.
- Sort data into order of temperature and of rainfall.
- Produce graphs to illustrate the comparisons.
- Combine all the lists and graphs with some written explanation in a final report.

Output will be the final report.

The solution

This requires:
- a spreadsheet to calculate averages;
- a database to produce lists of records and do the sorting;
- a business graphics package to produce pie charts, bar charts and line graphs (for details of which types of chart to use see Unit 14.5);
- a word processor for the final report.

An integrated package is the best solution to this problem. None of the tasks is too difficult for it and the data can be transferred between the different programs.

Quick test

1. Name *three* examples of applications software.

2. Give *three* examples of operations carried out by utility programs.

3. Give *three* functions of a computer operating system.

4. Give *one* function of a mainframe operating system which you would not expect to find in the operating system of a microcomputer.

5. Copy out the following statements and fill in the gaps (use a different word in each case).
   (a) A screen dump is an example of a _____ program.
   (b) A program which fails to validate input data is not _____.
   (c) A program which does not do what the manual says is not very _____.

6. Give *two* different ways in which data can be moved from one package to another.

7. What would you expect a desktop publisher to do that most word processors cannot?

8. What would you expect a spreadsheet to do that most databases cannot?

9. What would you expect a database to do that most spreadsheets cannot?

10. What would you expect a CAD package to do that most simple drawing packages cannot?

11. Name *four* different programs you would expect in an integrated package.

Summary

1. A **program** is a set of instructions which a computer carries out.

2. A **computer language** is the set of words and symbols used in writing a program.

3. A **macro** is an instruction which carries out several other instructions.

4 **Software** is a general term for programs which are written to help computer users. A computer system requires two types of software:
- systems programs which make the computer work efficiently;
- applications programs which help users to solve problems.

5 A **utility program** is a systems program which performs one task.

6 An **operating system** is systems software which controls the general operation of a computer. The functions of the operating system include:
- allowing users to run programs and organise files;
- dealing with errors;
- making the best use of the store and the peripherals;
- maintaining security.

7 Data can be moved from one package to another:
- by being exported as a file from one and imported into the other;
- by being cut or copied from one and pasted into the other.

8
- A **word processor** is a program for producing and editing text.
- A **desktop publisher** makes it possible to organise text and pictures together.
- A **database** is for handling files and retrieving information from them.
- A **spreadsheet** displays information in the form of a table. It allows calculations to be done on cells.

9 An **integrated package** consists of several general purpose applications programs which can use the same data.

Chapter 10
Presenting your work: word processing and desktop publishing

This chapter deals with the presentation of text using word processors and desktop publishers. See also Chapter 14 for other presentation methods.

10.1 Word processing

Introduction to word processing

KEY TERMS — **Word processing** means using IT to produce text such as letters and reports. A piece of text produced by a word processor is called a **document**.

ADVANTAGES: *of word processing*
1. It is easy to correct mistakes.
2. The results are easy to read and look professional.
3. Text can be stored on a disc for use again another time.
4. A word processor can be set so that the text moves along as you insert characters (see Unit 10.2 for **insert** and **overtype**).
5. Spellings can be checked automatically.
6. When a line is finished the cursor automatically goes to the next line (see Unit 10.2 for **word wrap**).

Requirements for word processing

A typical system for word processing consists of a PC with:
1. a word processing program – stored on ROM or hard disc;
2. a disk unit to store the documents. This may be a hard disc or the computer may be on a network. Floppy discs may be used as a 'backup';
3. a good quality screen;
4. a good quality printer – usually a laser printer.

Notes:
1. Some word processors use a GUI and mouse. The mouse can be useful for selecting blocks of text. However, a trained operator can often work faster using just a keyboard.
2. A word processor operator may also use:
   - a key-strip above the keys. The key strip shows short cut keys for the commands to avoid using the menus, which are slower;
   - a protective screen over the front of the monitor to cut down reflections, glare and radiation;
   - an adjustable chair to avoid injuries due to sitting in a poor position.

10.2 Entering, editing and improving text

Entering text

To enter text into a word processor the user simply types it. The user can end a paragraph by pressing the 'ENTER' key. At the end of a line this is not necessary because the word processor goes on to the next line automatically.

KEY TERMS

Word wrapping is the process of moving the cursor on to a new line automatically when the next word will not fit on the present one.

Note:
How far the word processor goes before wrapping around is decided by the width of the paper and the width of the left and right margins (see Unit 10.4).

Editing text

On most word processors if the user makes a mistake or wants to change anything he or she can move around the screen using the arrow keys or the mouse and simply alter it. Most word processors allow two ways to type a change:
- **overtype** – as you type you rub out the character your cursor is on;
- **insert** – the letters you type are inserted and all the rest of the text moves to make room for them.

Appearance and style

A word processor allows you to change the way text is displayed and printed. Common features are:
1. underlining text – drawing one or two lines under the text;
2. making text bold – letters are made thicker so that they stand out;
3. centring – a line is displayed and printed with the middle of the line of text in the middle of the page;
4. italics;
5. double line spacing – a blank line is left after each line of text.

> This line has been centred.
> **This line is in bold letters**.
> *This line is in italics.*
> And this line has been double underlined.

Fonts

Many word processors offer a choice of fonts, i.e. character designs.

KEY TERMS

A font is a set of printed characters of a particular size, style and design.

EXAMPLES: *of different fonts*
1. `This line is in Courier 12 cpi`
2. This line is in Times 12 pt
3. *This line is in Times 6 pt italic*
4. AND THIS LINE IS IN FRANKLIN GOTHIC 12 PT SMALL CAPS.

10.3 Spelling

KEY TERMS — A **spell checker** is a program which checks the spelling of words you have used against those in a dictionary.

Notes:

① The dictionary is a file of words stored with the spell checker.

② Usually you can also have your own dictionary to which you can add words which are not in the main dictionary. If a word is not in the dictionary, the spell checker stops for you to decide what to do.

Usually if a word is not found you are given a choice. You can:

① 'ignore' or 'skip' the word. If the word is someone's name or a number then you want the checker to go straight past it without doing anything, e.g. Fred, 123456, Southampton;

② add the word to your own dictionary. If you want to use a word regularly but it is not in the dictionary then you can add it, e.g. Reggae, IBM, soccer;

③ choose the right spelling from a list of suggestions. If a word is not in the dictionary, a list of similar words may be suggested which are in it. You can then select one from the list. For example, if you type 'socker' it might suggest 'shocker', 'soccer', 'soaker', 'socket';

④ correct a word. If you have spelt a word wrongly and the computer does not suggest the correct spelling then you can put it right yourself.

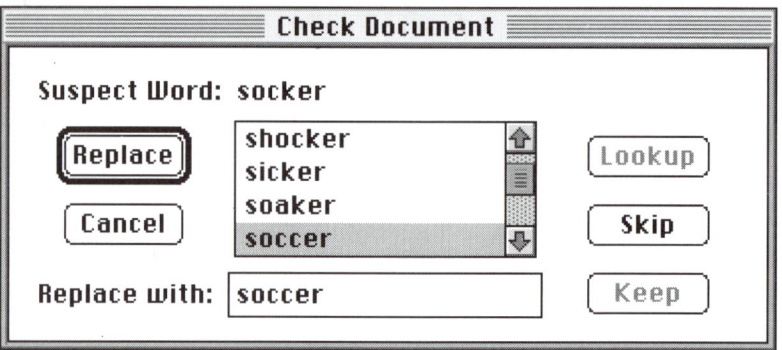

Fig. 10.1 Choice box on a spell checker screen

EXAMPLE: *of use of a spell check*

Ieuan carries out a spell check on a document containing the sentence 'Anthony Adams cannot apss GCSE Mathmatics'. The spell checker stops at each of 'Anthony', 'Adams', 'apss', 'GCSE' and 'Mathematics'. Ieuan
- tells it to ignore 'Anthony' and 'Adams';
- corrects 'apss' by hand because the spell checker does not guess the right word;
- adds 'GCSE' to the dictionary because it occurs several times in the document;
- the spell checker suggests the correct spelling of 'Mathematics'.

10.4 Tabs, margins and indents

Using the tab key

On any keyboard you have a **TAB key** (sometimes two). This is usually at the left of the keyboard. It is marked with the word TAB or with two arrows pointing in opposite directions.

When the TAB key is pressed, the cursor jumps across the page several positions at a time. The normal TAB positions are usually about 5 character widths apart.

EXAMPLES: *of using the TAB key*

1. To start the first line of each paragraph 5 spaces in from the edge of the page. The TAB key helps to always move the first line the same distance.
2. To present information set out in the form of a table with columns.
3. To key an address on a letter – so that one TAB will take the cursor to the right of the page.

Margins, indenting and justification

A word processor can change the way text fits on to a page.

KEY TERMS

The **margins** *are the limits which have been set for text near the edges of the page. They can be changed so that the text is nearer the edge or further away from it.*

Moving the **left** *or* **right** *margins makes the text wider or narrower. Moving the* **top** *or* **bottom** *margins makes it longer or shorter.*

The **indent** *is the distance text is moved in from the margin. You can indent part of the text without moving the actual margin.*

To **justify** *the text means to keep the letters in a straight line at the edge of the page.*

Note:
If the text is justified at both the left and the right the word processor has to put extra spaces in between the words to keep the ends of the lines straight.

EXAMPLES: *of margins, indents and justifying*
Entries from Jenny's diary for two days

1. As she saved it with:
   - left margin 0 centimetres and right margin 2.5 centimetres;
   - justified at the left but not the right;
   - no indenting.

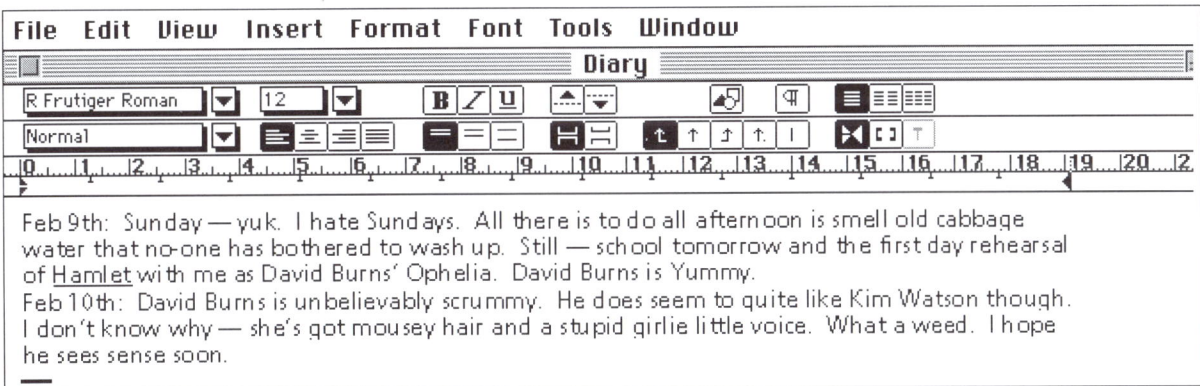

Fig. 10.2(a)

2. The same entry with:
   - Left margin 2.25 centimetres and right margin 5.0 centimetres;
   - Justified at both the left and the right;
   - Everything except the dates indented by 5 spaces.

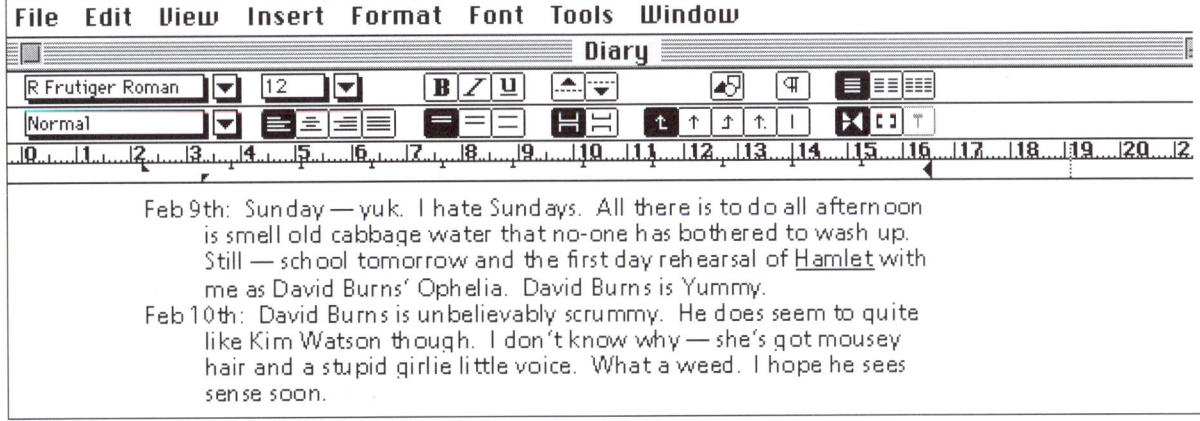

Fig. 10.2(b)

10.5 Working with blocks of text

Word processors allow you to mark a block of text. You can then:
- delete the whole block,

OR
- make a copy of the block of text somewhere else,

OR
- move the block somewhere else without making a copy.

EXAMPLE: *of deleting a block and of moving a block*
The next instalment of Jenny's diary

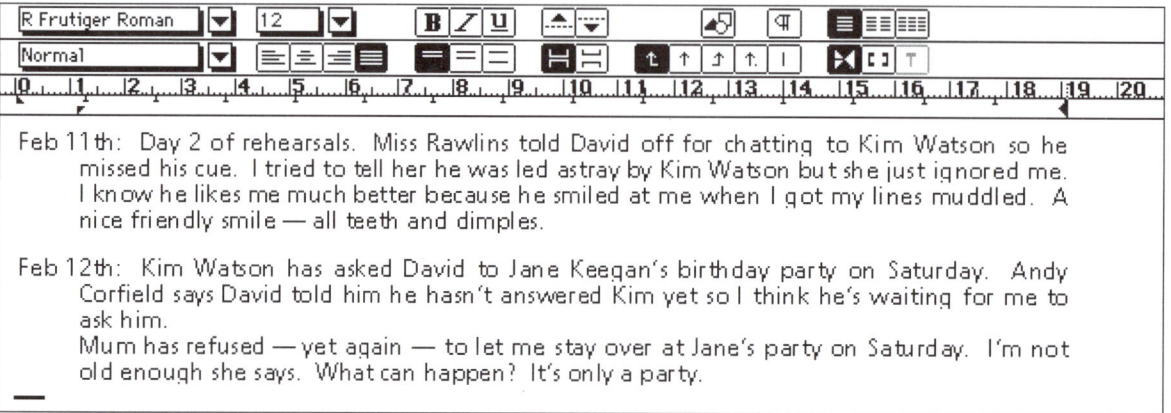

Fig. 10.3(a)

It is wrong so Jenny alters it

① Jenny has decided David's smile is not ' – all teeth and dimples' so she marked that as a block and deleted it.

② She has also remembered that Mum's refusal was on Tuesday the 11th, so she has marked that as a block and moved it to Tuesday.

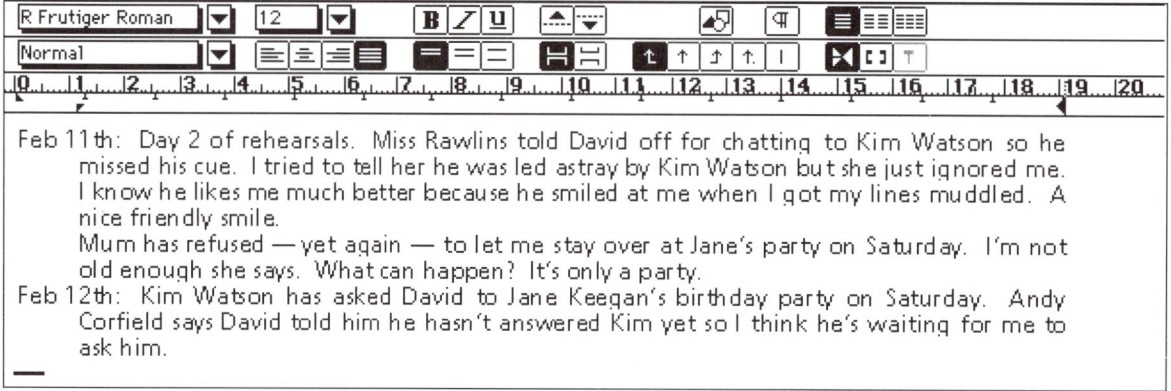

Fig. 10.3(b)

10.6 Further word processing techniques

Search and replace

A word processor allows you to:

① **search** for a word or words (sometimes this is called '**find**'). You simply key in the word and the cursor moves to the first place it occurs in the document.

❷ **search and replace.** The computer replaces one word by another one, wherever it finds it. Usually you have the choice of deciding whether to replace it or not when it is found.

EXAMPLE: *of search and replace*
Yet more of Jenny's diary
Jenny has decided it is a bit dangerous keeping her diary on the hard disc so she disguises David Burns' name. She does a search and replace – replacing 'David Burns' by 'H.' for 'Hamlet' or even 'Hero':

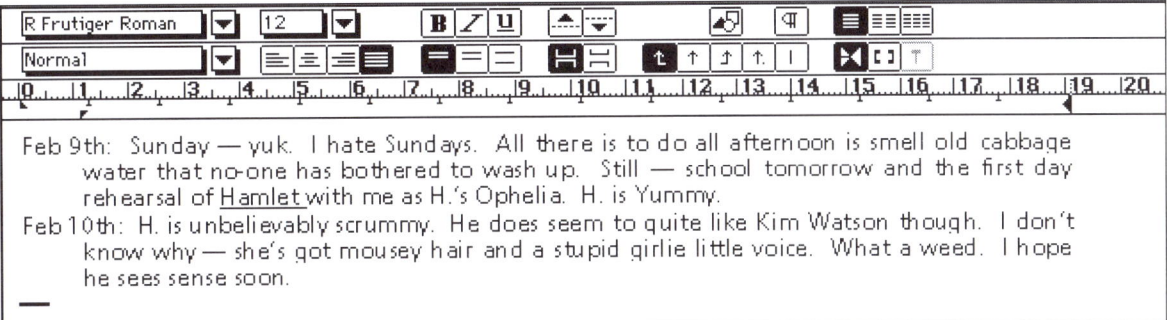

Fig. 10.4

Mail merge

Many word processors can produce a set of letters by adding to them the name and address of each person on a mailing list.

KEY TERMS

*A **standard letter** is a letter which an organisation stores on file because it is used frequently.*

*A **personalised letter** is a standard letter which is made to look like a personal letter by adding the recipient's name, address and possibly other details.*

*A **mail merge** is the operation of producing a set of personalised letters by merging the personal details with the standard letter.*

Notes:
❶ Other names for this technique include **mail shot** and **mass mailing**.
❷ The following are needed to carry out the mail merge:
- a file of names and addresses;
- the standard letter with gaps;
- the instructions on how to merge them – these may be codes within the standard letter.

APPLICATION: *involving a mail merge*
A building society is introducing a new type of account which pays very good interest for savings greater than £1000.
- A database program is used to search their mailing list of investors and produce a list of names and addresses of all those with savings above £1000.
- A letter is produced on a word processor explaining the advantages of the new account.
- The letter is merged with the mailing list and the personalised letters are sent out.

ADVANTAGE: *of a mail merge*
A mail merge allows an organisation to produce a large number of letters quickly and cheaply.

DISADVANTAGE: *of a mail merge*
A mail merge sometimes makes it too easy to produce letters which people do not want. They may be regarded as 'junk mail'.

10.7 Desktop publishing

For the production of leaflets, newsletters, magazines, etc. the facilities offered by a word processor are often not sufficient. A desktop publishing package is required.

KEY TERMS *Desktop publishing (DTP) is the use of a computer system to produce page layouts of high enough quality for printing or publication.*

CHARACTERISTICS: *of a DTP program*

1. Options within the package to produce text and graphics.

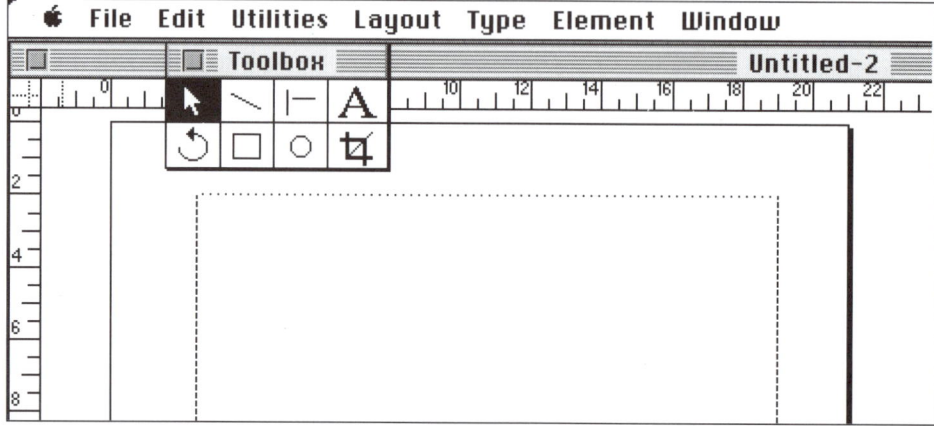

Fig. 10.5 Top of DTP screen showing menu and toolbox

2. Ability to import text and graphics from other packages.
3. Ability to divide the page into columns.
4. Facilities for moving pictures and pieces of text on the page and adjusting their size to fit spaces.
5. Guides to position text and graphics accurately.
6. A wide range of fonts, sizes and styles of text.
7. Flowing of text around objects and from page to page.

APPLICATIONS: *of DTP packages*

1. Production of leaflets and posters.
2. Producing newsletters and magazines.

Requirements for DTP

1. A DTP program.
2. A high-resolution monitor.
3. A mouse.
4. A laser printer.

It would also be advisable to have:

1. a word processor to prepare large quantities of text before importing them into the DTP package;
2. various specialist graphics packages for preparation of graphics which could not be produced using the limited drawing capability of the DTP package;
3. a library of clip art. **Clip art** is a set of standard graphic designs which can be imported into the work;
4. a scanner to copy pictures as another source of graphics.

Quick test

1. Which *two* of the following operations will move text away from the edge of the page:
   decreasing the margin   centring   changing font
   emboldening   indenting   justifying

2. Which *three* of the following may make text clearer to read:
   centring   emboldening   indenting   changing font
   justifying   italics   enlarging

3. What word processor function could you use to:
   (a) make headings more obvious,
   (b) type an address at the right of a letter,
   (c) produce a draft document with space between the lines for people to write comments.

4. Give the terms for:
   (a) adding a name and address to a standard letter,
   (b) producing a whole batch of similar letters using a mailing list.

5. Give *two* operations which a DTP package will do which a word processor often will not.

6. What type of package would you use to produce:
   (a) a poster   (b) a business letter   (c) a school newsletter
   (d) a CV?

Summary

1. **Word processing** means using IT to produce text.

2. The main advantages of word processing are:
   - it is easy to correct mistakes;
   - clear professional-looking results;
   - spellings can be checked automatically;
   - automatic **word wrap**.

3. A **font** is a set of printed characters of a particular size, style and design. Word processors usually offer a choice of fonts and sizes.

4. A **spell checker** is a program which checks the spelling of words you have used against those in a dictionary. A spell checker usually gives you choices. You can:
   - 'ignore' or 'skip' the word;
   - add the word to your own dictionary;
   - choose the right spelling from a list of suggestions;
   - correct the word yourself.

5. - A **personalised** letter is a standard letter made to look like a personal letter by adding a name and address.
   - A **mail merge** produces a set of personalised letters by merging personal details with a standard letter.

6. **Desktop publishing (DTP)** produces page layouts of high enough quality for printing or publication. DTP facilities include:
   - producing text and graphics;
   - importing text and graphics;
   - dividing the page into columns;
   - moving pictures and text and adjusting their size;
   - guides to position text and graphics accurately.

Chapter 11
Handling information: database programs

Before reading this chapter, check that you know the definitions in Unit 7.1. In particular you must be clear about the meanings of the words **file**, **record** and **field**.

KEY TERMS — *Information retrieval* means obtaining information you have specified from a set of stored data. The stored data is usually a data file or a database.

11.1 Database programs

KEY TERMS — *The word **database** is used with three slightly different meanings. The three meanings are given below. To each has been added a fuller term to describe the database more precisely.*

A database can be:
1. a large set of data containing all the information important to an organisation. This is an **organisational database**;
2. a program for handling files and retrieving information from them. This is a **database program**;
3. a file created by a database program. This is a **database file**.

This chapter is about database programs and database files.

When to use a database program

1. Use a database for your work when you have a lot of data about people, places or things and you want to find out something about them.
    A database program is particularly good at:
    - searching through a file and producing lists of records which fit certain conditions;
    - sorting a file into a different order;
    - producing statistics about the data in a file such as average height, etc.
2. If you want information about a certain topic you may find a database file on the subject which someone else has already created. This may have an information retrieval package with it or may be accessed by a standard database program.

Ready-made database files are available. Most will cost money but they may be available in a variety of forms:

1. on standard floppy disc. Some publishers produce sets of these for various subjects. Many of the database programs have sample database files supplied with them which are very useful for practice work;
2. on CD-ROM. These need a CD-ROM drive (similar to an ordinary music CD player but designed for use with a computer);
3. on-line databases (see also Unit 15.6). If the user has a terminal to a public network it is possible to access large databases on that.

EXAMPLE: *of a ready-made database*
The careers department of a school has access to files of jobs. A pupil can enter his or her personal details and interests and a database program produces a list of suggested jobs.

EXAMPLE: *of a database on CD-ROM or as a remote database*
A school or college with students who hope to go to university usually allows the students access to ECCTIS. This is an information retrieval package which gives details of university courses. A college using ECCTIS pays each year and the files are updated by:
EITHER
- the college is sent a CD-ROM containing the latest courses,

OR
- the college uses a modem and the telephone line to access the data from a remote database which is updated regularly.

ADVANTAGE: *of using remote on-line databases by modem*
If the user can afford the expense of using a public network by terminal, this allows access to databases from sources around the world (see Unit 15.6).

ADVANTAGE: *of a database on floppy disc*
Floppy disc is a cheap medium and can store quite large files.

ADVANTAGE: *of a database stored on CD-ROM*
Because CD-ROM allows a large amount of data to be stored cheaply a database can be 'multi-media' (see Unit 6.5) – and include sound, still pictures and video film as well as text.

EXAMPLE: *of a CD-ROM database*
A CD-ROM database of birds is available. If you look up a species in it you can hear the bird's song, see a photograph of it and its nest, and see film of the bird in flight.

11.2 Planning – how to design a database

Before you can put data into a database file you have to:
1. decide what data is required for the problem you are solving;
2. think of a name for your data file;
3. plan what fields you are going to have;
4. decide on a key field or sort field;
5. plan how to collect and record the data before it is typed in.

Deciding what data you require

1. Is the data in the best form for solving the problem? For example, if the data comes from asking people questions do you want:
   - YES/NO answers,

   OR
   - to give people a choice of several possibilities so that the data is 1, 2 or 3,

   OR
   - to let them write an answer in full.

2. Are you trying to put in too much data – or too little? You do not want to collect and type in data you are not going to use BUT it may be difficult to add another field later if you find you really need it.

③ Do you need to use codes for some of the data? For example, if one of your fields is SEX it is better to type just M or F rather than MALE or FEMALE.

A name for your data file

The database package may well ask you for a name straight away. In any case you will have to give it one when you save the data.

① Make sure the name you choose obeys the rules for the package, e.g. often you cannot have more than say eight letters in a name.
② Choose a name which will remind you what the data is, e.g. if the data is from the 1961 census then call the file CENSUS61. Do not call it BLUEGUM6 – even if it is the sixth file you have created since Blue Gum became your favourite group.

Planning what fields you are going to have

You will have to tell the database program what your fields are so write them down on paper first. For each field you usually have to:

① give the field a name;
② say what type of data the field is, e.g. **alphanumeric**, **numeric** or **date**;
③ say how much space it will take up, e.g. surname could be given 20 characters as this is the longest a surname is likely to be.

Field types (see Unit 1.2 for definitions)

Most databases allow:

① **alphanumeric** (may be called 'alpha' or 'string' or 'text'). This can include practically anything you can type on the keyboard. It is used for names, addresses and words.
② **numeric** (may be called 'number' or 'decimal'). This can be any number, e.g. -23.56. It is used for lengths, amounts of money, ages – any values you might do arithmetic with. If the field is numeric you may have to say how many decimal places are needed, e.g. for amounts of money you would usually say two.
③ **date** – usually in the form day/month/year, e.g. 23/10/92. Some databases allow United States dates which have the month first. If yours does, make sure you have set 'UK'.

Some databases also allow:

- **integer** – any whole number, positive or negative, e.g. 345;
- **logical** – these can have the value TRUE or FALSE;
- **label** (or 'heading') – so that you can put extra information on the screen.

It is also possible for data to include sound and graphics.

Deciding on a key field or sort field

Often a database package will ask you for a **sort field** or a key field (see Unit 7.1). This is so that your data does not have to be stored in the order in which you type it. Instead it can be stored in an order which is useful.

All you have to do is decide on a field which results in the file being in an order which is helpful when looking at it, e.g. alphabetical order of surname.

Planning how to capture the data

Before you can enter any data into a database you have to capture it.

① You will have to obtain the data from somewhere, e.g.:
  - by asking people questions;
  - by looking things up in books;
  - by doing an experiment.
② You or someone else will have to write it down.

You need a data capture form (see Unit 3.1). The form can be in
EITHER
① table format (also called column format). The form is marked in columns, with a field heading at the top of each column. Each record is written across the page, with a number of records on each form. This is useful if you are collecting the data yourself.

11.2 Planning – how to design a database

EXAMPLE: *of table or column format*

SOLENT SPORTS CLUB MEMBERSHIP					
Memb. No.	First name	Surname	Age	Sex (M/F)	Phone

Fig. 11.1

OR

❷ **form format** (also called **card format**). There is only one record on each form. The fields are spaced out on the form with suitable headings and explanations. This is useful if you are asking different people to fill in separate records.

EXAMPLE: *of form (or card) format*

SOLENT SPORTS CLUB MEMBERSHIP

Membership Number ....

First name ....   Surname ....

Age at 1/1/95 ....years   Sex (M or F) ....

Address ....   Phone ....

....

....

Fig. 11.2

To produce a data capture form you could of course draw it by hand but it would look better if you used a computer to produce it. If it was done as GCSE coursework it would also gain you more marks.

Possible methods are:

❶ use a word processor (see Chapter 10). Preferably you need one with an option to draw lines (the examples above were produced on a word processor with an option to draw tables);
❷ use a DTP package (see Unit 10.7). Lines will probably be easier to draw on this;
❸ use the database program. This may well have an option to print an empty file with grid lines.

11.3 Creating a database file

The main stages in creating a database are to:
1. produce a form to collect your data on – this can be done on a word processor;
2. collect and record the data to be keyed in;
3. run the database program;
4. name the data file;
5. key in for each field its name, type and possibly its length;
6. choose a sort field;
7. enter the data into the database – one record at a time;
8. save the database.

Saving database files

Some database programs save your data as you go along. If so, you have to **close** the file when you have finished entering data. On others you have to save the file when you have entered the data.

EXAMPLE: *the 'PEOPLE' database file – also used in later examples*
A database called 'People' has fields as follows:

'Forename'	– Alphanumeric	– Length 20
'Surname'	– Alphanumeric	– Length 20
'Date_of_birth'	– Date (or alphanumeric)	
'Height'	– Numeric	– Length 4

The following data has been collected and is keyed in:

Forename	Surname	Date_of_birth	Height
John	Smith	10/03/78	182
Janet	Smith	12/11/79	170
Bernard	Toms	01/09/77	180
Tracey	Hinds	23/02/79	176
David	Walker	19/02/78	189
Petra	Chaffey	21/08/79	178

Fig. 11.3 The PEOPLE database file

Editing database files

Most databases allow you to alter:
1. **the fields in your database.** You should be able to add fields and delete fields. You should also be able to change the names and length of fields and the type of data. You have to be careful, though, as you may lose some data in the process.

EXAMPLES: *of changing fields in the 'PEOPLE' database file*
- the name of the 'Date_of_birth' field could be changed to 'BirthDate'.
- the length of the Surname and Forename fields could be changed from 20 to 15.

2. **the actual data in your files.** You should be able to edit the data stored. You can probably display one record and then alter the contents of the fields in it.

EXAMPLES: *of changing data in the 'PEOPLE' database file*
- Janet Smith's name could be changed to Jane Smith.
- Bernard Toms' date of birth could be changed to 03/07/77.

11.4 Searches and queries

You can tell a database program to look for all the records in your database files which agree with certain conditions. This is called searching (see Unit 7.5).

KEY TERMS *A **query** (or **search string**) is the set of conditions you set for the computer to check the records against. A **match** happens when the computer finds a record which agrees with the query set.*

Query conditions

Usually you set a query and then tell the program to search. It produces a list of all the records which match the query.

A query can include comparisons which use any of the following to check for a match:
- = are they equal?
- < is the first less than the second?
- > is the first greater than the second?

Normally combinations of these symbols are also possible:
- <> not equal
- <= less than or equal
- >= greater than or equal

EXAMPLES: *of queries in the PEOPLE database*

① The query **Surname = 'Smith'** would give the matches:
John	Smith	10/03/78	182
Janet	Smith	12/11/79	170

② The query **Height > 180** would give:
John	Smith	10/03/78	182
David	Walker	19/02/78	189

③ The query **Height <= 180** would give:
Janet	Smith	12/11/79	170
Bernard	Toms	01/09/77	180
Tracey	Hinds	23/02/79	176
Petra	Chaffey	21/08/79	178

④ If the database is set to display only 'Forename' and 'Surname' then the query **Height <= 180** would give:
Janet	Smith
Bernard	Toms
Tracey	Hinds
Petra	Chaffey

⑤ The query **Height < 180** would give:
Janet	Smith	12/11/79	170
Tracey	Hinds	23/02/79	176
Petra	Chaffey	21/08/79	178

(The query would no longer match Bernard Toms because his height is equal to 180.)

Harder queries

KEY TERMS *The word **logical** applied to a statement or an expression means it is either **TRUE** or **FALSE**.*

Most databases allow queries to include:
① **NOT** to invert a logical expression;
② 'multiple queries' using **AND** or **OR** between logical expressions;
③ queries to check whether one string of characters is contained in another, i.e. whether one string is a **sub-string** of another.

EXAMPLES: *of a logical statement*
'Pigs can fly' is a logical statement which is FALSE.

of a logical expression
'$A = 6$' is a logical expression. (If A is 3 the expression is FALSE; if A is 6 it is TRUE.)

EXAMPLES: *of harder queries using the PUSSYCAT file*

COLOURING OF CAT BREEDS				
NAME	**COLOUR 1**	**COLOUR 2**	**COLOUR 3**	**EYES**
Birman	Blue	Chocolate		Blue
Blue-cream long-hair	Blue	Cream		Orange
Blue Persian	Blue			Orange
British Blue	Blue			Orange
Brown Burmese	Brown			Yellow
Calico	Black	Red	Cream	Orange
Chinchilla	White			Green
Havana Brown	Brown			Green

Fig. 11.4 The PUSSYCAT file

Here are some examples of searches of the PUSSYCAT file:

Query	Match (Names only)
COLOUR1 = 'Brown'	Brown Burmese, Havana Brown
Name (Contains) 'Brown'	Brown Burmese, Havana Brown
EYES = 'Blue' OR EYES = 'Green'	Birman, Chinchilla, Havana Brown
EYES = 'Blue' AND EYES = 'Green'	– (Eyes are Blue OR Green, not BOTH)
EYES = 'Blue' OR 'Green'	– (Probably gives an error message)
COLOUR1 = 'Blue' AND EYES = 'Blue'	Birman
NOT(COLOUR1='Blue') AND EYES = 'Orange'	Calico

Notes:
There is no set way of writing queries. Different database packages have different methods.

❶ In some packages a string has to be enclosed between quotes instead of apostrophes, e.g.
   "Smith" rather than **'Smith'**.
❷ Sometimes the words AND, NOT, OR are replaced by symbols or have to be between full stops, e.g.
   Surname = 'Smith' AND Forename = 'John'
   could be
   Surname = 'Smith' .AND. Forename = 'John'
   or it could be
   Surname = 'Smith' & Forename = 'John'
❸ Your database probably has a special query for 'contains'.
❹ Most databases do not allow the query:
   EYES = 'Blue' OR 'Green'
   You have to say:
   EYES = 'Blue' OR EYES = 'Green'
❺ Be careful about capital letters.
   The query   **EYES = 'Blue'** might give a different match from
               EYES = 'BLUE' or
               EYES = 'blue'

11.5 Statistics and sorts

Sorts

A database will usually allow a file to be sorted into ascending or descending order for one or more chosen fields (see Unit 7.5 for definitions). If two sort fields are chosen, then the second one will only be used if two records have the same value in the first sort field.

EXAMPLE: *of two sort fields*

The following names are to be sorted using SURNAME as the first sort field and FORENAME as the second sort field.

FORENAME	SURNAME
Alice	McDonald
Gina	Simpson
Bjorn	Ingerson
Cassidy	Simpson
Sachie	McDonald

The result would be:

FORENAME	SURNAME
Bjorn	Ingerson
Alice	McDonald
Sachie	McDonald
Cassidy	Simpson
Gina	Simpson

EXAMPLE: *of a sort*

The PUSSYCAT file is given in Fig. 11.4 in ascending alphabetical order of the names of the cats.

It can be sorted into descending alphabetical order of the names as follows:

NAME	COLOUR1	COLOUR2	COLOUR3	EYES
Havana Brown	Brown			Green
Chinchilla	White			Green
Calico	Black	Red	Cream	Orange
Brown Burmese	Brown			Yellow
British Blue	Blue			Orange
Blue Persian	Blue			Orange
Blue-cream long-hair	Blue	Cream		Orange
Birman	Blue	Chocolate		Blue

Statistics

Your database program will usually do calculations for you. These can be done:
EITHER
- on all the records in the database,

OR
- on just those records which have been selected by a query.

The statistics would operate on one of the numeric fields in your file. Examples are:
- **sum** or total – produced by adding up the value in that field for every record;
- **average** – the average for all values in that field;
- **maximum** or highest – the largest value in that field;
- **minimum** or least – the smallest value in that field;
- **count** – the number of records selected.

EXAMPLE: *of a count*

To find the number of cats in the PUSSYCAT file with blue eyes or with colour1 blue it would be necessary to:
- set the query **EYES = 'blue' OR COLOUR1 = 'blue'**;
- select the statistic for finding the number of records. (This might be under the heading COUNT in the menus.)

There are 4 records in the PUSSYCAT file which match this query so the result displayed should be 4.

11.6 More about databases

Generating a report

KEY TERMS A *database report* is a set of results from work on a database put together as a document for printing.

Instead of having to print out your results as you produce them, most database programs allow you to produce a report. You then print this out at the end, when you have finished. A report may include:

① lists of records – produced as the result of searches through your file;
② lists of records sorted into a different order from the original file;
③ statistics – calculations carried out on the data in the file;
④ text added by the user to link the results in the report and make it presentable. It may allow underlining, different fonts, page numbering, etc.

ADVANTAGES: *of a database report*
① It allows results to be printed out together as one document.
② It allows text to be added to link results together.

Note:
If your database does not have a report facility then export each result to a word processor file and produce a report using the word processor.

A query language

KEY TERMS A *query language* is the set of words and symbols which are used to retrieve information from a database.

Notes:
① Often a query language enables a user to retrieve information interactively.
② In the simplest case the language consists of single query statements.

EXAMPLE: *query language for the PEOPLE database* (see Fig. 11.3)
LIST Forename, Surname, Height FOR Height >= 180 .AND. Height <= 186
This will list the following:
John   Smith   182
Bernard   Toms   180

  A more complex language will allow the user to put instructions together in a sequence. This may be done by:
EITHER
● writing the sequence in the form of a program,
OR
● producing a macro (see Unit 9.1).

EXAMPLE: *of a program for the PEOPLE database* (see Fig. 11.3)
@ 1 , 5 SAY "Maximum height acceptable:"
@ 1 , 39 GET Max
@ 3 , 5 SAY "Minimum height acceptable:"
@ 3 , 39 GET Min
READ
LIST Forename, Surname, Height FOR Height >= Min .AND. Height <= Max
WAIT

Notes:
① The last two examples are both in the language which accompanies the database package dBASE (Version III PLUS).
② The program shown asks the user to type in values for Max and Min. It then displays the Forename, Surname and Height for all records with heights from Max to Min inclusive. The conversation might be as follows:

                    Maximum height acceptable: 186

                    Minimum height acceptable: 180

        John   Smith   182
        Bernard   Toms   180

❸ SAY causes text to be printed on the screen. GET causes the computer to expect input. The numbers after the @ symbol give the position on the screen where this will happen.

ADVANTAGES: *of a query language*

❶ It allows the user to retrieve information from a database without having to write a complicated program.
❷ If the query language allows the user to store a sequence of instructions then:
- the sequence stored can be used again;
- variables can be introduced. These enable the user to use the same sequence of instructions to retrieve different sets of data, e.g. in the example above Max and Min are variables to which the user can give values.

Linked files

Often an organisation has a number of files which have data in common. Database programs often allow the user to link files. Usually two files are linked by telling the program that one field in the first file is the same as a field in the second file.

APPLICATION: *of a database*

Estate agent

An estate agent's office has a small local network and a link to its other branch, which is in the next town. For its main customer service it has four sets of data.

❶ HOUSE – a database file of the houses for sale. The fields for this are:
House_Ref, House_Type, Price, Area, Beds, Recep, Garage, CH, Comments. Each house is given a house reference number when it is accepted on to the books. House_Type is a code which is based on the number of rooms and whether the house is detached, a bungalow, etc. Price is the amount the owner hopes to obtain for the house. Area is a code for the village or town the house is in. Beds is the number of bedrooms. Recep is the number of reception rooms. Garage is a code (0,1 or 2) for whether there is no garage or a single or a double garage. CH is a code for the type of central heating, if any.

House_Ref	House_Type	Price	Area	Beds	Recep	Garage	CH	Comments
32614	DH6	124950	Rich	4	2	2	G	Easy walk from centre
34612	AA3	93000	Rich	2	1	1	E	Spacious rooms, no gdn.
35478	TH5	53950	Bril	3	2	1	G	End terrace, small gdn.
36725	DH7	127950	Bril	5	2	2	G	Ground floor annexe w. 1 bd
37865	DH7	149950	Tile	4	3	2	G	Immaculate. Double glazed
37896	TH7	125000	Rich	5	2	0	N	3 storeys. Modernised

Fig. 11.5 Records from the HOUSE database

❷ OWNER – a database file of the owners of houses for sale. The fields for this are:
Name, Address, House_Ref, Comments.
House_Ref is the same field as in the HOUSE file. (See Fig. 11.6.)
❸ BUYER – a database file of prospective buyers. The fields for this are:
Name, Address, Max_Price, Area, House_Type1, House_Type2, Done.
Maximum price is the highest amount the customer is prepared to pay. Area is the town or village which the buyer is most interested in (an entry of ALL means they do not mind where it is). There are two fields for house type to allow clients more choice. Done contains the reference numbers of any houses the buyer knows about.

Name	Address	House_Ref	Comments
Sharma, H	6, Romer Grove, Richton	32614	Urgent - new job
Jarratt, P.T.	18, Railes Rd., Richton	34612	New instructions pending
Eisen, H	23, Forest Drive, Brillhurst	35478	
Mailer, T.V.	64, Wittering Lane, Brillhurst	36725	Contract ends 18/4
Seale, M.J.	Old Chapel, Rudd Lane, Tilemersh	37865	
Miraz, J.Z.	27, Compton Rd., Richton	37896	Quick sale required

Fig. 11.6 Records from the OWNER database

④ DTP files, one for each house. These are used to produce fact sheets giving house details to send to buyers. These are printed on a laser printer and each contains a scanned photograph of the house and word processed details of it. The name of each file is the same as the house reference number.

HOUSE and OWNER are linked files – linked by the field House_Ref. The database used has a query language which has been used to write several file enquiry programs. One of these programs is used as follows.

① A prospective buyer comes into the office.
② After a discussion, the estate agent runs the program and selects the screen display option.
③ The program then asks for a maximum price, an area (if any) and the house type. The estate agent is able to supply these following the discussion.
④ The program opens the house file and finds all the records which match. These are displayed one by one and the estate agent tags any which the buyer is interested in. The program matches prices in a range £5000 above and below the maximum – sometimes buyers are prepared to spend more if a house particularly suits them.
⑤ The computer prints out a list of the house reference numbers which is given to a secretary.
⑥ The secretary looks for copies of the fact sheets in a filing cabinet. Those which are not available he/she prints on the computer with the laser printer using the DTP program.
⑦ The house search program asks if the buyer wishes to be added to the BUYER file. If the answer is YES it asks for the buyer's name and address and adds another record to the file. This includes adding reference numbers of the houses chosen to the Done field.
⑧ At a later date the program can then be used to produce further lists for that buyer.

Quick test

1 Which of these would you use a database program for:
   (a) to work out your personal finances,
   (b) to store the details of all your tapes and CDs,
   (c) to write a letter to a friend?

2 Name *three* of the fields which would be in a database file of information about school pupils.

3 Give the name for the type of form used when collecting data for a database.

4 State *three* particular functions that a database program provides.

5 Give a reason why it is useful to have a database which has a report facility.

Quick test

Questions 6 to 9

The following are data types commonly available for data in databases:
- A Alphanumeric
- B Numeric
- C Date
- D Integer
- E Logical
- F Label

State which one would be used for each of the following:

6 a field on which statistics were being produced,
7 data which is either true or false,
8 names,
9 batting scores in a cricket database.

10 Look at the PEOPLE file (see Fig. 11.3). Write down the forenames and surnames of the people:
(a) in ascending order of surname,
(b) in descending order of height.

Summary

1 A database program can be used to:
   - **search** through a file to produce lists of records which fit certain conditions;
   - **sort** a file into a different order;
   - **produce statistics** about the data in a file.

2 Common **data types** used in databases are:
   - alphanumeric;
   - date;
   - logical;
   - numeric;
   - integer;
   - label.

3 To create a database you would normally have to:
   - produce a data capture form;
   - collect and record the data to be keyed in;
   - run the database program;
   - name the database file;
   - key in for each field its name, type and possibly its length;
   - choose a sort field;
   - enter the data into the database – one record at a time;
   - close or save the database.

4 To **retrieve information** from a file you set up a **query condition**. The program then searches for all records which **match** the condition.

5 Query conditions can include:
   - **comparisons** based on =,<,> and <>, >=, <=;
   - the **logical** operators AND, OR and NOT;
   - comparisons with **sub-strings**.

6 A **sort** rearranges a file into a given order.
   - A sort can be **numeric** or **alphabetic**.
   - A file can be sorted into **ascending** or **descending** order.

7 A **database report** is a set of results from work on a database put together as a document for printing.

Chapter 12
Models of situations

12.1 What is a model?

We are all familiar with the idea of a model as an imitation of an object, e.g. an architect's model of a building made to show what the finished building will look like.

We use the term in computing to mean rather more than that.

KEY TERMS

A **model** of a situation or an object is something which is made to appear and/or behave like the real thing.

A **computer model** of a situation or an object is a program and data which together behave like the real thing.

EXAMPLES: *of models*
1. A sculpture, a painting, a photograph or a film of a person.
2. A model car.

EXAMPLES: *of computer models*
1. A simulation of driving a car. The user controls the car with the keys or a joystick or a mock steering wheel. The car has to be kept on the road and has to avoid other cars which appear. The user can change gear and use the brakes and accelerator.
2. A graph of a company's profits. A spreadsheet is used to calculate the profits for each month. A chart package is then used to produce a line graph from these profits to show progress for the year.
3. A robot arm. The arm is made with a wrist, an elbow and a shoulder. It is then programmed to make movements similar to those of a person's arm.

CHARACTERISTICS: *of a computer model*
1. The behaviour of the model copies the actual situation, at least in some important ways. Usually only some of the situation is copied, e.g.
   (a) in the driving simulation example above:
   - if you hit something nothing too terrible happens;
   - you can see the road in front of you but you cannot look out of the side window at the pavement.
   (b) the robot arm may have a wrist, an elbow and a shoulder but only a grip instead of a hand.
2. The behaviour of the model is determined by rules which are built into the program. If you change the program or its data you can change the way the model behaves, e.g. in the driving simulation:
   - the program could be changed to make the car behave as though a tyre had a puncture,
   - the data could be changed so that the car goes faster.
3. The model can be studied to forecast what will happen in the real world, e.g. in the company profits example above a formula can be put into the spreadsheet to calculate

the likely profits for the next few months. This will allow the management to forecast future trends.

Reasons for using a model

1. To avoid danger, e.g. a computer model of a nuclear reactor to study the behaviour of the reactor if changes are made to the fuel rods.
2. To save money, e.g. a flight simulator. A pilot may learn a lot of flying techniques without the expense of actual flying.
3. To save time, e.g. a simulation of a biology experiment. A student may study the characteristics of a crop of peas. A computer can simulate the growth of several generations of hybrid peas. On the computer several seasons' growth can be simulated in a few minutes.
4. To help make difficult decisions, e.g. a model of the national economy. Ministers and Treasury officials can try various budget changes to see what their effect would be.
5. To improve designs, e.g. a simulation of an airport. Features can be incorporated into the model such as:
   - flow of people through the airport buildings;
   - flow of traffic on the proposed site and in the surrounding area;
   - the effects of the noise of the aircraft engines.
6. To stimulate interest, e.g. a learning game on a computer. A simulation of running a town can be made into a game. Students make policy decisions and are awarded points depending on whether or not the town thrives. They take more interest in the subject and learn more quickly.
7. To study behaviour of systems, e.g. the study into the origins of the universe. Theories such as the 'Big Bang' can be modelled and the consequences of the theory investigated.

ADVANTAGES: *of using a model*
1. A system can be studied without the danger or expense which may be involved in studying the real situation.
2. Predictions can be made about the future behaviour of a system.
3. The model can be run more quickly than the actual system to see how it will behave over a long period.
4. The model can be run slowly to study carefully effects which happen too quickly to observe clearly in the real system.

DISADVANTAGES *of using a model*
1. The model may not imitate the real system exactly. The model is only as good as the rules which govern its behaviour.
2. It may be difficult or expensive to produce a good model of a particular system.

Models and time

A model of an event may or may not take the same time as the actual event. It may operate:
1. at the same rate as the event – this is a **real time** model;
2. faster than the event;
3. slower than the event.

EXAMPLES: *of models with the same speed as the actual situation*
1. An aircraft flight simulation.
2. A computer animation when it is running.

EXAMPLES: *of models faster than the actual situation*
1. A computer simulation of the development of the Earth.
2. A time lapse film of a plant growing.

EXAMPLES: *of models slower than the actual situation*
1. An action replay of a hurdle race.
2. A computer animation while it is being produced.

Mathematical models

Many computer models have a mathematical basis:
1. the quantities in the actual situation are represented by variables in the program;
2. the rules which govern the model's behaviour are contained in formulae or program statements about these variables.

EXAMPLES: *of models using a mathematical formula*
1. A program which simulates on the screen a ball being thrown.
   - Here the quantities being modelled are the height, the horizontal distance covered by the ball and the time. They are represented by variables in the program statements.
   - The rules of the model are mathematical expressions in the program statements. For instance the horizontal distance is worked out by assuming that the speed is constant except for a reduction due to air resistance.
2. A spreadsheet.
   - The quantities in the actual situation are represented by cells in the spreadsheet.
   - The rules governing the behaviour of the model are built in formulae contained in the cells whose values can change.

Types of computer model

The main means of producing a computer model are:
1. Spreadsheets – these are dealt with in Chapter 13.
2. Computer graphics, including graphs and charts – see Chapter 14.
3. Simulation programs – see Unit 12.2.
4. Virtual reality systems – see Unit 12.3.
5. Expert systems – see Unit 12.3.

In the case of a spreadsheet or a computer graphics package, the user is creating the model by adding data to a general purpose package. With a simulation or an expert system the model has been created for them.

Stages in producing a model

1. Analyse the problem thoroughly – collect data from the real-life situation if possible.
2. Design the model – work out what the variables and the rules are.
3. Produce the model, e.g write a computer program or formulae in a spreadsheet.
4. Test and improve the model – until it produces the same results as are observed in the actual system.
5. Validate the model – over a period of time, check that it does produce the same results as the actual system.
6. Use the model to make predictions – it is now ready to answer 'What if … ?' questions and predict what would happen to the real system in a new situation.
   - Change the values of the variables.
   - Make changes to the rules governing the model.

12.2 Simulations

KEY TERMS *A computer **simulation** of a system is a program which models that system.*

CHARACTERISTICS: A computer simulation has the same characteristics as other models:
1. it mimics a real-life situation;
2. the behaviour of the model is determined by rules. These are usually mathematical formulae built into the program;
3. the behaviour of the model can be studied to find out how the actual system would behave in similar circumstances.

APPLICATIONS: *of computer simulations in brief*

① Military operational research
A program can simulate battle conditions to assess weapons and tactics under various conditions, e.g. difficult terrain, adverse weather.

② International relations
A program simulates the behaviour of different countries of the world, e.g. to predict how neighbouring countries will react to a particular decision by one country.

③ Circuit testing
It is no longer necessary to make an actual test circuit for any new chip which is designed. The new designs are instead tested by simulation. The design is first produced using a special drawing program. From these drawings a computer can produce a model which works out the output of the circuit for different combinations of inputs. If the results of the simulation are satisfactory then production can be started.

APPLICATIONS: *of computer simulations in detail*

① A computer model of a nuclear power plant

The situation
National Power is the national body who run nuclear power stations. They use a simulation of each power station to improve the performance of the actual station.

What the computer does
The computer model calculates temperatures, pressures and flows of gases and liquids at different points in the plant.

For each power station there is a different version of the model. The purpose of each model is to:
- check each day whether the plant is producing as much power as could be expected;
- find what conditions give the most economic running of the plant;
- find what changes could be made to the plant to improve output;
- predict what the temperatures, pressures and flows are in parts of the plant where there are no instruments.

Testing
The model is continually tested by checking its results against the values shown on actual instruments in the plant. If the model does not agree with the instruments, then the programs are improved.

② Flight simulation
As early as the 1940s pilots were given some training in mock-ups of real aircraft cockpits. Later, when the first multi-engined jet airliners were introduced, computer-controlled flight simulators were employed. The 'cockpit' was mounted on hydraulic rams. The rams were under the control of a computer whose program simulated various flying conditions. The crew under training had to respond by referring to their instruments and operating their controls. In these early simulations the 'view outside' was not very realistic. Advances in computer graphics have meant that visual images are now available to improve the authenticity of the simulations.

Techniques have improved so much that it is now possible for the training of military pilots to include the experience of enemy attacks. The attacks have a random factor in them so that the pilot is forced to respond not only quickly, but in a flexible way.

Civil pilots are able to practise landing and taking off. Accurate images of real airports appear in the simulation. Again random elements are introduced into the simulation so that the pilot has to respond to, say, a burst tyre on landing.

Flight simulation programs of a less complex nature are available for microcomputers. Some merely provide amusement, but others provide a serious exercise for would-be pilots.

12.3 Other computer models

Virtual reality

In recent years some simulations have been improved by allowing the user to experience the model rather than just look at it.

Chapter 12 Models of situations

KEY TERMS *A **virtual reality** system is a computer simulation which the user can interact with in such a way that the experience appears real.*

CHARACTERISTICS: *of virtual reality systems*

1. The user feels a part of the simulation.
2. The model may be experienced through any or all of the senses – hearing, smell, touch, sight, taste. The user's body may be physically moved.
3. Various devices may be used to improve the interaction including:
   - a helmet to improve the visual and hearing effects;
   - a glove which can be used both to receive touch sensations and to control the model;
   - a joystick for more detailed control of the simulation.

APPLICATIONS: *of virtual reality*

Virtual reality is proving very popular for games but the system will clearly also be an important tool for the future.

Exploring a building

A 3-D database model is created of a building. The users can move around in the model using:
- stereoscopic helmets to see the building in 3-D;
- tracking devices so that they know where they are;
- special joysticks to navigate their way around.

This technique has been used with:
- an abbey which is now ruined but the computer model is a reconstruction of the original abbey;
- a theatre which has not yet been built so that people can wander round the model and make comments about the design. If necessary, changes can be made to the model – and the plans.

Expert systems

Ways are being found to store the knowledge of experts so that others may call on their expertise without them having to be present.

KEY TERMS *An **expert system** is a computer program which simulates the knowledge and experience of a human expert.*

CHARACTERISTICS: *of a typical expert system*

1. It deals with only one particular type of problem.
2. It interacts with the user by question and answer. The computer asks one question, the user replies and the computer's next question depends on that answer.
3. It can cope with incomplete answers. The user may not be able to answer some questions but still needs help.
4. It explains how it arrived at its conclusions. The user may have misunderstood a question and this becomes clear from the computer's comments. The user can then **backtrack** – go back through some questions and answer them again.

How an expert system works

The expert system consists of:
- **a knowledge base.** This contains facts about this particular application and rules about how to apply them;
- **an inference engine.** This is a program which gradually works towards a solution of the user's problem using the expert's knowledge and the user's replies.

The expert system is constructed by:
- a specialist in expert systems (a **knowledge engineer**) working with the expert whose knowledge is going to be used;
- using an **expert system shell**. This is an expert system without a knowledge base. The knowledge engineer and the expert add the facts and rules which form the knowledge base.

APPLICATIONS: *of expert systems*

❶ Tax/benefits advice
The expert system contains all the facts and rules relating to the current tax and benefit allowances. This includes who qualifies for them and how to claim them. The computer asks questions about the user's circumstances and gives information and advice.

❷ Identifying rocks
The user collects rock samples and then uses a program which asks about their characteristics. Answering the questions may involve performing various analyses of each rock sample to determine its basic structure and the constituent minerals and their properties.

❸ Medical diagnosis
The computer asks the patient about his or her symptoms and the patient replies. For most questions, the computer offers the patient a choice of answers. The program does not replace the doctor. The computer provides the doctor with suggested causes of the symptoms and the reasons for these deductions. The doctor can then decide on the correct diagnosis and suitable treatment.

ADVANTAGES: *of computer assisted diagnosis*
- Some patients are happier describing symptoms to an impersonal computer than to a person.
- The computer interaction can take place while the doctor is seeing another patient. Patient and doctor can then discuss the computer's findings later.
- The computer can call on specialist knowledge which the doctor does not have.

Quick test

1 Choose *three* of the following which are computer models:
 (a) a graph showing a firm's profits for a year,
 (b) a word processed letter,
 (c) a flight simulation,
 (d) a compiler,
 (e) a virtual reality system.

2 Give *three* reasons for using a model instead of the real thing.

3 Which *two* of the following are real time models:
 (a) a virtual reality system,
 (b) a time lapse film,
 (c) an action replay,
 (d) a flight simulation,
 (e) a spreadsheet?

4 Put the following steps into order:
 (a) validate the model,
 (b) test and improve the model,
 (c) produce the model,
 (d) analyse the problem,
 (e) design the model.

For each of the examples in questions **5** to **9** say which, if any, of the following terms applies to it:
 (a) a computer model (b) a simulation
 (c) an expert system (d) virtual reality

5 A game in which two players using interconnected computers see images of each other and feel they are taking part in a sword-fight.

139

6 An electronic book.
7 A company's sales drawn up on a spreadsheet.
8 A robot which walks and talks like a human being.
9 A system which diagnoses why a car will not start by asking a set of questions.

10 Why would a virtual reality program use a viewer in a headpiece rather than an ordinary television screen?

Summary

1 A **computer model** of a system is a program and data which behaves like the real thing, e.g. a driving simulation, a graph of business profits, a robot arm.

2 A model:
   - may copy only part of the actual system;
   - is determined by rules usually built into the program;
   - can be used to forecast what will happen in the real world.

3 A model can be used in order to:
   - avoid danger;
   - save money;
   - save time;
   - help make difficult decisions;
   - improve designs;
   - stimulate interest in learning;
   - study behaviour of real systems.

4 A computer model may run at the same rate, faster or slower than the real system.

5 In practice computer models can be produced using:
   - spreadsheets;
   - computer graphics, including charts;
   - simulation programs;
   - virtual reality systems;
   - expert systems.

6 The stages in producing a model are:
   - analyse the problem;
   - design the model;
   - produce the model;
   - test and improve the model;
   - validate the model;
   - use the model to make predictions.

7 A computer **simulation** of a system is a program which models the system.

8 A **virtual reality** system is a simulation which appears real.
   - The user feels a part of the simulation.
   - The simulation may be experienced through all the senses.

9 An **expert system** is a computer program which simulates the knowledge and experience of a human expert.

10 An expert system consists of:
   - a **knowledge base** of rules and facts;
   - a program to work out a solution of the user's problem.

Chapter 13
Creating models: spreadsheets

13.1 Introduction to spreadsheets

If you want to use a computer to model a situation involving numeric data, then a spreadsheet is often the simplest way to do it. (Simulations and expert systems require a lot of knowledge and time to produce.)

KEY TERMS

A **spreadsheet** program gives you a table on the screen in which you can move around and in which you can place data.
   The table consists of rectangular slots called **cells**.
   The cells are arranged in **rows** across the page and **columns** down the page.

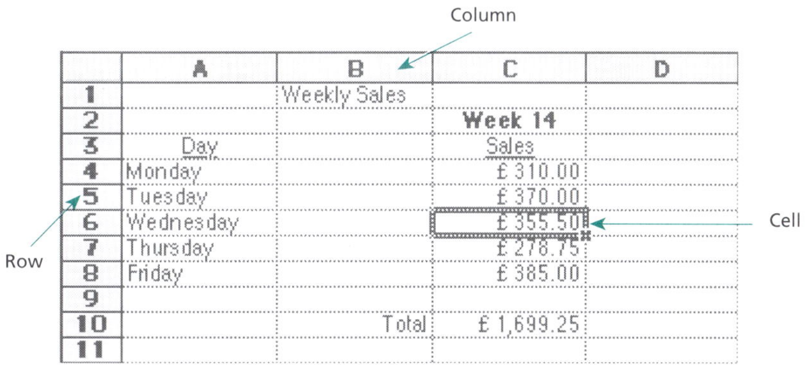

	A	B	C	D
1		Weekly Sales		
2			Week 14	
3		Day	Sales	
4		Monday	£ 310.00	
5		Tuesday	£ 370.00	
6		Wednesday	£ 355.50	
7		Thursday	£ 278.75	
8		Friday	£ 385.00	
9				
10		Total	£ 1,699.25	
11				

Fig. 13.1 A spreadsheet screen

Labelling cells

The user can refer to any cell or group of cells by using a label. Usually a label for a cell consists of the column followed by the row. Different programs have different ways of labelling the rows and columns.
   This label is called a **reference** (see Unit 13.4).

Entering data

The data placed in the cells can be:
- numbers;
- words and other text;
- formulae which make it possible to do calculations on the numbers.

Fig. 13.2 A spreadsheet with 123.4 being entered into C3

Data is usually entered by moving to the cell you want using the cursor keys or the mouse and then keying it in.

EXAMPLE: *of a simple spreadsheet*
The SHOP SALES spreadsheet
Gratesby School Shop is run mainly by the teachers and pupils and is open at break times and in the lunch hour. It sells anything useful which cannot be supplied free by the school. This includes pens and pencils, floppy discs for computers, T-shirts, etc. The pupils who help to run it learn as they work and they record a summary of each week's takings on a spreadsheet. This gives a summary of the sales for the week. The columns show:

Day	–	the day of the week;
I.C.	–	the person in charge for that day;
Sales	–	the number of items sold;
Cost	–	the cost to the shop of the items which were sold;
Income	–	the amount of money taken for the day.

	A	B	C	D	E	F
1		Shop Sales - Week Ending 3rd Feb 1995				
2						
3						
4	Day	I.C.	Sales	Cost	Income	
5	Monday	William	45	15.5	19.7	
6	Tuesday	Kath	53	18.63	24.45	
7	Wednesda	Jenny	37	11.48	15.45	
8	Thursday	Chris	72	21.2	26.65	
9	Friday	Jo	64	19.25	24.9	
10						

Fig. 13.3 The original SHOP SALES spreadsheet with the data keyed in and no attempt made to improve the format

Note:
The text in each of cells B1 and A7 is too long for the cell. In the case of B1 the spreadsheet has let the text overflow out of the right of the cell. For cell A7 however, the 'y' of Wednesday has been cut off because there is something in B7. One solution to this is to widen column A.

13.2 Improving the look of a spreadsheet

You should be able to improve a spreadsheet as follows.

Changing the column widths
You can make the columns wider or narrower.

Underlining and bold
Many packages will allow you to use underlining, bold and often to change fonts. Underlining is useful to:
- emphasise headings;
- put a line under a column of figures which is being totalled.

Centring and justifying

Most spreadsheets put text at the left of a cell and numbers at the right. However, if you want to you can change this so that data is at the left, the right or in the centre of a cell. The spreadsheet will probably allow you to do this to columns or rows or whole blocks of cells.

Changing the formats of numbers

A spreadsheet will allow you to change the formats of numbers:
- to make them amounts of money or percentages;
- to change the number of decimal places.

Note: Entering amounts of money
If you type a £ sign the spreadsheet will take what you type as a string instead of an amount of money. The amount should be entered as an ordinary number. The format can then be changed to pounds later.

13.3 Formulae

The contents of a cell can be text or a number but they can also be a formula. It is these formulae which allow spreadsheets to do calculations and to model real situations.

KEY TERMS *A **formula** is a mathematical expression which allows the value in one cell to be worked out from the values in other cells.*

Note:
There are different ways of letting the spreadsheet know that the contents of a cell are a formula. Often this is done by starting the formula with an '=' sign.

EXAMPLE: *of a simple formula*
A spreadsheet has the following data in it:
- cell C2 contains 11, cell D2 contains 2.5;
- the formula = C2 + D2 is put in E2.

When the ENTER (or RETURN) key is pressed the value 13.5 appears (see Fig. 13.4).

Note:
The cell E2 contains the formula = C2 + D2 but what you see in it is the result 13.5.

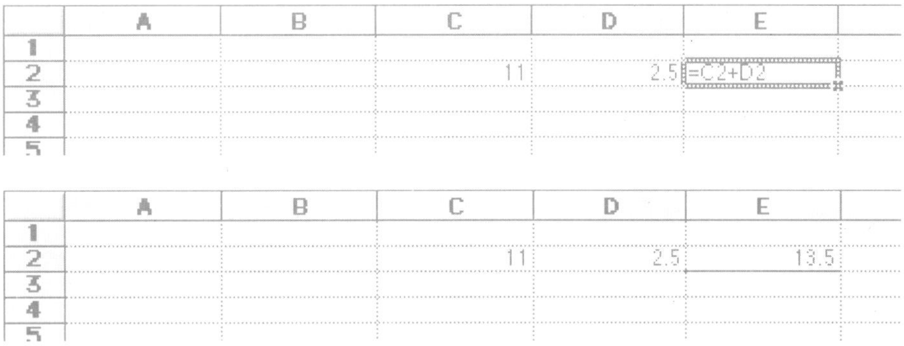

Fig. 13.4 A spreadsheet with the formula = C2 + D2 entered in E2

EXAMPLES: *of formulae*

The SHOP SALES spreadsheet
Fig. 13.5 shows the original spreadsheet (Fig. 13.3) improved by changing the money formats and adding simple formulae as follows:
- in C10 a formula for the total sales which adds the five cells above it:
  = C5 + C6 + C7 + C8 + C9;
- in D10 a similar formula for the total cost:
  = D5 + D6 + D7 + D8 + D9;
- and in E10 a similar formula for the total income:
  = E5 + E6 + E7 + E8 + E9.

	A	B	C	D	E	F
1		Shop Sales - Week Ending 3rd Feb 1995				
2						
3						
4	Day	I.C.	Sales	Cost	Income	
5	Monday	William	45	£15.50	£19.70	
6	Tuesday	Katherine	53	£18.63	£24.45	
7	Wednesday	Jennifer	37	£11.48	£15.45	
8	Thursday	Christopher	72	£21.20	£26.65	
9	Friday	Joanna	64	£19.25	£24.90	
10		Totals	271	£86.06	£111.15	
11						

Fig. 13.5 SHOP SALES spreadsheet with the Sales, Cost and Income columns totalled

Range of cells

KEY TERMS *A **range of cells** is a group of cells referred to as a unit.*

On many spreadsheets a range of cells is referred to using a colon (:).

EXAMPLES: *of ranges of cells*
1. C5:C16 is all the cells in the column C between C5 and C16 inclusive. Including C5 and C16 this covers 12 cells.
2. C2:D3 is the block of cells C2, C3, D2, D3.

Functions

On most spreadsheets the user can include mathematical functions in a formulae.

EXAMPLES: *of functions*
1. SUM – the result of adding the numbers in the cells given.
2. AVERAGE – the average of the numbers in the cells given.
3. COUNT – the number of cells in the range given.
4. MAXIMUM – the largest value in the cells given.
5. MINIMUM – the smallest value in the cells given.
6. More complex mathematical functions such as SINE, COSINE, etc.

Different spreadsheets will have different ways of doing these and the words may be abbreviated, e.g. AVG for AVERAGE, MAX for MAXIMUM.

EXAMPLES: *of functions in use*

The SHOP SALES spreadsheet
1. The formulae in cells C10, D10 and E10 calculate the totals of sales, cost and income. To do this they use the SUM function.
   The formulae used to produce the totals in Fig. 13.5 can be replaced by:
   - in C10 – = SUM(C5:C9)
   - in D10 – = SUM(D5:D9)
   - in E10 – = SUM(E5:E9)
2. In Fig. 13.6 averages for the sales, cost and income totals have been calculated using:
   - in C11 – = AVG(C5:C9)
   - in D11 – = AVG(D5:D9)
   - in E11 – = AVG(E5:E9)

	A	B	C	D	E	F
1		Shop Sales - Week Ending 3rd Feb 1995				
2						
3						
4	Day	I.C.	Sales	Cost	Income	
5	Monday	William	45	£15.50	£19.70	
6	Tuesday	Katherine	53	£18.63	£24.45	
7	Wednesday	Jennifer	37	£11.48	£15.45	
8	Thursday	Christopher	72	£21.20	£26.65	
9	Friday	Joanna	64	£19.25	£24.90	
10		Totals	271	£86.06	£111.15	
11		Averages	54.2	£17.21	£22.23	
12						

Fig. 13.6 The SHOP SALES spreadsheet with functions used

	A	B	C	D	E
1		Shop Sales - Week Ending 3rd Feb 1995			
2					
3					
4	Day	I.C.	Sales	Cost	Income
5	Monday	William	45	15.5	19.7
6	Tuesday	Katherine	53	18.63	24.45
7	Wednesday	Jennifer	37	11.48	15.45
8	Thursday	Christopher	72	21.2	26.65
9	Friday	Joanna	64	19.25	24.9
10		Totals	=SUM(C5:C9)	=SUM(D5:D9)	=SUM(E5:E9)
11		Averages	=AVG(C5:C9)	=AVG(D5:D9)	=AVG(E5:E9)
12					

Fig. 13.7 The SHOP SALES spreadsheet with functions used and the formulae shown

13.4 Copying cells

One of the most powerful features of a spreadsheet is its ability to copy data and formulae.

EXAMPLES: *of copying formulae*

The SHOP SALES spreadsheet

The pupils who run the Gratesby School Shop are very keen to know their profits. They add columns into the SHOP SALES spreadsheet for Profit and for Profit%:
- Profit is worked out by subtracting the Cost from the Income;
- Profit% is worked out by dividing the Profit by the cost and then expressing it as a percentage.

The spreadsheet's COPY CELLS option is then used to copy the formulae into other cells.
  In Fig. 13.8 the previous SHOP SALES spreadsheet has been improved as follows:

❶ only two formulae were actually typed in. These were:
- in cell F5: = E5 − D5 and
- in cell G5: = F5 / D5

❷ the other profits and percentages were produced by copying formulae down the columns:
- copy cell F5 down the range F6:F11 and
- copy G5 down the range G6:G10
  (The value in G10 is the overall percentage profit.)

❸ the columns were then tidied up:
- the numbers in column F were reformatted by marking them as a block and making them into amounts of money;
- in the same way the numbers in column G were reformatted to be percentages and to have only two places of decimals.

	A	B	C	D	E	F	G	H
1		Shop Sales - Week Ending 3rd Feb 1995						
2								
3								
4	Day	I.C.	Sales	Cost	Income	Profit	Profit%	
5	Monday	William	45	£15.50	£19.70	£4.20	27.10%	
6	Tuesday	Katherine	53	£18.63	£24.45	£5.82	31.24%	
7	Wednesday	Jennifer	37	£11.48	£15.45	£3.97	34.58%	
8	Thursday	Christopher	72	£21.20	£26.65	£5.45	25.71%	
9	Friday	Joanna	64	£19.25	£24.90	£5.65	29.35%	
10		Totals	271	£86.06	£111.15	£25.09	29.15%	
11		Averages	54.2	£17.21	£22.23	£5.02		
12								

Fig. 13.8 The SHOP SALES spreadsheet with two extra columns for Profit and Profit% added to the right

Chapter 13 Creating models: spreadsheets

	A	B	C	D	E	F	G
1		Shop Sales - Week Ending 3rd Feb 1995					
2							
3							
4	Day	I.C.	Sales	Cost	Income	Profit	Profit%
5	Monday	William	45	15.5	19.7	=E5-D5	=F5/D5
6	Tuesday	Katherine	53	18.63	24.45	=E6-D6	=F6/D6
7	Wednesday	Jennifer	37	11.48	15.45	=E7-D7	=F7/D7
8	Thursday	Christopher	72	21.2	26.65	=E8-D8	=F8/D8
9	Friday	Joanna	64	19.25	24.9	=E9-D9	=F9/D9
10		Totals	=SUM(C5:C9)	=SUM(D5:D9)	=SUM(E5:E9)	=E10-D10	=F10/D10
11		Averages	=AVG(C5:C9)	=AVG(D5:D9)	=AVG(E5:E9)	=E11-D11	
12							

Fig. 13.9 The SHOP SALES spreadsheet showing formulae for the Profit and Profit% columns

Note:
The spreadsheet has not copied the formulae exactly, e.g. the formula = E5 − D5 has been changed to = E6 − D6 and then to = E7 − D7, etc. as we go down. As it happened this was just what was needed in this case. Most spreadsheets allow for formulae to change as they are copied, or to stay the same, as the user requires.

KEY TERMS A *reference* means the label given to a cell in a formula, e.g. C5, G6.
A *relative reference* is a label which changes when the formula is copied.
An *absolute reference* is a label which does not change when the formula is copied.

EXAMPLES: *of absolute reference and relative reference*
In many spreadsheets an absolute reference is formed by adding a $ sign.
C5 is an absolute reference and will not be changed by copying.
C5 is a relative reference and will change when it is copied.
In the case of C$5, the C can change but the 5 cannot.

EXAMPLE: *of an absolute reference*
The SHOP SALES spreadsheet
The Gratesby School Shop gives a percentage of its profits to charity. This percentage is changed from time to time but at the moment it is 20%.
- Column H has been reserved for the donations to charity.
- In Fig. 13.10 the percentage (20%) has been put in cell H2.
- Each day's donation is then worked out by multiplying the profit for the day by the contents of H2.
- The formula for H5 is = H$2 * F5.

Notes:
① The $ sign has been used to make the number 2 an absolute reference so that it does not change when the formula is copied down column H (see Fig. 13.11).
② In most computer packages an asterisk is used as a multiplication sign.

	A	B	C	D	E	F	G	H
1		Shop Sales - Week Ending 3rd Feb 1995						
2							Charity	20.00%
3								
4	Day	I.C.	Sales	Cost	Income	Profit	Profit%	Donation
5	Monday	William	45	£15.50	£19.70	£4.20	27.10%	£0.84
6	Tuesday	Katherine	53	£18.63	£24.45	£5.82	31.24%	£1.16
7	Wednesday	Jennifer	37	£11.48	£15.45	£3.97	34.58%	£0.79
8	Thursday	Christopher	72	£21.20	£26.65	£5.45	25.71%	£1.09
9	Friday	Joanna	64	£19.25	£24.90	£5.65	29.35%	£1.13
10		Totals	271	£86.06	£111.15	£25.09	29.15%	£5.02
11		Averages	54.2	£17.21	£22.23	£5.02		
12								

Fig. 13.10 The SHOP SALES spreadsheet with the charity percentage and the donations column added

	A	B	C	D	E	F	G	H
1		Shop Sales - Week Ending 3rd Feb 1995						
2							Charity	0.2
3								
4	Day	I.C.	Sales	Cost	Income	Profit	Profit%	Donation
5	Monday	William	45	15.5	19.7	=E5-D5	=F5/D5	=H$2*F5
6	Tuesday	Katherine	53	18.63	24.45	=E6-D6	=F6/D6	=H$2*F6
7	Wednesday	Jennifer	37	11.48	15.45	=E7-D7	=F7/D7	=H$2*F7
8	Thursday	Christopher	72	21.2	26.65	=E8-D8	=F8/D8	=H$2*F8
9	Friday	Joanna	64	19.25	24.9	=E9-D9	=F9/D9	=H$2*F9
10		Totals	271	86.06	111.15	=E10-D10	=F10/D10	=H$2*F10
11		Averages	=AVG(C5:C9)	=AVG(D5:D9)	=AVG(E5:E9)	=E11-D11		
12								

Fig. 13.11 The SHOP SALES spreadsheet showing formulae for column H

13.5 A spreadsheet as a model

A spreadsheet is a model of the situation it represents.

1. The behaviour of the model copies the actual situation. If the data produced in the actual situation changes then the spreadsheet can be changed to show this.
2. The behaviour of the model is determined by a set of rules. In the spreadsheet these rules are produced by formulae.
3. The model can be studied to forecast what will happen in the real world. You can try putting values into the spreadsheet just to see what will happen. The formulae will make other values change.

EXAMPLE: *of changing a spreadsheet to see what will happen*

The SHOP SALES spreadsheet

The pupils who run the Gratesby School Shop want to increase the amount given to charity. They try various values for the charity percentage to see what will happen.

A value of 25% increases all the daily donations and increases the total donation for that week to £6.27.

	A	B	C	D	E	F	G	H
1		Shop Sales - Week Ending 3rd Feb 1995						
2							Charity	25.00%
3								
4	Day	I.C.	Sales	Cost	Income	Profit	Profit%	Donation
5	Monday	William	45	£15.50	£19.70	£4.20	27.10%	£1.05
6	Tuesday	Katherine	53	£18.63	£24.45	£5.82	31.24%	£1.46
7	Wednesday	Jennifer	37	£11.48	£15.45	£3.97	34.58%	£0.99
8	Thursday	Christopher	72	£21.20	£26.65	£5.45	25.71%	£1.36
9	Friday	Joanna	64	£19.25	£24.90	£5.65	29.35%	£1.41
10		Totals	271	£86.06	£111.15	£25.09	29.15%	£6.27
11		Averages	54.2	£17.21	£22.23	£5.02		
12								

Fig. 13.12 The SHOP SALES spreadsheet showing the result of changing the charity percentage to 25%

Quick test

Questions **1** to **4** refer to a spreadsheet which has its columns labelled A, B, C ... and its rows labelled 1, 2, 3 ...

1. Give a label for:
   (a) the cell below G5,
   (b) the cell to the right of A4.

2 If the range of cells from A4 to A8 is A4:A8 give the ranges for:
   (a) the five cells to the right of G7,
   (b) the four cells below G7,
   (c) the four cells to the left of G7.

3 Use the function SUM to give:
   (a) the total of the five cells below G6,
   (b) total profits for the year if January's profits are in C5, February's in C6, and so on.

4 In a spreadsheet, cell B5 contains the cost of an item excluding VAT and cell C5 contains the amount of VAT to be paid. Cell D5 contains a formula for the total including VAT. Is it:
   (a) = C5 + D5   (b) = B5 + C5
   (c) = B5 + 100 * C5   (d) = B5 * C5

5 What else can you put in spreadsheet cells besides text and numbers?

6 Name *three* different operations which you would expect to be able to carry out on text in a spreadsheet cell.

7 Name *three* different types of number format you would expect in a spreadsheet cell.

8 If a spreadsheet is used to produce a model of a situation:
   (a) where are the variables of the model?
   (b) how are the rules which govern the behaviour of the model written?

Summary

1 A **spreadsheet** program provides a table consisting of vertical columns and horizontal rows of cells. Each cell has a label called a **reference**, e.g. C6.

2 The data placed in the cells can be:
   - numbers;
   - words and other text;
   - formulae to do calculations on the numbers.

3 The format of numbers can be changed including:
   - making them amounts of money or percentages;
   - changing the number of decimal places.

4 A **formula** is a mathematical expression which allows the value in one cell to be worked out from the values in other cells.

5 Most spreadsheets allow functions in formulae including: SUM, AVERAGE, COUNT, MAXIMUM and MINIMUM.

6 A spreadsheet is a simple example of a computer model.
   - The variables of the model are cells containing formulae.
   - The rules of the model are made by the formulae.

Chapter 14
Presenting your work: graphics and charts

14.1 Graphics

KEY TERMS *The term computer **graphics** refers to any pictures or graphs produced using a computer.*

EXAMPLES: *of computer graphics*
1. The computer-produced landscape in a simulation game.
2. A mathematically generated pattern.
3. Business graphics – graphs and charts produced to show results in an easily understood way.
4. CAD graphics – designs produced by interacting with a computer and drawing on the screen.

Drawing and design packages

Programs which allow you to produce pictures include packages which allow:

1. **freehand drawing and 'painting'**
   This is usually done with a **'paint'** package which allows lines to be drawn freehand with 'pens' and 'brushes'.
2. **computer aided design (CAD)**
   Accurate drawings are produced with a sophisticated CAD package.
3. **image manipulation**
   Images produced by scanning, using a digital camera, or by using a drawing package are improved and changed.
4. **3-D modelling**
   Pictures are built up from their coordinates using triangles or polygons. They are given a 3-D appearance by mathematical operations to produce the appearance of shadows and highlights.
5. **animation**
   A number of gradually changing images are produced to give the appearance of movement. Techniques include **morphing** where the computer calculates the intermediate images to make one image appear to change smoothly into another.

Storage of pictures

Pictures are stored in a computer in two different ways.

KEY TERMS *A **pixel based** package stores a picture as a set of dots. This is also known as **bit-mapped**.*
*An **object based** package stores each picture as a set of shapes, storing the coordinates of each shape. This is also called **vector based** or **line based**.*

Note:
An enlargement of an object based drawing is more accurate than a pixel based one. This is because when you enlarge a pixel based picture you see the pixels and it appears as a set of squares.

14.2 Paint packages

KEY TERMS *Paint package is a general term for any program which allows freehand drawing and colouring.*

CHARACTERISTICS: *of paint packages*

1. Drawing is done on the screen using a mouse.
2. Storage of the picture is in pixel based form. A 'zoom' facility allows you to enlarge part of the picture and change individual pixels.
3. Selections are made from various icons and menus around the edges of the screen. Options usually include:
   - different thicknesses of pen or brush;
   - different ways the pen or brush can draw – in blobs or stipple or lines;
   - colours – the set of colours which you select from is called a **palette**;
   - patterns – you can usually fill shapes with a pattern as well as with plain colours;
   - a rubber for rubbing out mistakes;
   - standard shapes you can draw – such as oval, circle, square, rectangle, curve;
   - some scissors or a net – something you can mark an area of the picture with.

   When you have done this you can usually:
   (a) delete that part of the picture, OR
   (b) move it to somewhere else, OR
   (c) make a copy of it;
   - limited ability to key text.

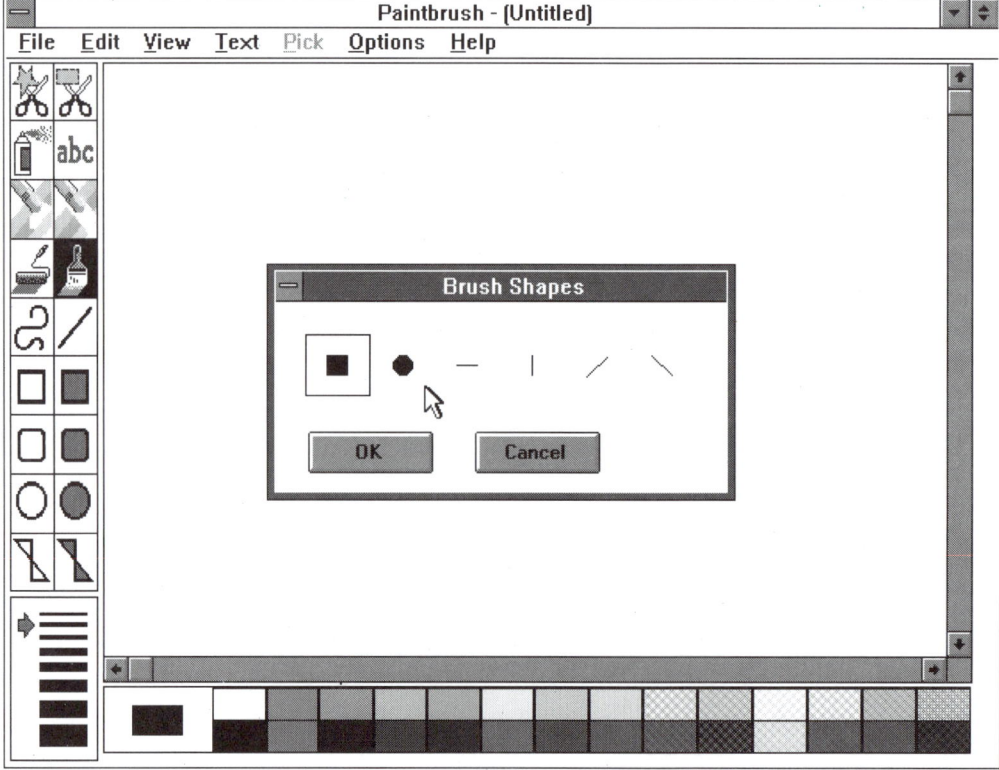

Fig. 14.1 The screen and icons from a paint package

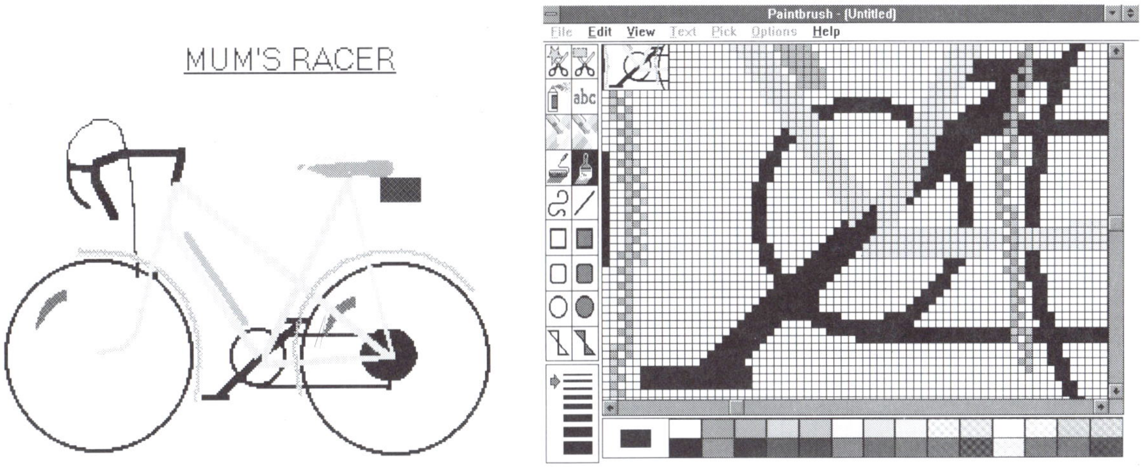

Fig. 14.2 'Mum's racer' produced using a paint package. The set shapes were used – a circle for the wheels, a rectangle for the saddle bag. The frame was drawn using thick lines and curve shapes. The 'zoom' facility was used to get the details right

ADVANTAGES: *of pixel based paint packages*
1. Drawing can be done freehand.
2. Small areas of the drawing can be improved by zooming and retouching.
3. Operations such as copying and erasing can be done on parts of shapes.
4. Use can be made of scanned pictures.

DISADVANTAGES: *of pixel based paint packages*
1. Stored pictures take up a great deal of memory.
2. Enlarged images have ragged outlines.

14.3 CAD graphics

KEY TERMS A *computer aided design (CAD)* system allows the user to produce accurate drawings. It is also known as *computer aided draughting*.

CHARACTERISTICS: *of CAD systems*
1. Usually object based, i.e. storing lines and shapes rather than pixels.
2. Aids to accurate positioning and drawing:
   - a grid of guide lines;
   - an accurate measuring system on the screen.
3. Powerful facilities for changing drawings, e.g. scaling, rotation and reflection.
4. Libraries of standard components, e.g. kitchen furniture and appliances, electronic components.
5. Software to do calculations from the drawing, e.g. calculation of length and area, calculating the cost of standard components used in a design.
6. Specialised computing equipment.

Hardware for CAD

A CAD system is demanding for processing, input, output and storage.

1. **Processing**
   CAD requires fast processing. Operations like scaling and rotation require a mathematical operation to be carried out on every object in the drawing. However, the more powerful microcomputers are quite adequate for this.
2. **Input** (see also Unit 4.5)
   A mouse is not really adequate as an input device. A graphics tablet can be used with a puck or a stylus:
   - for selection of shapes and options from a template;
   - for accurate digitising of existing drawings.

Chapter 14 Presenting your work: graphics and charts

③ Output (see also Unit 5.3)
- A high resolution monitor is required for close work.
- A plotter, or at least a laser printer, is needed for hard copies.

④ Storage
Storage is required for:
- **drawings**
  With an object based system a simple drawing uses very little store. However, for practical applications drawings are complicated and require a large amount of storage.
- **CAD software**
  Professional CAD programs are large and complex.
- **component databases**.

A CAD system requires large amounts of:
- hard disc;
- RAM in the main store.

Software facilities on CAD systems

KEY TERMS

① *Grid lines* – *a set of horizontal and vertical lines which help to place objects accurately:*
- *the distance between the grid lines can be changed to fit the scale of the drawing;*
- *the program can be set to 'snap' to the grid lines. This allows objects and points to be positioned accurately.*

Fig. 14.3 'Mum's racer' produced using a CAD package. This time a grid was drawn and the centres and bases of the wheels were placed on grid lines to ensure that the wheels are the same diameter and the bicycle is horizontal

② *Scaling*
The whole drawing or objects in it can be made larger or smaller. Usually you have to:
- *select the object or objects to be scaled;*
- *choose a scale factor;*
- *choose a point from which the objects are scaled.*

Note:
Scaling is not the same as zooming. You zoom an area to alter it and then return it to its normal size.

③ *Rotation*
A part of the drawing can be rotated about a point on the screen. Usually you have to:
- *select the object to be rotated;*
- *select a point as a centre for the rotation;*
- *indicate how far round to rotate the object – usually with the mouse.*

④ *Reflection*
An object is reflected by using a line as an imaginary mirror. Each part of the object is copied to be the same distance from the mirror but on the other side of it. The effect is to turn the object round to face the other way.

14.3 CAD graphics

EXAMPLE: *of rotation*

Fig. 14.4 'Mum's racer' rotated to go uphill. The centre used for the rotation was the bottom of the hill

EXAMPLE: *of reflection*

A car fan belt

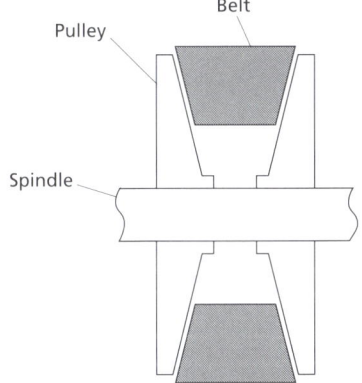

This picture was produced using reflections as follows:
- the top left quarter of the pulley was drawn;
- this was reflected about a vertical 'mirror' to produce the top right quarter;
- the top of the picture was then completed by drawing in the top section of the belt;
- the top of the picture was then reflected in a horizontal mirror to produce the bottom of the picture;
- the spindle and the labelling were added.

ADVANTAGES: *of CAD systems*
1. Wider range of operations than a simple paint package.
2. More accurate drawing. CAD packages are object based:
   - drawings can be enlarged without losing detail;
   - accuracy is possible without using too much storage.
3. Wide range of standard shapes available.
4. Calculations can be done from drawings.

DISADVANTAGES: *of CAD systems*
1. Professional CAD software is expensive.
2. CAD requires high quality input, output and storage.

APPLICATION: *of CAD*

Design of heating appliances
A heating firm makes various types of heaters, radiators, fires, kettles, etc. Until a few years ago all their designs were drawn on paper by draughtsmen. Gradually this work has been taken over by design engineers producing drawings themselves using the CAD package AUTOCAD. The work involves:
- creating new designs;
- adapting old designs to produce new drawings;
- digitising paper drawings using a graphics tablet so that old designs are gradually all available for CAD work.

Adapting old designs has meant:
- a wider range of heaters is made and it is possible to fit customer needs more closely;

Chapter 14 Presenting your work: graphics and charts

- it takes far less time to create a new design.

A further bonus has been that manuals can be produced by adapting the CAD drawings and adding them to word processor text using a DTP package.

CAD/CAM

KEY TERMS

CAM is computer aided manufacture. A machine tool such as a lathe is controlled by a computer which sends it instructions to select tools and to use them to make metal components.

CAD/CAM is computer aided design/computer aided manufacture, in which a CAD system and a CAM system are integrated.

In CAD/CAM, data from the CAD system is converted to a set of instructions for the processor controlling the CAM equipment. Once a part has been designed using the CAD software the other processes are automatic:

1. conversion of the data into a set of machine tool instructions;
2. operation of the CAM system:
   - selection of tools (e.g. cutters or drills);
   - selection of speeds (e.g. for a drill or a lathe);
   - movement of the tool to machine the part being manufactured.

14.4 Graphs and charts

Business graphics

Graphs and charts are often referred to as 'business graphics'. They are usually produced by using either:

1. a special Business Graphics package,

OR

2. the chart option on a spreadsheet package,

OR

3. a graphics option in an integrated package.

Usually the data for the graph or chart comes from rows or columns of a spreadsheet by:

1. 'Cut' or 'Copy' from the spreadsheet and 'Paste' into the chart,

OR

2. Exporting the data from the spreadsheet as a file and importing it into a chart package.

Information required to produce a graph

To produce a clear graph you need:

1. data
   - This may be referred to by the chart package as 'Data' or 'Series' or 'Values'.
   - It is usually obtained from the rows or columns of a spreadsheet.
2. titles for the graph
   - A main title to state what the graph is, e.g. COMPARISON OF TEMPERATURES.
   - A sub-title to give more detail to the title, e.g. Average Monthly Temperatures for 1995.
3. titles for the axes (except on pie charts)
   These explain what the axes represent, e.g. on the vertical axis: Temp °C, on the horizontal axis: Month.
4. labels on the axes
   Labels to tell you the size of the values shown on the graph, e.g. on the vertical axis: 5, 10, 15, 20, 25, 30 etc., on the horizontal axis: January, February etc.
5. a legend
   Any information added to a chart or graph other than on the axes is often called a **legend**. For example, if there are two temperature graphs on the same chart, one with squares and one with circles, the legends might be:

   --o-- Maximum   --■-- Minimum

14.4 Graphs and charts

Notes:

① Many chart packages refer to the vertical axis as the *y*-axis and the horizontal axis as the *x*-axis.

② Often the package works out the scales for the axes automatically.

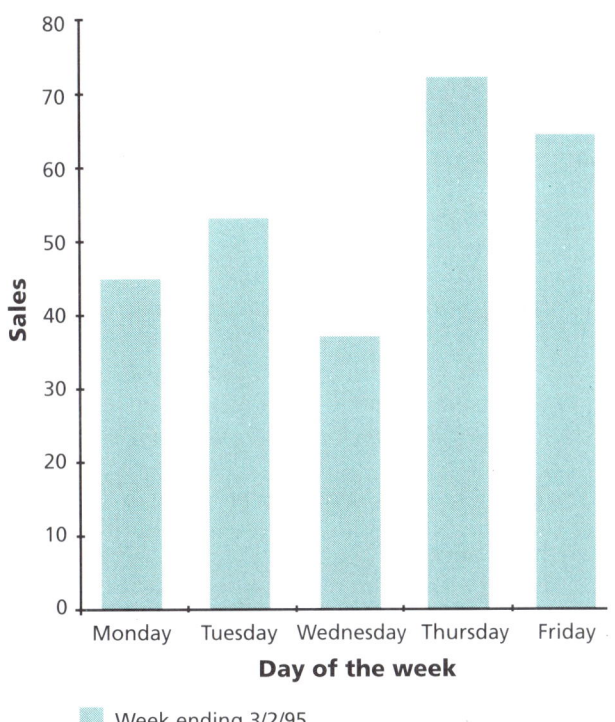

Fig. 14.5 Bar chart showing sales for the week at Gratesby School Shop. The titles and labels for this graph are as follows:
Title   – GRATESBY SCHOOL SHOP
Sub-title   – Sales for week ending 3/2/95
x-axis title – Day of the week
y-axis title – Sales
x-axis labels – Monday, Tuesday, Wednesday, Thursday, Friday
y-axis labels – 0, 10, 20, 30, 40, 50, 60, 70, 80
Legend   – Week ending 3/2/95

Preparing to produce a chart

As the information required for a graph is complicated it is best to prepare it beforehand. A suitable form can be produced on the word processor and filled in before the graph is started.

```
Name .....WILLIAM HUTTON......................... Date ......6TH FEB. 1995.............
Graph title ......GRATESBY SCHOOL SHOP........................
Sub-title ........SALES FOR WEEK ENDING 3/2/95.............
Graph type ...........BAR.........................
Axis titles:
Horizontal ......DAY OF THE WEEK........................... Vertical ..... SALES......................
Axis labels:
Horizontal .....B5:B9...................
Vertical ...........................
Data:
1st series .........D5:D9..............
2nd series .........................................
3rd series .........................................
Other details .........................................
.........................................
```

Fig. 14.6 Graph form filled in for the Gratesby School Shop bar chart

155

Notes:

❶ No labels have been put in for the vertical axis as these are worked out automatically.

❷ No 2nd and 3rd series have been put in as the graph is based on just one set of numbers (the sales).

14.5 Types of chart

KEY TERMS

A **bar chart** is made up of rectangular blocks or bars. The length or height of a bar shows the size of the number it represents.

A **pie chart** is in the form of a circle with lines drawn out from the centre. It looks like a pie which has been cut into uneven slices. Each slice represents a number – the bigger the slice, the bigger the number. A pie chart shows what each of the values is as a fraction or a percentage of the total.

A **line graph** has a set of points joined by a line.

A **scatter graph** is produced when two different quantities are plotted against one another to find out if they are related in some way. The scatter graph simply consists of a set of points.

Which type of chart to use

Bar chart
Used to show the relative sizes of a set of separate values. For example, a graph to show the amount of support for each political party at one election.

Line graph
Used to show how a quantity is changing. Often the horizontal axis represents a time scale. For example, a graph to show how support for the different political parties has changed over the past ten years.

Pie chart
Used to show how something is shared. For example, a graph to show the number of votes for each political party as a percentage of the whole electorate.

Scatter graph
Used to show how two different quantities are related. For example, a graph of unemployment numbers against crime numbers for different towns to see if there is a connection between crime and unemployment.

Quick test

1. What type of graphics package would you use to:
   (a) make an accurate drawing,
   (b) draw a graph of a mathematical function,
   (c) produce a freehand drawing,
   (d) scan a photograph and improve it?

2. Name *three* types of peripheral that you would need for CAD work which you would often not have on a PC.

3. Name *two* methods which a graphics package can use to store pictures.

4. Which method of picture storage would probably be used for:
   (a) a CAD package,
   (b) a paint package.

5. State *two* functions which a CAD package has which most paint packages do not.

6 Why can a CAD package enlarge pictures without losing accuracy whereas a paint package cannot?

7 What is the general term for the type of system which integrates a CAD system with a lathe or similar machine?

8 Where does a chart program often obtain its data?

9 What type of chart would you normally use to show:
   (a) the changing temperature over a year,
   (b) the percentage of taxes being used for health, education, roads, defence and other items,
   (c) the amount of rainfall in each month,
   (d) whether the number of flowers on a plant is related to its height.

Summary

1 **Computer graphics** refers to any pictures or graphs produced using a computer.

2 Drawing and design packages include packages for:
   - freehand drawing and 'painting';
   - computer aided design (CAD);
   - image manipulation;
   - 3-D modelling;
   - animation.

3 Storage of pictures can be:
   - **pixel based** (bit-mapped) – a picture is stored as a set of dots;
   - **object based** (vector based or line based) – each picture is stored as a set of shapes.

4 A **paint package** is a general term for any program which allows freehand drawing and colouring.

5 A **computer aided design (CAD)** system allows the user to produce accurate drawings.

6 Hardware for CAD usually includes:
   - a microcomputer with large hard disc and main store;
   - a graphics tablet with a puck or a stylus;
   - a high resolution monitor;
   - a plotter, or at least a laser printer.

7 - **CAM** is computer aided manufacture.
   - **CAD/CAM** is computer aided design/computer aided manufacture. It involves a CAD system integrated with a CAM system.

8 Types of graph or chart include:
   - a **bar chart**, made up of rectangular blocks or bars;
   - a **pie chart**, in the form of a circle with lines drawn out from the centre;
   - a **line graph**, which has a set of points joined by a line;
   - a **scatter graph**, produced when two different quantities are plotted against one another.

Chapter 15
Communications

15.1 Introduction to communications

KEY TERMS

Generally **communication** means sending information between one person or device and another.

The term **data communication** is used particularly when the data is being sent between a user and a computer or between computers.

Telecommunications are data communications over large distances.

EXAMPLES: *of communications*
1. Two people speaking on the telephone.
2. A sales department sending a fax to a customer.
3. Using a modem and a terminal to contact a remote computer.

Videotex

KEY TERMS

Videotex is a term for any information system which uses a computer to transmit data to users' screens.

Teletext and **viewdata** are both examples of videotex.

Teletext is a system for sending out information using ordinary television signals. The customer has an adapted television set and the information is displayed as pages of text. The user can receive data but cannot send it back.

Viewdata is an interactive information system where the telephone is used to link users to the host computer. Normally the user has a modem used with a terminal or a microcomputer. The user can send messages back to the computer.

A **page** is one screenful of information and is sent as a unit. For some viewdata systems, the user has to pay for each page which is viewed.

Fax

KEY TERMS

Fax (short for facsimile) is a widely-used method of transmitting the contents of documents using ordinary telephone lines.

The fax machine at one end scans the document and converts the image into telephone signals. The fax machine at the receiving end uses these signals to reproduce a copy of the document. The document sent can include both pictures and text.

ADVANTAGES: *of fax*
1. High speed compared with letters.
2. Convenience and simplicity – a mixture of written messages and prepared information can be sent with no more trouble than making a phone call.

DISADVANTAGES: *of fax*
1. Faxed printouts are sometimes of poor quality.
2. It is relatively difficult to computerise faxed information.

Note:
Normally a computer is not involved in fax transmissions. However, it is now possible to buy a fax modem and suitable software to transmit and receive computer information via fax.

15.2 Teletext

EXAMPLES: *of teletext systems*
1. The BBC system – called CEEFAX. This appears in full on BBC2, with a shorter, fast-access version on BBC1.
2. The ITV system – called TELETEXT. Part of the information for this appears on ITV and part on Channel 4.
3. Similar systems on satellite channels.

CHARACTERISTICS: *of teletext systems*
1. Teletext can only be viewed on specially adapted televisions.
2. Teletext systems are not interactive. The user cannot send messages back to the computer.
3. For a given television channel, the same pages are sent out repeatedly one after the other. All the user can do is to select which page to look at and wait for it to arrive.
4. The user has a keypad (usually remote and hand-held) and keys in the numbers of selected pages.

Hardware requirements for teletext
1. A television set adapted to receive the data.
2. A remote keypad which includes buttons for teletext operations.

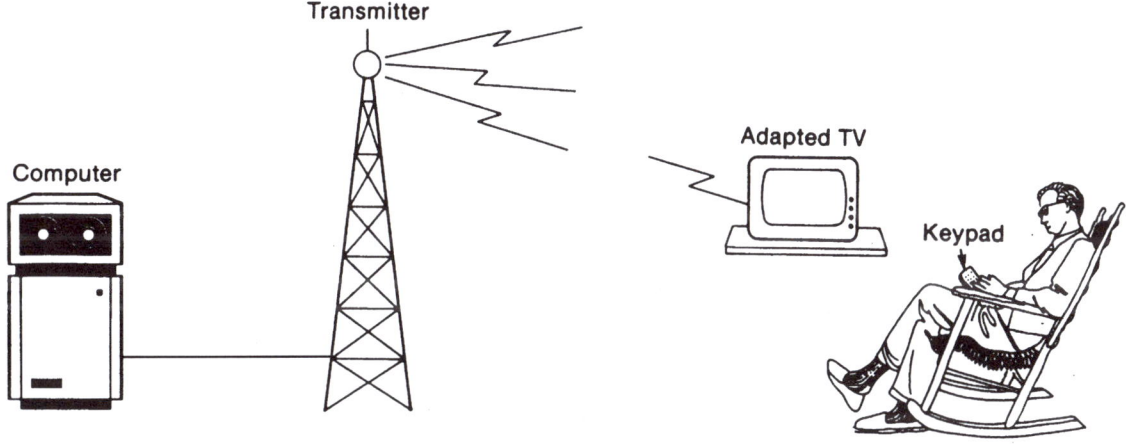

Fig. 15.1 A teletext system

EXAMPLES: *of information available from teletext systems*
1. Up-to-date news.
2. Latest sports results.
3. Weather information.
4. Details of radio and TV programmes.
5. Stock exchange prices.

APPLICATIONS: *of teletext*
1. **Use of sub-titles by deaf people**
   The teletext systems supply a number of services to deaf people including subtitles on many programs. As people on a program are talking, what they are saying appears in large letters in a rectangular box near the bottom of the screen. The user:
   - selects the channel showing the program,
   - selects teletext,
   - selects the subtitle page.
2. **Contributions from viewers**
   Both CEEFAX and TELETEXT run teletext pages written by contributors. Users can send items of news, reviews, stories and other items and these are included in special magazine pages.

ADVANTAGES: *of teletext*
1. It is relatively easy to select the information you want.
2. The equipment required is fairly inexpensive.
3. Once you have the equipment, using it costs nothing extra.
4. Teletext data can be added to ordinary television pictures, e.g. subtitles added to programmes for deaf people.
5. Pages can be changed easily so information is up-to-date.

DISADVANTAGES: *of teletext*
1. There are only a limited number of pages to look at.
2. The user cannot interact with the computer.

15.3 Networks

KEY TERMS (For network see Unit 2.5.)

A **local area network (LAN)** is a network which is all on one site, such as a school or block of offices. The work stations in a local area network are usually connected directly by cables (see Unit 15.4).

A **wide area network (WAN)** is a network which connects large numbers of computers and terminals over long distances. The work stations in a wide area network are connected by telephone or similar data links (see Unit 15.5).

EXAMPLES: *of networks*
1. Local area networks:
   - an interconnected set of computers in a doctor's surgery;
   - a network of computers in a school.
2. Wide area networks:
   - a public viewdata network such as Campus;
   - a chain of banks with terminals connected to the bank's headquarters.

Means of communication

Data can be transmitted by:
1. **wire cable**
   This conducts data as electrical signals and may be:
   - co-axial cable with only one wire in the middle for sending and receiving data;
   - parallel cable which has a number of wires and allows several signals to be sent at the same time;
   - standard telephone lines.
2. **fibre optic cable** (also known as **optical fibre cable**)
   This contains glass fibres and data is transmitted as light signals. It can transmit far more data than wire cables but is expensive and not so flexible.
3. **transmitted signals without cables**
   - Radio waves – including the use of satellites.
   - Microwaves – very useful over relatively short distances.

Communications hardware

Communication to wide area networks is usually achieved using a terminal and a modem with a telephone line (see Unit 2.5 for terminals).

KEY TERMS A **modem** (MOdulator-DEModulator) is a device which allows a computer or a terminal to use the telephone line for communication.

EXAMPLE: *of the use of a modem*
If a terminal user is using a modem to access a public network the modem:
- converts digital signals from the terminal into analogue signals and sends them along the telephone line to the host computer;
- receives analogue signals from the telephone line and converts them back into digital signals for the terminal.

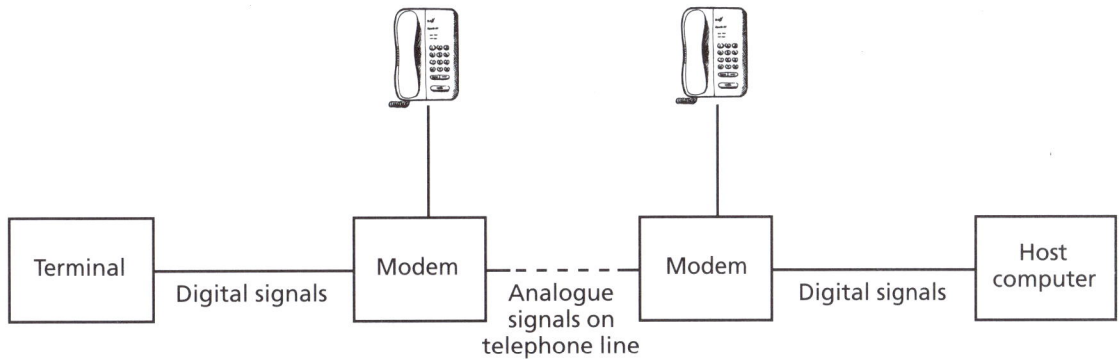

Fig. 15.2 Diagram showing modems being used to connect a terminal to a host computer

15.4 Local area networks

CHARACTERISTICS: *of local area networks*
1. The workstations are normally microcomputers.
2. The communication between workstations is usually along cables.
3. The network contains peripherals such as hard disc units and printers to which all users have access via the network.
4. To use a program, the user loads it into his/her own workstation and runs it there. This contrasts with many wide area networks where the user has only a terminal and all the programs run in a central 'host' computer.
5. The network has special computers called servers to control the main disc units and printers.

KEY TERMS
A *print server* is a computer on a network which controls a printer.
A *file server* is a computer on a network dedicated to controlling a hard disc and handling users' files.

Note:
The file server deals with the security of the files it controls. This includes checking passwords and user identities.

APPLICATION: *using local area networks*
A school network (see Fig. 15.3)
A school has two networks each with its own file server which also acts as a print server. The file servers are connected together by a fibre optic cable. This enables pupils in one area to use the other file server, so that they can access their files from any station in the school. The two networks have slightly different facilities:

- **in the IT area**
  Each station is a microcomputer with a floppy disc drive and a mouse. The pupils access software mainly through a graphical user interface using the mouse. The network has two inkjet printers. Most of the computers are in two classrooms but the file server and hard disc unit are in a separate office. There is also one workstation at the front of a classroom with a large screen so that the teacher can show it to a whole class. The network is used by Information Technology pupils to do coursework and also by classes in other subjects.

- **in the Business Studies department**
  The workstations are microcomputers used mainly for word processing. The computers do not have mice as the pupils work from the keyboards. The network has a laser printer for high-quality printing of letters and a dot matrix printer for draft copies. A hard disc unit is used mainly for storing files of text.

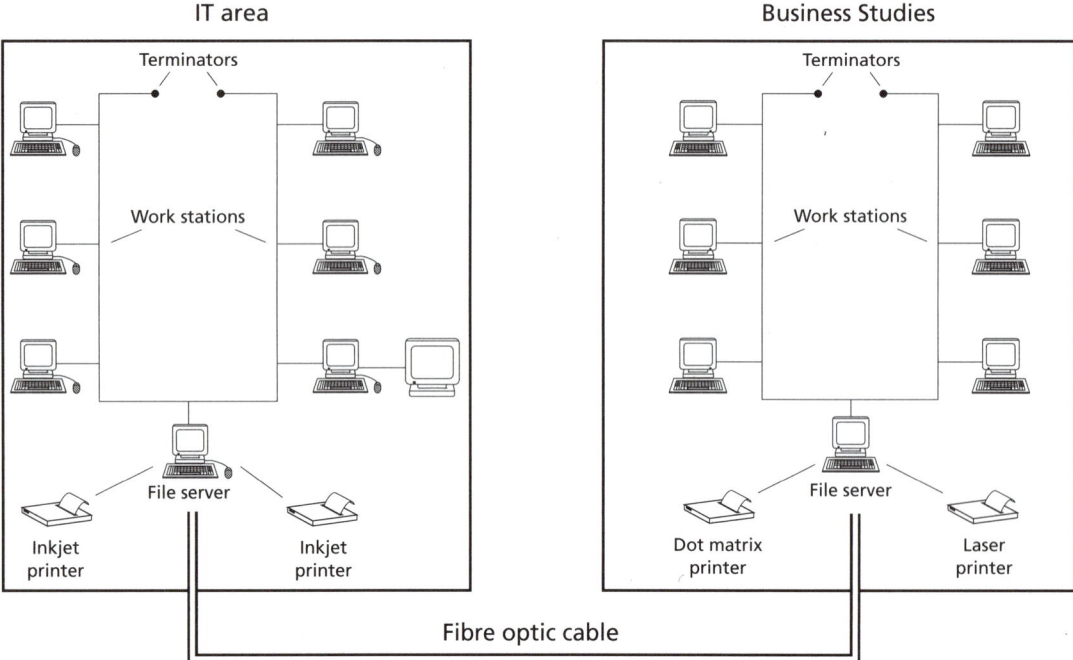

Fig. 15.3 Diagram of a school network

ADVANTAGES: *of local area networks*
1. The stations can share peripherals. Disc units and printers can be of better quality because they do not have to be bought for each station.
2. Users do not need to use floppy discs for data files. They can sit at any of the work stations and access their own files from the file server.
3. A user's files cannot be accessed by other people.
4. A user can use any software from any station. A number of stations can access and run the same program at the same time.
5. The stations can communicate with one another – either directly or using an electronic mail system through the file server.

DISADVANTAGES: *of local area networks*
1. If the file server for a network breaks down, the users may have no data files or software to work with.
2. A network with only a small number of stations is expensive. The file server has to be quite a powerful computer and cannot usually be used for anything else while the network is running.

Requirements for a local area network

Hardware
1. The stations – these can be ordinary PCs:
   - each needs an interface to the network – probably a circuit board;
   - each also needs a cable to connect it to the network;
   - they will have fewer requirements for disc drives than a standalone computer.
2. A file server. This needs to be a powerful computer with:
   - a large hard disc unit;
   - a large main store;
   - some means of backing up the hard disc – probably a tape streamer;
   - possibly some CD-ROM facility.
3. A printer or printers:
   - these need to be robust and faster than a printer for a standalone computer;
   - with a computer to act as print server.
4. A cabling system – securely fitted.

Software
1. Network management software to:
   - organise the files into user areas and maintain security;

- organise backup and printing;
- keep data and programs going to the right places;
- allow the system manager to oversee and control the network;
- enable users to interact with the system.

❷ Applications software

All the programs being used need network or site licences to allow a number of users to access them at the same time.

People

❶ A system manager to install software and oversee backups and changes.

❷ Technicians to maintain hardware and call in engineers if necessary.

15.5 Wide area networks

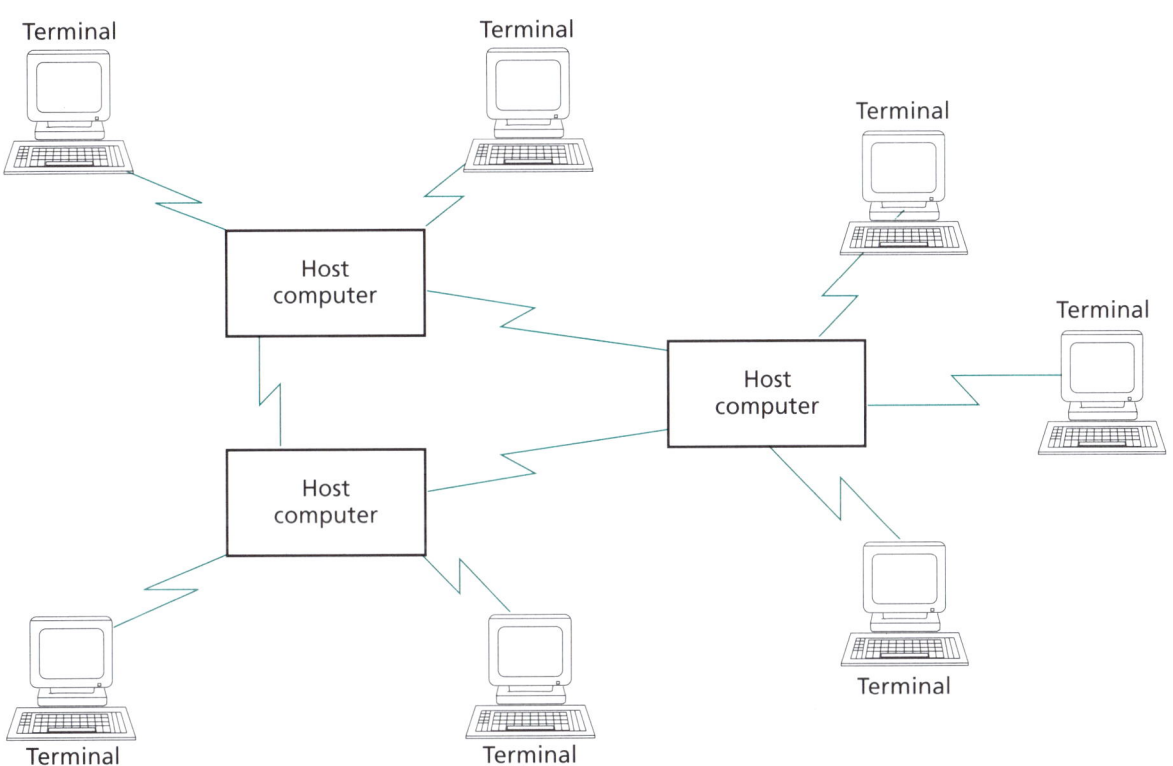

Fig. 15.4 Diagram of a typical wide area network. The network shown has three host computers. A user connects to the nearest host and can then be connected to any other host

CHARACTERISTICS: *of wide area networks*

❶ Computing power for the network is usually provided by one or more 'host' computers. These may be remote from one another, connected by high-speed data links.

❷ The workstations are terminals or microcomputers. Often the host computers run the programs and the stations simply act as a means of communication.

❸ The network may be nationwide or even worldwide.

❹ Users usually connect to a point on the network near to them. A user connected by telephone will often be able to make a local call.

15.6 Public viewdata networks

In Britain, and in other countries, there are a number of viewdata networks available to the public. They are usually accessed using the telephone system. The user needs a terminal and a modem and has to pay a subscription.

Hardware requirements

1. A terminal. This can be:
   - a visual display terminal,
   OR
   - a microcomputer running a communication program so that it behaves as a terminal.
2. A telephone line which can be used for fairly long periods.
3. A modem.

Software requirements

1. Users have to decide which viewdata service or services they wish to use and pay subscriptions to them. For each service they will usually be given:
   - a manual of instructions and lists of services available;
   - a telephone number for the service;
   - an account number and password (this password can be changed by the user later).
2. Users with microcomputers need the software to make their computers behave as terminals. This software, known as **communications software**, will usually enable the computer to:
   - make the phone call automatically;
   - carry out most of the logging-in conversation – the user still has to type in a password;
   - send and receive data in the same way as an ordinary visual display terminal;
   - carry out the logging-out sequence and disconnect the phone.

Services available on viewdata networks

KEY TERMS

Telesoftware is software which is made available to users of a viewdata network. Programs can be received in the same way as data.

A **bulletin board** is an area where one user of a viewdata system can leave messages and information which is then available to all other users.

Electronic conferencing involves a group of people having a debate or a discussion using terminals.

Electronic mail (E-mail) is a system which allows users to send messages to one another. Each user has a 'mailbox' – an area of the main computer's store containing messages sent to them.

A user can usually:
- send a message to another user;
- send a message to a group of users;
- scan the mailbox and display a list of the messages in it;
- read any message which seems important;
- print messages out on paper;
- send a reply to a message;
- delete or retain messages which have been dealt with.

Notes on electronic mail:
- A long letter can be typed beforehand, using a word processor, and stored on disc. This is done with the terminal off-line to save a long telephone call. The user then logs on to the computer and the letter is transmitted quickly.
- Two people using electronic mail do not have a direct conversation. One person sends a message and the other receives it later. It is rather like sending letters but is faster.

Gateways to other networks
A viewdata network often provides its users with an option to access another network without logging out. This is called a **gateway** to the other network.

Access to databases
A user can search files of data for information. The files may be provided:
- by groups of users;
OR
- by professional information providers.

Ordering goods and services
A user can use a viewdata service to:

15.6 Public viewdata networks

- book holidays;
- order theatre tickets.

EXAMPLES: *of viewdata services available*

❶ Campus

Campus is a British educational network used by schools and colleges. It is run by BT (British Telecom) and *The Times* and uses normal telephone lines.

The data providers are local authorities, schools themselves but also organisations such as the stock exchange and the army. During the summer, the universities use Campus to publish details of places available for prospective students.

Its facilities include:
- an electronic mail service to schools and colleges in the UK and many other countries;
- databases produced for and by schools;
- up-to-date text from British newspapers;
- commercial databases including travel and leisure, government information and weather data;
- an electronic conferencing service;
- information on other users and Campus services;
- a gateway to Télétel, the French on-line service.

❷ Télétel

The French on-line information service has about 7 million users in schools, homes and businesses. This is partly because the terminals are provided free. However, the services have to be paid for. There are nearly twenty thousand different services available including:
- looking up telephone numbers – this was the original use of Télétel;
- booking tickets – such as from Paris to London on Eurostar;
- shopping – you can order a wide variety of goods;
- electronic mail to users in France and other countries;
- information on shows, films and other events in Paris;
- information about the regions of France.

❸ Internet

The Internet is a world-wide network with millions of users.
It includes:
- An E-mail service which allows users to contact one another anywhere in the world. For this each user has a unique **E-mail address**. This is made up of strings of characters separated by full stops. The address includes information like the user's chosen name, the host computer their mail is stored in, their type of organisation and the country they live in.
- A huge network of sources of information and software known as the **World Wide Web**. Each individual source is called a **Web site**. Many of these sites are provided free of charge by individuals and by organisations such as universities.

To use the Internet, as well as the usual computer, telephone and modem the user needs a subscription to an **Internet access provider**. This is a company which provides:
- A number of exchanges so that most users can access the network with a local telephone call.
- Software to interface with the network. This includes a **browser** - a program to search the Web for information.

ADVANTAGES: *of viewdata*
1. A wide variety of interactive services.
2. Access to large databases and other mainframe facilities.

DISADVANTAGES: *of viewdata*
1. The cost:
   - initial cost of equipment;
   - cost of telephone calls;
   - charges for using some pages;
   - annual subscription for the use of the service.
2. On some systems response is slow and the method of searching is cumbersome.

Chapter 15 Communications

ADVANTAGES: *of electronic mail over post*

1. Less use of paper:
   - mail can be read and replies made without printing;
   - a letter can be written using a word processor and transmitted direct – again without use of paper.
2. Fast delivery – messages can be received almost immediately after they are sent.
3. The cost is usually the same to anywhere in the world.
4. Uncomplicated system. If an employee of one company sends a letter by post to an employee of another, a chain of people is involved. Electronic mail only involves the computer system and the two people concerned.

DISADVANTAGES: *of electronic mail compared with post*

1. Electronic mail can only be sent to people who subscribe to the service and use it regularly.
2. A user does not know any mail has been received until he/she logs on.
3. It is expensive to use a public network.
4. Widespread use of electronic mail might threaten the jobs of postal and office workers.

Quick test

1. Give *two* advantages of teletext over viewdata.

2. Give *two* advantages of viewdata over teletext.

3. Give *two* ways of selecting a page on teletext.

4. What teletext services could help someone who is:
   (a) housebound,
   (b) disabled in some other way?

5. Choose *three* of the following which make it easier for people to work from home:
   teletext   cheap PCs   MICR   electronic mail
   local area networks   bar codes   fax

6. (a) What is the difference between a LAN and a WAN?
   (b) Which of the two is more likely to need a modem to use it?

In questions **7** to **11** state what videotex service is being described:

7. three people typing messages to one another so that all three see both the messages and the replies,
8. accessing one viewdata network while logged on to another one,
9. one person sending a message to another person which they then find when they log in,
10. selecting pages of information on an adapted television,
11. leaving a message where all users of the network can see it.

12. Give *three* different tasks an electronic mail system carries out.

Summary

1. **Fax** is a widely used method of transmitting the contents of documents using ordinary telephone lines. Fax transmission does not usually involve use of computers.

2 **Videotex** systems use a computer to transmit data to users' screens. The main systems are:
- **teletext**, which sends out information using ordinary television signals;
- **viewdata**, which uses the telephone to link users to a host computer.

3 Teletext:
- can only be viewed on specially adapted televisions;
- is not interactive. The user cannot send messages back to the computer.

4 Viewdata:
- requires a modem and a terminal or a microcomputer;
- is interactive. The user can send messages back to the computer.

5 A computer **network** is a system of computers and workstations connected together.

6 A **local area network (LAN)** is a network in a small area, often one building, usually connected by cables.

7 A **wide area network (WAN)** is a network operating over long distances using telephone or similar data links.

Chapter 16
Measurement and control

16.1 Control systems

KEY TERMS

Device control refers to one piece of equipment controlling the operation of another piece of equipment by sending signals to it. The controlling equipment is usually
- a computer, OR
- a circuit containing a microprocessor.

A **control system** consists of everything involved in the control of a device – the processor, the programs, the interfaces and the devices themselves.

EXAMPLE: *of device control*

A disc unit in a computer system is controlled by the processor which sends it:
- data to be stored;
- control signals to rotate the disc and operate the heads so that the data is stored in the right places.

Note:
The disc unit also sends control signals back to the processor. It does this when it has finished the present task and is ready for another.

EXAMPLES: *of control systems*

1 A washing machine
The user selects a sequence which a microprocessor in the machine carries out in order. It sends signals to switch the heater, pumps and motors on and off at the right time intervals.

2 A fully automatic camera
A processor receives light readings from light sensors. When the shutter release button is partly pressed, the processor sends control signals to adjust the aperture and shutter speed. Then when the shutter release button is completely depressed the film will be correctly exposed.

Output signals from the processor

KEY TERMS

The signals sent by a computer to a device are called **control signals**. They may be in the form of:
- short electrical pulses sent down a cable, OR
- a simple voltage in a cable, OR
- radio, microwave, laser or infra-red pulses.

An **output port** is a connecting point on a computer through which it can send control signals.

A PC usually has a choice of ports on the back of it allowing:
- different types of signal;
- different types of cable connection.

A **relay** is a switch which can be switched on and off by an electrical signal. It can be used in the device being controlled to switch lights and motors on and off.

16.1 Control systems

*An **actuator** is a device which can produce a movement when given an electrical signal. It receives the control signals and converts them into movement.*

*A **transistor** is a device which can be used to switch current on and off without any mechanical movement.*

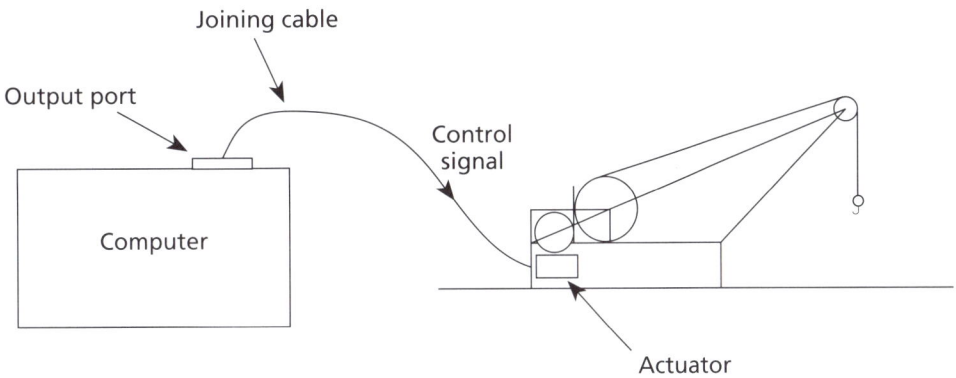

Fig. 16.1 Diagram of a simple control system

Motors

Large movements are achieved using motors.

KEY TERMS

*A **motor** converts electrical energy into movement.*

*A **stepper motor** is a type of motor which only moves a small amount for each control pulse it receives. Whereas most motors run continuously once switched on, stepper motors have to be sent repeated pulses to keep them going.*

ADVANTAGE: *of a stepper motor*

A stepper motor can be controlled precisely. For a given number of pulses received, it will always move exactly the same distance.

Interfaces

KEY TERMS

*An **interface** is some hardware, and possibly also some software, that is used to connect two devices or systems to enable them to communicate.*

An interface may have to:
- control and check the data being transmitted;
- convert data from one form or one code to another;
- allow for a difference in speed between two devices.

EXAMPLES: *of interfaces*

1. A graphical user interface consisting of a mouse and some windows software.
2. When a new disc drive is fitted into a microcomputer, a disc interface is also fitted. This usually consists of an integrated circuit board inside the computer.
3. A modem forms the interface between a computer and the telephone system when a public network is used (see Unit 15.3).

Control interfaces

Control systems often need interfaces between the computer and the controlled device. This happens if the type of signal sent or received by the computer is not the same type as that of the device. In particular the interface may need to include analogue-to-digital or digital-to-analogue converters.

KEY TERMS

*A **digital-to-analogue (D–A) converter** is an interface to convert a digital signal to an analogue one. It converts a set of binary signals to one single varying voltage. (See Fig. 16.2.)*

EXAMPLE: *of use of a D–A converter*

A computer operated lathe

The speed of the motor driving the lathe is proportional to the voltage of the analogue

169

control signal it receives. The computer sends a pattern of control signals representing a binary number. A D–A converter changes this to the actual voltage needed to control the speed of the lathe.

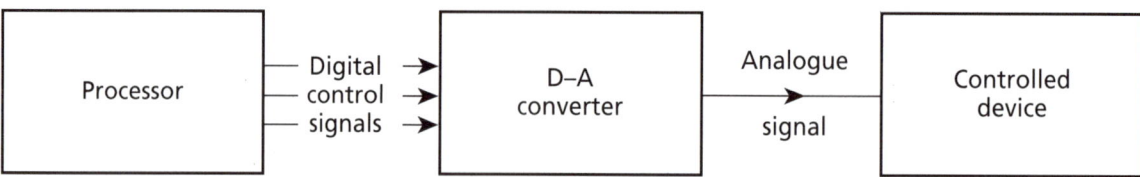

Fig. 16.2 A digital-to-analogue converter in use

KEY TERMS *An **analogue-to-digital (A–D) converter** is an interface to convert an analogue signal to a digital one.*

Usually an A–D converter consists of an integrated circuit which inputs a voltage. It outputs a set of binary signals. These represent a binary number which is roughly proportional to the input voltage.

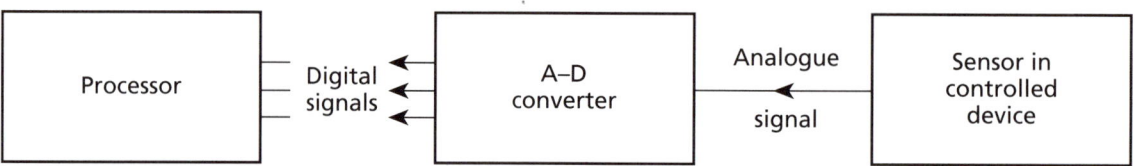

Fig. 16.3 An analogue-to-digital converter in use

EXAMPLE: *of use of a A–D converter*

A light-seeking robot
The robot has a light sensor. This produces a voltage which is proportional to the amount of light which falls on it. An A–D converter in the robot converts this to a set of binary signals. These are sent to a computer which sends back signals to change the direction in which the robot is moving.

16.2 Sensors and feedback

A simple control system can work by a processor sending control signals to a device which then operates accordingly (see Fig. 16.1). However, in most control systems the computer also receives signals back. These help the processor to decide what to do next. Such signals may come from:
- sensors or instruments, e.g. an infra-red sensor which sends a signal if a beam across a gateway is broken;
- switches or buttons used by a user or an operator, e.g. a button pushed by a pedestrian waiting to cross at traffic lights.

KEY TERMS *A **sensor** is a monitoring device which measures some physical quantity and sends signals back to the processor.*
*An **input port** is a connecting point on a computer through which it can receive signals from sensors and switches.*

Note:
The sensors used may be:
- simple digital devices sending a binary 0 or 1 signal;
- analogue devices giving a varying value which has to be converted into binary signals.

EXAMPLES: *of sensors*

❶ A thermocouple for measuring temperature
This is a device which produces a voltage proportional to its temperature. It is an analogue sensor because it produces a continuous range of voltages.

16.2 Sensors and feedback

② A pressure pad at a traffic light
This produces a signal if a car goes over it. It is a digital sensor because it is either on or off.

③ An infra-red sensor on a camera
An infra-red beam is produced by the camera and reflected back from an object. The reflection is detected by a sensor on the camera and the processor in the camera can work out whether or not the object is in focus.

④ An analogue light sensor (which uses a light-resistant diode)
This responds to the amount of light falling on it. The voltage produced is greater as more light falls on it.

APPLICATION: *of sensors*

A burglar alarm system (see also Unit 17.2).
The following types of sensor are set up in a house to help the alarm system detect burglars:

① A small switch in the hinge of the outside door and opening window which sends a signal when it is opened.

② An infra-red sensor in the kitchen doorway which sends a signal when the beam is interrupted.

③ A heat sensitive sensor in a corner of the lounge which reacts to the presence of a person in the room.

KEY TERMS *Feedback generally means using output from a system to influence the input.*
Data from sensors is received by the processor and these data help it to decide what control signals to send. The processor uses feedback to keep the control system stable.
Feedback which is used to keep a system stable is called **negative feedback**.

EXAMPLES: *of feedback in everyday life*

① A cyclist
A cyclist starts to overbalance to the right. This is sensed and a message goes to the brain. The cyclist unconsciously shifts his weight towards the left and steers slightly to the right. This corrects the overbalancing.

② A loudspeaker system
Sound from a microphone is amplified and fed through loudspeakers. The person holding the microphone moves in front of one of the speakers without thinking. Sound output from the speaker is input by the microphone. This sound is amplified and output again – louder. The sound very quickly becomes too loud for the speakers to cope with and a loud whistle results.

Note:
In the second example the feedback actually makes the system unstable. This is called **positive feedback.**

Components of a control system (See Fig. 16.4.)

A control system normally requires a processor which has:
- storage for program and data (for a small microprocessor just a ROM for the program and a small amount of RAM for the data);
- a control program which can send control signals and deal with feedback from sensors;
- input ports to receive data from sensors;
- output ports to send control signals;
- interfaces to convert signals between the processor and the rest of the system. It may also have to allow for timing differences between devices.

APPLICATION: *of sensors and feedback*

① Automatic control of a greenhouse
The situation
A large nursery has a number of greenhouses which need constant attention. To save workers having to continually check them, an automatic computer-controlled system is introduced.

Chapter 16 Measurement and control

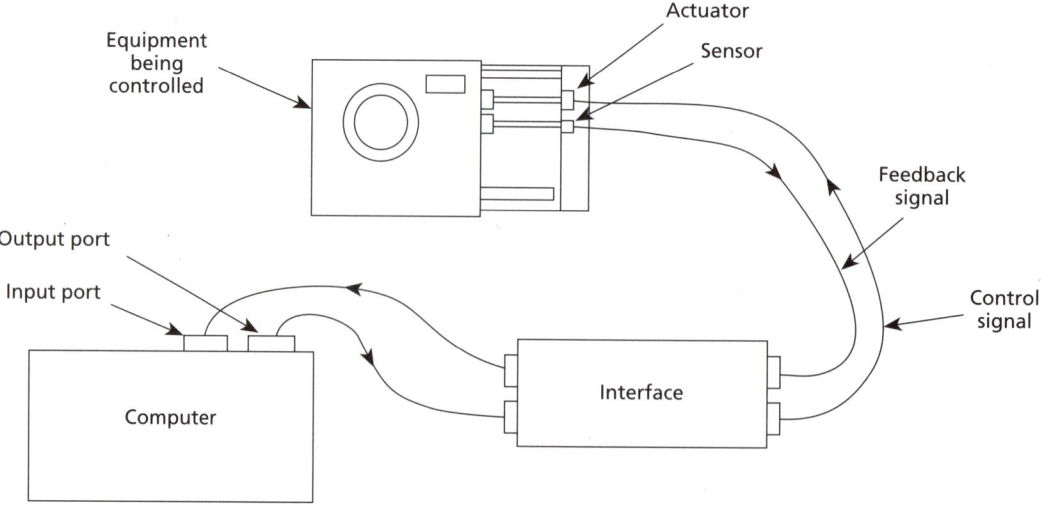

Fig. 16.4 Diagram of a control system showing sensors

Each greenhouse needs to be kept at constant temperature and constant humidity. These can be controlled by:
- opening or closing overhead ventilators – opening the ventilators decreases temperature and humidity, while closing the ventilators increases them;
- switching a fan on or off – on decreases temperature;
- switching a heater on or off – on increases temperature;
- putting misters on or off – on increases humidity.

Data capture

The greenhouse has suitably placed sensors to measure:
- temperature;
- humidity.

The temperature sensor is digital but the humidity sensor is analogue.

Role of the computer

The computer receives readings from the sensors. Readings from the humidity sensor are passed through an analogue-to-digital converter. It is programmed to check humidity and temperature at 10-second intervals and take appropriate actions, e.g.
- if temperature is too low, then:
  switch the heater on,
  shut the ventilators slowly, checking humidity and temperature,
  switch the fan off if necessary;
- if humidity is too low, then:
  put the misters on until humidity recovers.

16.3 Process control

KEY TERMS *Process control* means automatic control of an industrial process.

A computer is used to control an operation by monitoring readings from sensors and sending control signals when necessary.

CHARACTERISTICS: *of process control*

1. It is a real time operation – input from sensors is processed and control signals are sent back almost immediately.
2. It is an example of the use of feedback – the sensor input is used to adjust the process if it is out of balance.
3. The computer usually controls the supply of materials and the timing of each part of the process.
4. Some more sophisticated systems allow for 'learning' to take place. The computer 'remembers' how the best results were obtained and attempts to reproduce those results.

16.3 Process controls

Requirements for process control
In a computerised process control application the following items are generally required:
1. a controller – usually a dedicated computer or a microprocessor-based circuit;
2. sensors to provide information on the process under control. If a sensor is analogue an analogue-to-digital converter is needed;
3. actuators to carry out control actions in response to signals from the processor. If the actuator is analogue a digital-to-analogue converter is required;
4. display devices (e.g. monitor screens, LED or LCD displays) so that a human operator can check the system;
5. a printer to provide hard copy when required.

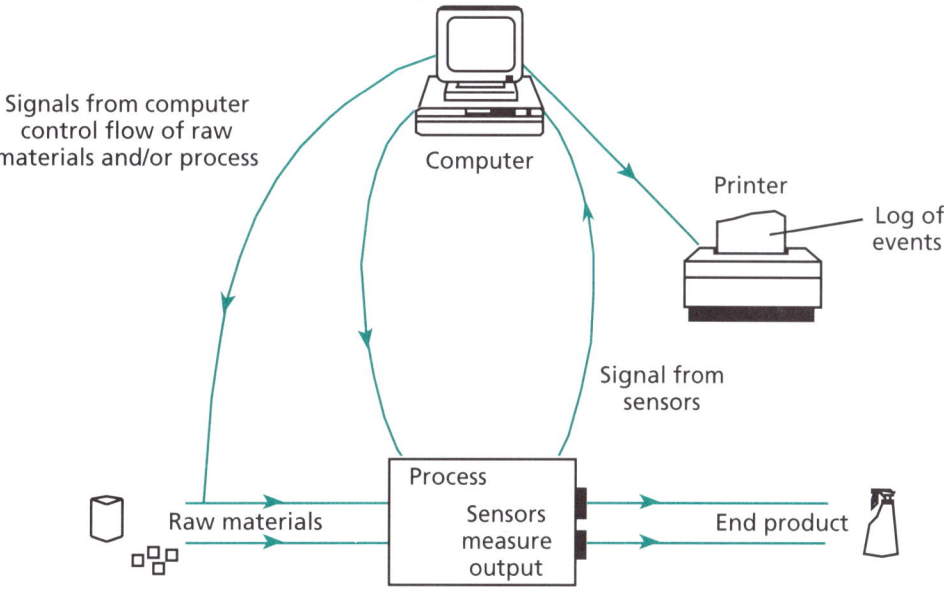

Fig. 16.5 A process control system

APPLICATION: *involving process control*

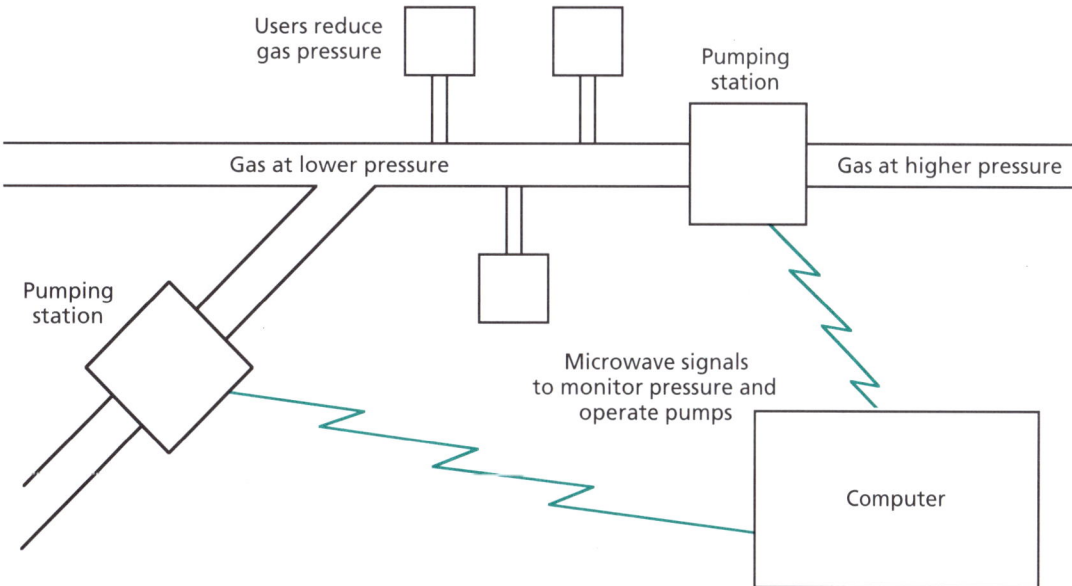

Fig. 16.5 A process control system

Control of gas pipelines and pumping stations
The situation
As consumers use gas, the pressure has to be maintained at a fixed level throughout the grid. This is done by pumping gas to those areas where the pressure is dropping.

Chapter 16 Measurement and control

Data capture

Each pumping station has a microprocessor and pressure sensors. Signals are sent from these by microwaves.

The role of the computer

The whole grid is controlled by a computer at the board's headquarters. It sends a microwave signal to a pumping station asking for pressure readings. The microprocessor there sends results back. These are analysed and the main computer sends signals to the microprocessor to adjust the pumps.

ADVANTAGES: *of introducing computers to control processes*

1. Lower labour costs:
   - fewer operators and maintenance staff are required;
   - maintenance work can be put out to contract.
2. A more flexible system:
   - the product can be changed to suit the customer.
3. More reliable:
   - microprocessors rarely fail and are easily replaced.
4. Better quality:
   - quality of raw materials can more easily be monitored;
   - tests can be carried out at various stages of the process.
5. Improved safety:
   - control is improved at all stages;
   - 'fail safes' can be included in the programs to avoid dangerous conditions;
   - sensors can be put in places where it would be unpleasant or dangerous for a person to go.
6. Better conditions for workers:
   - more interesting work;
   - possibly higher pay;
   - cleaner, less hostile conditions.

DISADVANTAGES: *of introducing computers to control processes*

1. Less staff required – meaning redundancy for some.
2. Remaining staff will need retraining.
3. Other skilled staff will be required and may be difficult to find.
4. High cost of initial investment in the new control equipment and software.

16.4 Robots

KEY TERMS — A *robot* is a device which can be programmed to do work which otherwise has to be done by people. An *android* is a robot which looks like a human being.

Notes:
1. Robot comes from *robotnik* which is Czech for a workman.
2. Androids feature a lot in science fiction films. However, most modern robots are not androids but they do often copy movements and parts of the human body, particularly the arm.

Robot locomotion

Many robots cannot move bodily from place to place. Those which can may use:
1. **wheels**

EXAMPLE: *of a robot with wheels*

A robot for moving parts around a factory.

2. **caterpillar tracks** (continuous belts, as on a tank):
   - for slow movement, possibly over difficult terrain;
   - allow accurate control of movement.

EXAMPLE: *of a robot with caterpillar tracks*
A robot used by the army to detonate bombs.

❸ **legs**:
- a robot cannot easily walk on two legs because every time it raises one leg it has to balance on the other one;
- robots with several legs are used for slow movement over very rough ground.

EXAMPLE: *of a robot with legs*
A spider-like robot used to investigate the craters of volcanoes.

Stationary robots

Many industrial robots are fixed in position. Often the parts and movements are similar to those of a human arm. They have:
- a waist;
- a shoulder;
- a wrist and
- a hand.

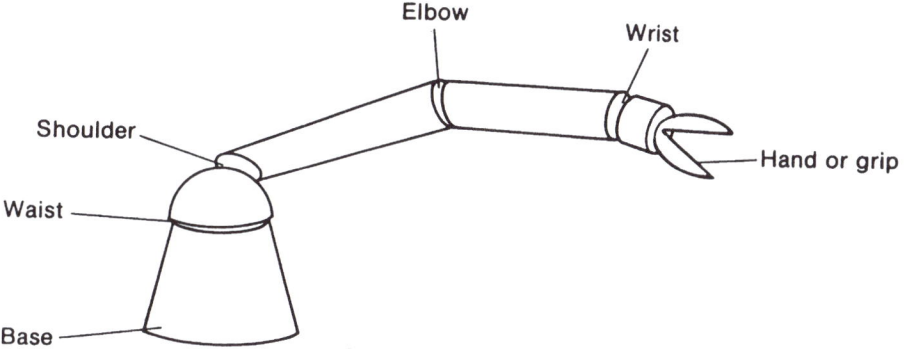

Fig. 16.7 A robot arm showing the main parts

EXAMPLES: *of stationary robots*

❶ **A robot to test cash-issuing terminals**
The situation
Before it is installed in the wall of a bank, a cash-issuing terminal has to be thoroughly tested. This is done by getting a robot to operate it for several hours.
The role of the robot
The robot inserts cards and presses the appropriate buttons on the terminal, taking the money and stacking it. It selects a card from ten different cards and carries out different types of transactions so that the test simulates real use by customers. The terminal does not have to be positioned very carefully as the robot can find the terminal and memorise where it is.
Safety
This robot will only work when no one is near it. To avoid hurting anyone the robot moves to a safe point and stops when anyone approaches.

❷ **A robot used in car manufacture**
A car factory may contain a number of robots. Often many of them are of the same type, but they may have different hands and each one is separately programmed for its own task (such as welding).

Use of sensors in robots

Sensors can be installed in a robot:

❶ **to improve safety**
Many robots are programmed to stop working if an unknown object is sensed within their field of operation.

❷ **to allow feedback and adaptability**
The computer controlling a robot which is fitted with sensors can react to a changed situation.

Chapter 16 Measurement and control

EXAMPLE: *of the use of sensors to give feedback*

A mobile robot carrying parts in a car factory

The situation

The factory has a large warehouse containing parts at one end. Parts have to be transported from here to the various work areas.

The role of the robot

The robot has a light sensor and uses it to follow a white line on the factory floor. If the sensor shows a low light reading the robot is not properly following the line. The processor adjusts the direction until the light level rises again, showing that the line is being followed.

Methods of operating robots

1. The processor controlling a robot may be contained in the robot or it may be separate. If separate, the processor may:
   - be connected by a cable, OR
   - send signals to the robot, e.g. by radio waves or microwaves.
2. A robot may be programmed:
   - by switching the robot into 'learn' mode. An operator leads it through the necessary sequence of movements by hand or using a joystick. The computer memorises the movements and carries them out repeatedly to perform the required task;
   - by inputting the sequence of operations required as a program.

EXAMPLES: *of programming a robot*

1. **A simple robot designed to paint metal panels**

   This robot will only paint the shape it has learnt to paint. When a new shape of panel is required, it has be led through the sequence of movements. This robot has no feedback system. If a panel is incorrectly placed on the conveyor it may paint thin air.

2. **A more complex robot used to paint metal panels**

   This robot is fitted with a video camera to record the shape of a panel. The processor controlling it decodes the video picture and memorises the shape. It can paint panels of different shapes and at different angles. Its sprayer is automatically switched off if no panel is present.

ADVANTAGES: *of robots*

1. They can carry out a task repeatedly for hours without stopping.
2. They can operate where humans cannot easily go, e.g.
   - on other planets;
   - deep in the ocean;
   - probing explosives.
3. They do not make errors due to tiredness or lack of concentration.

DISADVANTAGES: *of robots*

1. High cost of purchase.
2. Not as versatile as people – they can only cope with the particular situations they are built and programmed for.

16.5 Data logging

KEY TERMS

Data logging is the automatic recording of data as it is produced.

Data acquisition is the capture and storage of data for a data logging system.

CHARACTERISTICS: *of a data logging system*

1. A process is monitored by instruments or sensors.
2. Often the sensors are connected to an interface board which in turn is connected to the computer.
3. The computer controlling the system samples the readings at regular time intervals.

16.5 Data logging

④ The readings are recorded, usually by storing them on backing store.
⑤ The data is analysed. This may happen continuously or after the data has been collected.
⑥ Results may be displayed continuously:
- as a set of numbers on a printer, OR
- as a constantly changing screen display, OR
- as a graph produced on a drum plotter or a chart recorder.

KEY TERMS *The **time interval** for a data logging system is the time between one reading and the next.*
*The **period of logging** is the total length of time over which readings are taken.*

The time interval and period of logging have to be carefully thought out when designing a data logging system. The period may be determined by the subject being studied. The time interval is more likely to be decided by the equipment being used to record and analyse the data.

EXAMPLE: *of a time interval and a period of logging*
Temperature of a liquid
A computer is being used to produce a graph of the rate of cooling of a liquid from its boiling point. The computer is connected, via a suitable interface, to a digital thermometer placed in the liquid. It has been observed that the liquid cools to room temperature at least within 20 minutes. The software package used to produce the graph has a maximum of 50 plot positions across the screen.
It is decided that:
$$\text{Period of logging} = 20 \text{ minutes}$$
$$\text{Time interval} = 20 \text{ minutes} / 50$$
$$= 24 \text{ seconds}$$

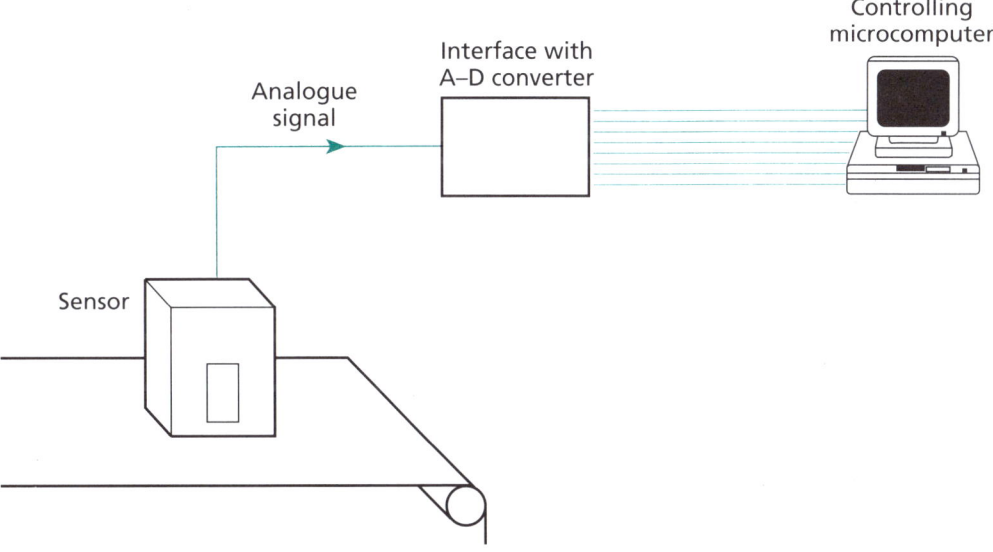

Fig. 16.8 A simple data logging system

APPLICATION: *involving data logging*

Monitoring conditions inside a petrochemical plant
Data acquisition
Sensors monitor the temperature in the boiler, the flow at two critical points and the output produced by the plant.
The role of the computer
The computer takes a sample of each of the four readings at one minute intervals. These values are stored in a disc file. Graphs of each the readings are displayed all the time on the computer's screen. The four graphs are adjusted each minute to take account of the new reading.
Each hour the values stored are used to produce statistics of the performance of the plant.

Note:
In this case the time interval is 1 minute and the period of logging for each session is 1 hour.

Chapter 16 Measurement and control

Quick test

1. Select *two* of the following which are control applications:
   (a) stock control
   (b) the exit barrier in a car park
   (c) a CD-ROM disc
   (d) a burglar alarm system
   (e) a supermarket checkout.

2. Give *two* inputs which might be received by a computer controlling a pedestrian crossing with traffic lights.

3. A computer has inputs from a thermocouple measuring temperature and a light sensor detecting the presence or absence of light. It drives a continuous motor at various speeds and a stepper motor. Where in this system might there be
   (a) a D–A converter
   (b) an A–D converter?

4. Give *two* different methods of getting a robot to perform a fixed sequence of tasks.

5. State which *three* of the following are necessary for a data logging system:
   (a) a processor
   (b) a compiler
   (c) a keyboard
   (d) sensors
   (e) backing store
   (f) actuators.

6. Why might you use sensors for:
   (a) a computer-controlled central heating system,
   (b) street lamps,
   (c) a traffic light system?

7. Which *two* of the following systems most need to use feedback:
   (a) a cyclist to balance a bicycle,
   (b) a bar code reader inputting bar codes,
   (c) a plotter drawing a diagram,
   (d) a computer-controlled rolling mill producing steel sheets of equal quality?

Summary

1. A **control system** usually consists of a processor, a control program, interfaces and a device under the processor's control.

2. An **interface** is used to connect two devices or systems to enable them to communicate. Control systems often need to include:
   - analogue-to-digital (A–D), OR
   - digital-to-analogue (D–A) converters.

3. A **sensor** is a monitoring device which sends signals back to the processor via an **input port**. There are many types of sensor including:
   - a thermocouple for measuring temperature;
   - a pressure pad (e.g. at a traffic light);
   - an infra-red sensor (e.g. on a house alarm system);
   - an analogue light sensor (which uses a light-resistant diode).

4. **Feedback** means using output from a system to affect the input.

5. **Process control** means automatic control of an industrial process.

6. - A **robot** is a device programmed to do work otherwise done by people.
   - An **android** is a robot which looks like a human being.

7. - **Data logging** is automatic recording of data as it is produced.
   - **Data acquisition** is capture and storage of data for data logging.
   - Data logging systems may display results continually and/or analyse them later.

Chapter 17
Programming for control systems

17.1 Controlling a turtle with LOGO

Some of the ideas of control programming can be understood by using a language like LOGO. LOGO includes a set of commands to move a turtle to produce patterns.

KEY TERMS

A *floor turtle* is a simple robot which can move about the floor and carry out operations in response to LOGO instructions.

A *screen turtle* is a shape drawn on the screen to represent a turtle. It can be programmed to move and draw on the screen using the same instructions used to move a floor turtle on the floor. It may be represented on the screen by an arrow shape. This is all that is needed to show the direction the turtle is facing.

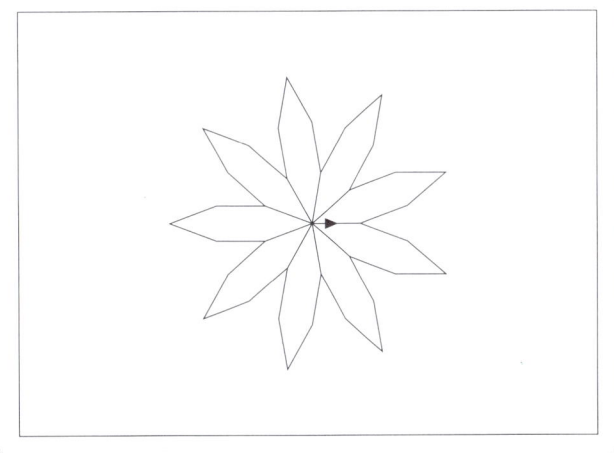

Fig. 17.1 A floor turtle and a screen turtle

A floor turtle needs:
- a means of moving forwards or backwards a precise distance in the direction it is pointed, e.g. a wheel or wheels driven by stepper motors;
- a means of turning through an exact number of degrees to face in another direction; e.g. a guide wheel driven by a stepper motor;
- a pen which can be moved down to write a line, or up for the turtle to move without writing;
- interfaces, cables and software so that a computer running LOGO can control its movement.

Simple LOGO instructions

The basic instructions for operating a turtle are as follows.

PEN DOWN — Lowers the pen. All movements of the turtle will draw a line until a PEN UP command is received.

PEN UP — Raises the pen. No line will now be drawn until there is a PEN DOWN instruction.

FORWARD n — Moves the turtle n steps forward in the direction it is pointing, e.g. FORWARD 15 moves the turtle 15 steps forward.

BACKWARD n — Moves the turtle n steps backwards – that is in the opposite direction to the way it is pointing, e.g. BACKWARD 25 moves the turtle 25 steps backwards.

LEFT b — Rotates the turtle to the left by an angle of b degrees, e.g. LEFT 90 turns it left through a right angle.

RIGHT b — Rotates the turtle to the right by an angle of b degrees, e.g. RIGHT 180 would turn it to the right by 180° – right round to face in the opposite direction.

REPEAT n [ ] — This allows you to repeat a set of instructions without having to keep writing them out. Whatever is in the square brackets is repeated n times.

EXAMPLE: *of use of REPEAT*

A square

PROGRAM: To draw a square with side 40 and leave the turtle facing in the original direction.

This could be drawn by:
```
PEN DOWN
FORWARD 40     RIGHT 90
FORWARD 40     RIGHT 90
FORWARD 40     RIGHT 90
FORWARD 40     RIGHT 90
PEN UP
```

This could be done by a much shorter program using REPEAT:
```
PEN DOWN
REPEAT 4 [FORWARD 40 RIGHT 90]
PEN UP
```

Note:

If the turtle is facing diagonally across the screen to begin with these instructions will still draw a square. It will however, stand on a point rather than on one side.

Defining new instructions – procedures

In many computer languages, it is possible to put together a sequence of instructions and give it a name as a new instruction.

KEY TERMS *A **procedure** is a new instruction defined by putting together a group of the existing instructions.*

The programmer usually defines a new procedure for each task which is frequently used.

EXAMPLE: *of using a procedure*

A procedure PETAL is defined as follows.
```
PEN DOWN
LEFT 20        FORWARD 15
RIGHT 20       FORWARD 15
RIGHT 20       FORWARD 15
RIGHT 140      FORWARD 15
RIGHT 20       FORWARD 15
RIGHT 20       FORWARD 15
RIGHT 160
PEN UP
```

This draws a rough petal shape and brings the turtle back to the direction it faced first. A program can then be written to show a flower shape using the procedure PETAL (see the screen in Fig. 17.1):

REPEAT 9 [PETAL RIGHT 40]

Note:
Many application packages, such as spreadsheets or word processors, can also have one new instruction which is formed by putting together existing instructions. In these situations it is usually called a **macro** (see Unit 9.1).

17.2 Programming control systems

In control work the processor has to be given a program of instructions. Each problem to be solved requires a different program.

Control algorithms

It helps to understand a control situation and to design a program for it if the structure of the program is first written in simple English. The language used needs to be:
- precise – using clear language;
- set out so that it is easy to read.

EXAMPLE 1: *of a control algorithm*

Burglar alarm
A burglar alarm has two sensor systems, one using touch sensors in the doors and windows and the other using infra-red beams inside. Both these sensors are normally on all the time that the burglar alarm system is on. If either of these sensors is off the processor switches on an alarm and also switches on the outside lights.

The program to do this could be represented as:
```
REPEAT
    CHECK touch sensor.
    CHECK infra-red sensor.
    IF touch sensor OFF OR infra-red sensor OFF THEN
        SWITCH ON alarm
        SWITCH ON lights
UNTIL alarm system switch OFF
```

Notes:
1. The language is English but it is precise.
   - Every time the same operation is done the same words are used (e.g. SWITCH ON).
   - To emphasise the regularly used words, they have been written in capital letters.
2. Where statements should be grouped together this has been done by indenting them from the margin, e.g.
   - SWITCH ON alarm and SWITCH ON lights have been indented together to make it clear they are both governed by the IF condition;
   - all the statements between REPEAT and UNTIL have been indented to make it clear they are all to be repeated.

EXAMPLE 2: *of a control algorithm*

A pedestrian crossing
The lights are normally green for cars and red for pedestrians. The lights can be changed by a pedestrian pushing the button so that they go into the crossing sequence. However, it has been observed that they will not change if in the last 10 seconds:
- a car has passed over the pressure pad, OR
- a pedestrian has already crossed.

Chapter 17 Programming for control systems

The processor controlling the lights seems to follow the sequence:
```
REPEAT
    Set pedestrian's lights RED, driver's lights GREEN
    REPEAT
        If pressure pad down set time = 0
    UNTIL pedestrian button has been pushed AND time > 10
    Go through crossing sequence
    Wait 10 seconds
UNTIL system switched off
```

The crossing sequence of lights is as follows:

Motorist's light	Pedestrian's light
AMBER	RED
RED	GREEN
FLASHING AMBER	FLASHING GREEN

Control tables

The pattern of inputs or outputs or control signals for a control system can be shown in a table. This is usually done using a table of binary digits (0's and 1's - see Unit 1.3).

EXAMPLE: *of a control table*

The lights in the pedestrian crossing example can only occur in certain combinations. These can be shown in a table where 0 represents OFF and 1 represents ON:

MOTORIST			PEDESTRIAN			
GREEN	AMBER	RED	GREEN	AMBER	RED	
0	1	0	0	0	1	Start crossing sequence
0	0	1	1	0	0	Pedestrian can go
0	1	0	1	0	0	Flashing
0	0	0	0	0	0	The other flash
1	0	0	0	0	1	Motorist can go

Notes:
1. It has been assumed that when the lights flash they are either both ON or both OFF.
2. There are a lot of other combinations but they are not allowed, e.g. 1 0 0 1 0 0 would mean that both the pedestrian and the motorist had GREEN lights.

Control equipment for a personal computer

Control equipment is available which enables users to simulate control systems – or to control real systems. Typically it includes (see Fig. 17.2):
- a control interface connected to the computer's input and output ports. This would have sockets for a number of input and output leads;
- various sensors;
- push buttons;
- lights of various colours;
- motors.

It also contains software with a control language for:
- switching outputs on and off;
- receiving input from sensors.

EXAMPLE: *of programming control equipment*

A particular set of control equipment has some software which includes the following control instructions for making up programs. Instructions which can be used include:

OUT n x –   send to output port number n
                      x is the value sent to it, often just ON or OFF

IN n x –   read from input port number n
                      x is the value read from it – it may be ON or OFF

Fig. 17.2 Control equipment

WAIT n	–	wait for n seconds
SETTIME n	–	set the clock to n seconds
GETTIME x	–	read the time on the clock into x
REPEAT ... UNTIL ...		

This is used to simulate the pedestrian traffic lights in Example 3 above. The lights are made up and plugged into output ports as follows:

1. Motorist's red
2. Motorist's amber
3. Motorist's green
4. Pedestrian's red
5. Pedestrian's green

The part of the program to simulate the crossing sequence is as follows:

Instruction	Explanation
OUT 2 ON	Amber ON for motorist
OUT 4 ON	Red ON for pedestrian (in case it is not on)
WAIT 5	Wait 5 seconds for any motorists to stop
OUT 2 OFF	Amber OFF for motorist
OUT 1 ON	Red ON for motorist
OUT 4 OFF	Red OFF for pedestrian
OUT 5 ON	Green ON for pedestrian
WAIT 20	Wait 20 seconds for pedestrians to cross
SETTIME 0	Set the clock to zero
REPEAT	
OUT 2 ON	
OUT 5 ON	Flash amber for motorist
OUT 2 OFF	and green for pedestrian
OUT 5 OFF	for 10 seconds
GETTIME T	
UNTIL $T = 10$	

17.3 Solving control problems

Using information systems to solve problems is dealt with in Chapter 18. Documentation of the solutions is dealt with in Chapter 19. However, there are special aspects of solving control problems so those are dealt with here.

The sequence of steps should follow the general sequence for problem solving explained in Chapter 18. For control projects it is important to read your instructions carefully to see what you need to do and what you need to hand in. However, the sequence will usually be as follows.

Problem recognition

If you are allowed a choice of topic do not start by deciding straight away on a control system you are going to construct.

Instead, try considering different situations. All kinds of systems can be simulated:
- at home: burglar alarms, washing machines, central heating systems, devices for switching lights on and off, greenhouses, car door, window and seat belt systems;
- at school: theatre lights, disco lights;
- outside: traffic lights, level crossings, pedestrian crossings, security systems.

But you do not just need a situation, you need a problem to solve. You probably need more than one problem – because until you investigate you do not know that a control system is the best solution for a given problem.

Feasibility study

For most projects you now need to produce a project proposal. You investigate the situation briefly and write out a summary for your teacher giving a brief paragraph on each of:
- *the situation and the problem;*
- *hardware for the solution;*
- *what the program will do.*

Your teacher will probably make comments on whether this is suitable.

Analysis of the problem

You now need to study the problem more carefully:
- talk to the people involved, e.g. for the pedestrian crossing, talk to drivers and pedestrians. It would be too dangerous to actually stop people at the crossing, you need friends and neighbours who use it.
- make written notes based on observations, e.g. timings of lights, traffic queues, etc.

Design of a new system

1. Before you start writing any programs or building anything you need to do some work on paper.
2. If this is an assessed project, look at the mark scheme. You may well find that designing the system merits more marks than making it.
3. At the very least you will need to produce:
   - a diagram of the hardware required;
   - a diagram or written description of what the system does;
   - a flowchart or structure diagram showing how the program carries this out.
4. Make sure that the hardware you propose is available and that the program is possible.

Construction of the new system

1. If this is an assessed project, look at the mark scheme again. If the hardware cannot gain many marks, there is no point in spending all your time constructing models.
2. Make sure your program not only works but is easy to understand:
   - it should have an obvious structure, broken up into procedures;
   - put in comments and choose names which make it clear what everything is. In particular, it should be easy to tell by looking at the program which output devices are being switched on and off and which sensors are being read.

Testing

For each of the following do the test and sort out any problems before going on to the next one.

1. Test that the interface and the software have been set up correctly. You can usually do this by putting small lights (or LEDs) in the output sockets and running a simple program which flashes all the lights on and off.
2. Test the rest of the hardware. With all your equipment set up, run a test program to check the sensors and the output devices.
3. Test the whole system. Devise tests so that when each sensor or switch is operated you can forecast what will happen. Check for each one that what does happen is as predicted.

Evaluation

You will probably be expected to produce an evaluation report as part of the project. You should take the following into account:

1. Evaluate the whole system – does it work to the specification in your design?
2. Have you solved the problem? You may have to run the system and make detailed observations to help solve the original problem.
3. Could it be done better if you had more time and equipment or better software?
4. Does what you have done have any practical application?

Quick test

1. Give *six* instructions that a turtle normally has.

2. Of the six instructions in question **1** give a set of *four* instructions which would be enough to draw all the patterns you can draw with the six.

3. The following turtle program is supposed to draw a 60° triangle but it does not. Correct the mistake.
   PEN DOWN
   FORWARD 30   RIGHT 60
   FORWARD 30   RIGHT 120
   FORWARD 30   RIGHT 120
   PEN UP

4. Describe in words the shape drawn by:
   REPEAT 6 [FORWARD 50 RIGHT 60]

5. An alarm in a bank vault should be switched on if either the outer door or the inner door is open. What is wrong with the following program statement to describe this?
   IF outer door OPEN AND inner door OPEN THEN SWITCH ON alarm

6. Name *two* types of diagram necessary in the design documentation of a project to create a control system.

7. State *three* parts of testing a control system once it is finished.

Summary

1. - A **floor turtle** is a simple robot which can move about the floor and responds to LOGO instructions.
   - A **screen turtle** is a shape on the screen which can carry out the same instructions as a floor turtle.

2
- A turtle can usually obey:
  PEN DOWN, PEN UP, FORWARD n, BACKWARD n, LEFT b, RIGHT b.
- A set of instructions can be repeated using REPEAT n [...].

3 Actual control equipment will have a control language with instructions for:
- switching outputs on and off;
- receiving input from sensors.

4 A project on control work involves:
- finding a problem to solve;
- producing a project proposal and having it accepted;
- investigating the problem further;
- producing a design for a solution including a diagram of the hardware, a description of what the system will do and a program flowchart or structure diagram;
- constructing the hardware but not spending too long on it;
- writing the program in a way that is easy to understand;
- testing the interface, the rest of the hardware and then the whole system including the program;
- evaluating the project.

Chapter 18
Solving problems using IT

18.1 Introduction to problem solving

Computers are used in all areas of business, industry, government, education, transport, medicine, everywhere. Each one of these applications arose as someone's solution to a problem.

Solving a problem may be seen as a number of main stages. In producing a solution, a new information system is developed.

KEY TERMS

*The **system life cycle** is the set of steps which it is necessary to go through in developing a new system to solve a problem.*

*A **systems analyst** is a person whose job it is to analyse an existing system and develop a new one.*

Note:
The system life cycle is described below as it would be carried out professionally by a systems analyst. However, in doing a GCSE project or assignment you should go through as many of these steps as are practical. You are the systems analyst.

Steps in the system life cycle
Developing a new system usually involves the following steps:
1. problem recognition;
2. feasibility study;
3. analysis of the problem;
4. design of a new system;
5. construction of the new system;
6. conversion from the old system to the new;
7. maintenance and review of the new system.

Note:
Different people often number these stages differently and do not always give them exactly these names, e.g. Stages 5 and 6 (construction and conversion) are often put together and called **implementation**.

18.2 The professional way – the system life cycle

Problem recognition
- Carry out a preliminary study of the situation.
- Decide exactly what the problem is.

Chapter 18 Solving problems using IT

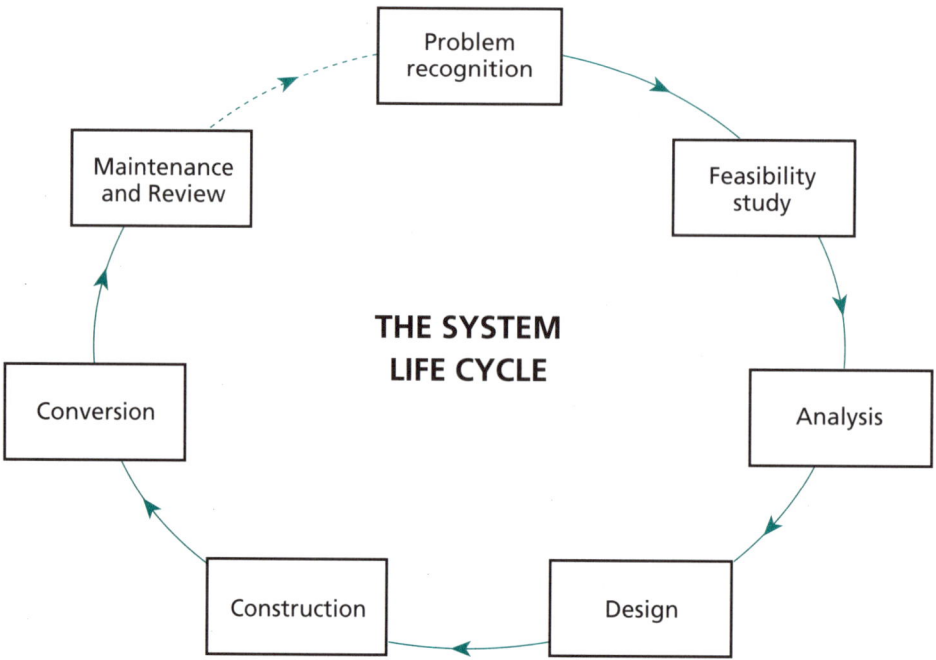

Fig. 18.1 The system life cycle

Feasibility study

This is an investigation into whether a new system is realistic. It will enable the people requiring the new system to decide whether to go ahead with it.
At this stage the management
- decides whether or not to continue with the project;
- suggests changes if it is going ahead.

Analysis of the problem

Now that permission has been given to go ahead and investigate more thoroughly you should:
1. study the existing system if there is one:
   - interview users of the current system – find out what is wrong with it;
   - read any manuals or instructions which are in use;
   - observe the current system in operation.
2. work out what the new system requires.
3. decide what the new system has to do.

(At this stage no decisions have been made about what hardware and software to use.)

Design of a new system

This is the stage at which all parts of the new system must be thought out. The new system should make good use of the skills of existing employees. It should be 'user friendly'.
1. Consider possible solutions which fit the analysis.
2. Consider whether new hardware is required.
3. Consider whether new software is required. Possibilities are:
   - use an existing general purpose application package;
   - buy a new general purpose application package;
   - buy a specialised program for this application which is already on sale;
   - have a program written specially for this application.
4. Prepare a design of the new system. Each of the following has to be worked out:
   - data capture – forms have to be designed if necessary;
   - the type of user interface;
   - validation methods – how is input data going to be checked?;
   - data files;
   - programs – if some new programs have to be written then they have to be designed at this stage;

18.2 The professional way – the system life cycle

- output of data – decide what data is to be output on screens and printers;
- security – decide on arrangements for backup of data files.

5 Produce diagrams and written designs to explain all these items clearly, e.g.
- a system flowchart would show how the inputs, outputs, files and programs relate to one another;
- programs or sequences of instructions can be shown on flowcharts or structure diagrams.

As far as possible new systems are designed **top-down**.

KEY TERMS

Top-down design is a method of solving a problem by breaking it down into tasks and then into gradually smaller and smaller tasks.

The process of breaking a task down into smaller and smaller parts is called **stepwise refinement**.

In top-down design the main function of a program is expressed as simply as possible. This function is then split up into more detailed separate procedures. These are then split further and so on. The process finishes when the program has been split down to the level of separate computer operations.

Construction of the new system

The new system has to be created and tested according to the specifications set out in the design:

1 any new programs have to be written;

2 **system testing** – programs and methods have to be tested and debugged:
- test data is designed and the results are forecast. The data has to be chosen carefully to include:
  (a) typical data like that which would be used in normal situations;
  (b) abnormal data – of a type which would not crop up very often but could cause the system to fail when it did;
- the tests are carried out;
- programs are debugged and the tests repeated as necessary;

3 **acceptance testing** – the users of the new system check it to see that it does what they wanted;

4 user documentation is prepared;

5 users are trained to use the new system;

6 technical documentation is prepared so that the new system can be maintained.

Conversion to the new system

1 File conversion – data needed for the new system may have to be keyed in or converted from some existing files.

2 Software and hardware installation.

3 System conversion – people will have to change their work methods. This can be done in several ways including:
- a direct changeover – the old system is scrapped and replaced by the new straight away, OR
- parallel working – the two methods are both kept working until the new one has proved reliable.

4 Evaluation – the users feed back comments and the analyst produces a report on the success of the system and on any difficulties which arise.

DISADVANTAGE: *of parallel working*

Having two systems going at once is expensive and needs twice the staff time.

DISADVANTAGE: *of a direct changeover*

If something is wrong with the new system and the old one has been abandoned there is nothing to fall back on.

System maintenance and review

The new system has to be monitored and problems solved as they arise.
- Keep watch on the new system – there should be regular reports.
- Repair faults in both hardware and software.
- Upgrade the system as requirements change.

18.3 A coursework project – what to do

Tackling GCSE coursework

The above account deals mainly with the solving of commercial problems. However, many of the same principles apply to GCSE coursework.

- The coursework requirements for the various GCSE syllabuses are dealt with in the Introduction to this book.
- Many coursework tasks in Information Technology consist of using IT to solve a problem. You are put in the role of systems analyst and you have to go through the steps of the system life cycle.

In this section we go through the steps usually needed in producing a piece of coursework. Remember:

- each piece of coursework has a set of instructions – keep referring to it and do what it says;
- most coursework is an exercise in problem-solving, not just in using a computer;
- if you have a copy of the mark scheme, make sure you are producing evidence of the skills it requires;
- produce any printouts and documentation as you do the work – not in a mad rush at the end.

Problem recognition

If the topic of the coursework is your decision then you need:

- a situation,
- a user and
- a problem.

You are looking for a situation and a person with a problem to solve which involves data to reorganise in some way.

EXAMPLES: *of situations and users with problems to solve*

- Your work if you do a part time job.
- Your own hobbies or those of friends.
- The work of your parents or other relatives.
- Local businesses.
- Your other subject teachers at school, e.g. storing results of experiments, producing graphs or statistics.
- Someone else in the school, e.g. in the office or the library.
- Estate agents – details of houses, lists for customers.
- Home collection of video tapes – storing tape contents, looking for space on tape.
- Cassette or CD labels – storing details of music, printing labels.
- A sports club – recording players in a tournament.
- Holidays – working with details from holiday brochures.

Feasibility study

You then have to describe the situation, the prospective user and the problem. This will be needed as part of the documentation of your coursework and may be needed for a project proposal. Your teacher may have to agree this before you can carry on.

Analysis of the problem

It is important at this stage to concentrate on the problem and *not* on how you are going to solve it. You need to:

- interview the prospective users to find out what they want;
- decide what the new system needs – what data will be input, what will be stored and what output;
- decide on what you intend the project to achieve.

Design of a new system

You now have to decide how to solve the problem.

① Investigate possible solutions

Where you have a choice consider:
- hardware – choice of computer, whether to use a mouse or a keyboard;
- software – whether to use a spreadsheet, a database, a word processor or a desktop publisher (see Chapter 9 for choice of software); whether to write a program yourself.

② Choose a solution and work out details

- Input data – what data is to be input and how to collect it; what data capture forms you need.
- How the input data will be checked to see that it is accurate.
- What data will be stored in files – will it be in the form of spreadsheets or databases?
- What fields are required? Draw a table to show how the records will be structured:

EXAMPLE: *of a table showing record structure*

Field name	Type	Length
Surname	String	20
Forename	String	20
Year	Number	1
Tutor	String	3
Mark1	Number	2
Mark2	Number	2
Total	Number	3

- Algorithm required – this may be:
  (a) a program which you write, e.g. a control program, OR
  (b) the sequence which has to be followed to solve the problem.

At this point you will probably have to produce a flowchart or a structure diagram (see Units 19.3 and 19.4).

- Outputs – any screens or printouts which your work is going to produce should be planned out first.
- Security arrangements – usually the most important consideration here is how important files are going to be backed up. You may also have to consider the problem of the wrong people being able to change or delete files.

Usually for your design you will need to produce a system flowchart (see Unit 19.2). This will show all that you have worked out for the design, particularly:
- how the data is captured and checked;
- what the programs do;
- what data is stored and where;
- what data is output and how.

Construction of the new system

What you do here will depend entirely on what the work is. You may have to:
- write a program, AND/OR
- create a set of macro instructions (see Unit 9.1), AND/OR
- go through a sequence of operations using your chosen software, writing the operations down in order so that they can be repeated or included in user documentation.

If you are writing a program remember:
- computer programs should be easy to use. They should not irritate users by printing out too few instructions and headings, or too many;
- if a user enters the wrong data it should be easy to recover the situation and correct the data.

Testing the system

It is very important to do this thoroughly and to work to a plan. You need to:
- work out what needs to be tested;
- design and write out a set of test data. These should be designed:
  (a) to test the system with normal data;
  (b) to test that when given incorrect data the system warns the user and does not break down;
- forecast the results of running the system with the test data;
- check that these results are correct – and print out tests. Write on each printout what it shows OR number it so that your evaluation can refer to it.

Note:

These instructions for testing are easy to carry out if you have written a program (see Unit 17.3 for testing a control system). If you are simply using a software package there is less to test. However, you can and should test:
- formulae in spreadsheets;
- sorting procedures;
- any calculations such as average or totals.

To do this select some test data which it is easy to forecast results for, so that you can easily see that the software is working correctly.

Documentation

The coursework instructions may require you to produce:
- **documentation for a user**. It is important that this should not just be a list of instructions on how to interact with a program (see Unit 19.6).
- **technical documentation**. If you have written your design well this should not be difficult (see Unit 19.7).

Evaluation

Any coursework should be evaluated and a report written. This should be factual and should include:
- **reference to your tests**. If any of the results differ from your forecasts, explain why. If you had to change anything because the tests did not work explain that as well.
- **reference to the original objectives**. Comment on whether you have achieved what you set out in your analysis.
- **limitations of the work**. Comment on any operations you would like to carry out but cannot because the software you used cannot do them. Suggest what you could have done with more time to improve the work.
- **comments on the success of the work**. Be factual – there is no point being boastful. Give an honest analysis of whether or not the project was a good idea.

Quick test

In questions **1** and **2** put the stages of problem solving in their correct order.

1. (a) Design
   (b) Analysis
   (c) Problem definition
   (d) Feasibility study

2. (a) System maintenance
   (b) Staff training
   (c) Conversion
   (d) Construction

3. Give *three* types of diagram which could be produced in carrying out the design of a new system.

Questions **4** to **6** are based on the following steps of the system life cycle:
(a) Problem definition
(b) Analysis
(c) Design
(d) Implementation
(e) Maintenance and review.

4 Between which two stages would you do a feasibility study?

5 At which stage would you write a program?

6 At which stage would you carry out staff training?

Summary

1
- The sequence of steps in developing a new system to solve a problem is called the **system life cycle**.
- A **systems analyst** analyses existing systems and develops new ones.

2 The main steps in the system life cycle are:
- problem recognition;
- feasibility study;
- analysis of the problem;
- design of a new system;
- construction of the new system;
- conversion from the old system to the new;
- maintenance and review of the new system.

3
- A **feasibility study** establishes whether or not a new system is a good idea, and estimates the time and resources required to develop it.
- Management has to approve the **feasibility report** before the project can go ahead.

4 An analysis is done to:
- study the existing system;
- work out what the new system requires.

5 At the design stage:
- it is decided whether new hardware and software is required;
- a design is prepared of the new system including: data capture, the type of user interface, validation methods, data files, output and security. Any new programs are designed at this stage.

6 Construction of the new system includes:
- writing any new programs;
- **system testing** and debugging;
- producing technical and user documentation.

7 Conversion can be carried out as:
- a direct changeover;
- parallel working.

Chapter 19
Documentation

19.1 Documentation and diagrams

KEY TERMS *The term **documentation** refers to any information which has been prepared to help people who are using or trying to adapt a computer system or some software.*

Usually documentation consists of any or all of:
- notes;
- diagrams;
- manuals;
- instructions.

Documentation of some kind is required at each stage of the system life cycle:
1. to help the people designing and constructing a system to work together better;
2. to help analysts and programmers maintain or modify a system after it has been installed;
3. to explain how to install a program or a system;
4. to explain to the users what to do.

In this chapter we concentrate on documentation of two main types:
- **technical documentation** – that is documentation about how a system or a program works;
- **user documentation** – in particular documentation explaining how to install and use software.

Use of diagrams in documentation

Diagrams are used a great deal in documenting information systems. There are a number of recognised types. They are used in communicating:
EITHER
- a design, OR
- a solution.

Diagrams can be drawn which represent:
EITHER
- the devices in a hardware system, OR
- an information system, OR
- the way an algorithm or a program works, OR
- the design of a data structure – such as a file.

In this chapter we concentrate on the:
- **system flowchart** – which represents a whole information system;
- **program flowchart** – which represents how a program works;
- **structure diagram** – which represents the structure of a program.

Flowcharts

KEY TERMS *A **flowchart** is a diagram representing the operations involved in a process.*

A flowchart consists of:
- **symbols (or boxes)** to represent the operations. There are standard shapes for the different types of operations and these should be remembered and used;

- messages in the boxes. These state briefly what the operations are;
- lines connecting the symbols. These lines may have arrows on them.

Notes:

❶ A flowchart can also have notes in the margin (usually at the right of the flowchart). These are useful because they allow operations to be explained while keeping the messages in the boxes short.

❷ A plastic template can be used to draw flowcharts. This has box shapes on it which you can draw round.

KEY TERMS *A **system flowchart** represents the operations on data in an information processing system.*
*A **program flowchart** represents the sequence of operations in a program.*

Notes:

❶ The system flowchart and the program flowchart are quite different from one another. In particular:
- the arrows in a system flowchart represent the flow of data;
- the arrows in a program flowchart represent the order of the instructions.

❷ There are no STOP and START boxes in a system flowchart.
This is because the arrows on it do not represent moving through time. A system does not really have a beginning and an end so there is not a first and a last operation.

19.2 System flowcharts

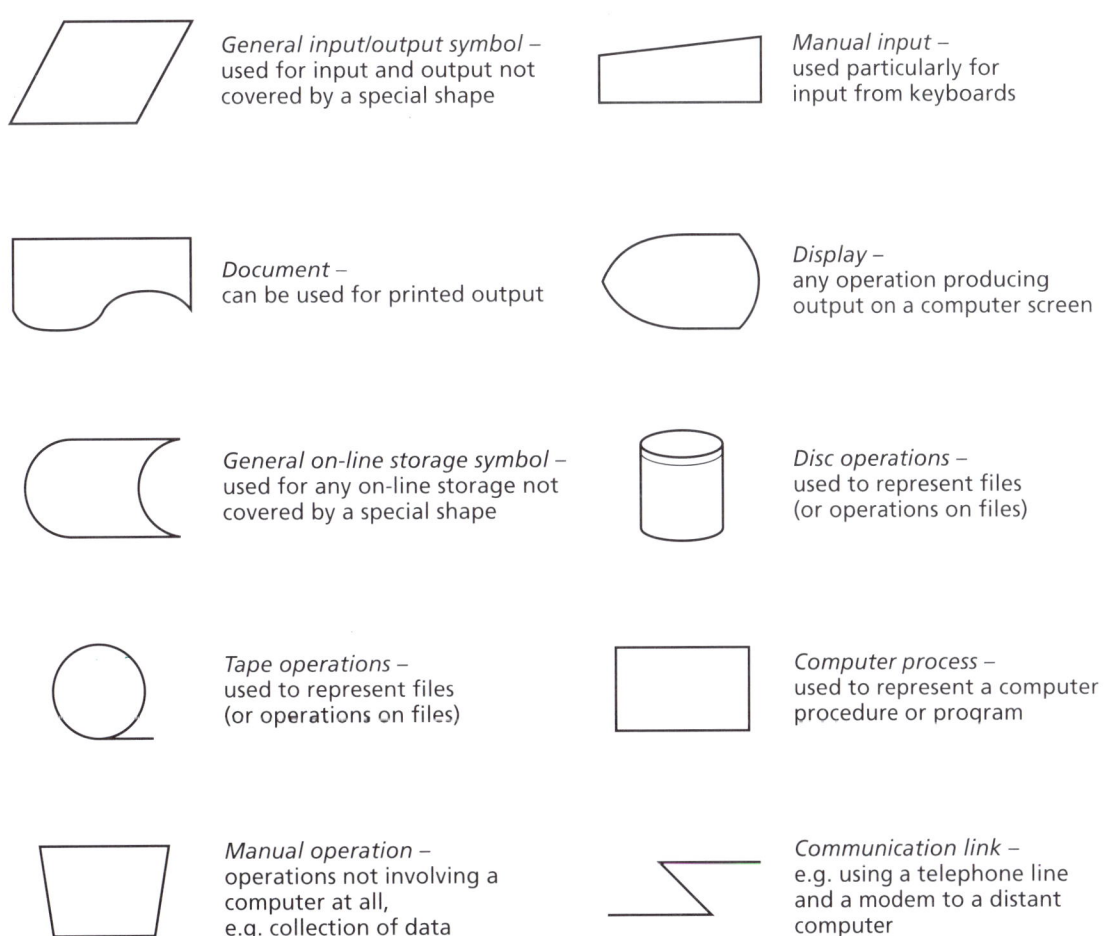

Fig. 19.1 Standard shapes of symbols used in system flowcharts

On a system flowchart:
- the symbols represent operations on data. In fact each box usually looks like the medium used for the operation;
- the arrows represent the direction in which data is moved.

Notes:
The general symbols for input/output and for on-line storage can be used:
- when the operations do not have their own shapes, e.g. CD-ROM storage or plotter output;
- for all input/output or storage instead of using the special shapes.

Drawing system flowcharts

❶ System flowcharts are quite different from other flowcharts.
- There are no details of how a program works, e.g. there are no START symbols, STOP symbols or decision boxes.
- The arrows and lines show the flow of data within the system. They do **not necessarily** show the order in which operations are carried out, e.g. the line joining two boxes may well have arrows going both ways if the data flows both ways.

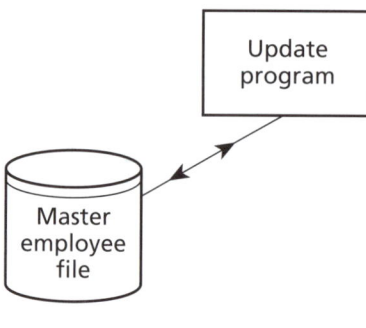

Fig. 19.2

❷ A system flowchart looks neater if you obey the following rules:
- Represent programs in process boxes (rectangles) down the middle of the page.
- Show data capture operations at the top left.
- Put boxes for files and output towards the sides of the page.
- Make messages in the boxes very brief and add comments at the far right of the page.

EXAMPLES: *of system flowcharts*

A pupil records system for a school
The system is described in words below. This description should be checked against the system flowchart in Fig. 19.3.

Hardware
- The school office has a microcomputer with both a hard and a floppy disc unit and a printer.
- Data communication with the main computer is achieved using modems. The school's microcomputer acts as an intelligent terminal to the main computer.

Software
The records are maintained using a database program. There are also separate programs for tasks such as:
- validating data as it is typed in;
- updating all the records at the beginning of each year so that first year pupils become second year pupils, etc;
- connecting the microcomputer to the local authority's main computer.

Data capture
- Part of the data on the pupils comes from the local authority's main computer via the modem.
- The rest comes from forms completed by the pupils and their teachers:
    (a) most of this data is sent to a local computer bureau at the start of the year and keyed to disc;
    (b) changes during the year are keyed in by office staff at a terminal.

Data validation
- The forms are checked for accuracy by the teachers.
- Data is also validated by the computer as it is input.

Files
The main data file includes for each pupil at the school:
name, year of entry, date of birth, address, phone numbers, medical problems, test result from the previous school, year of study, subjects studied, form tutor.

19.2 System flowcharts

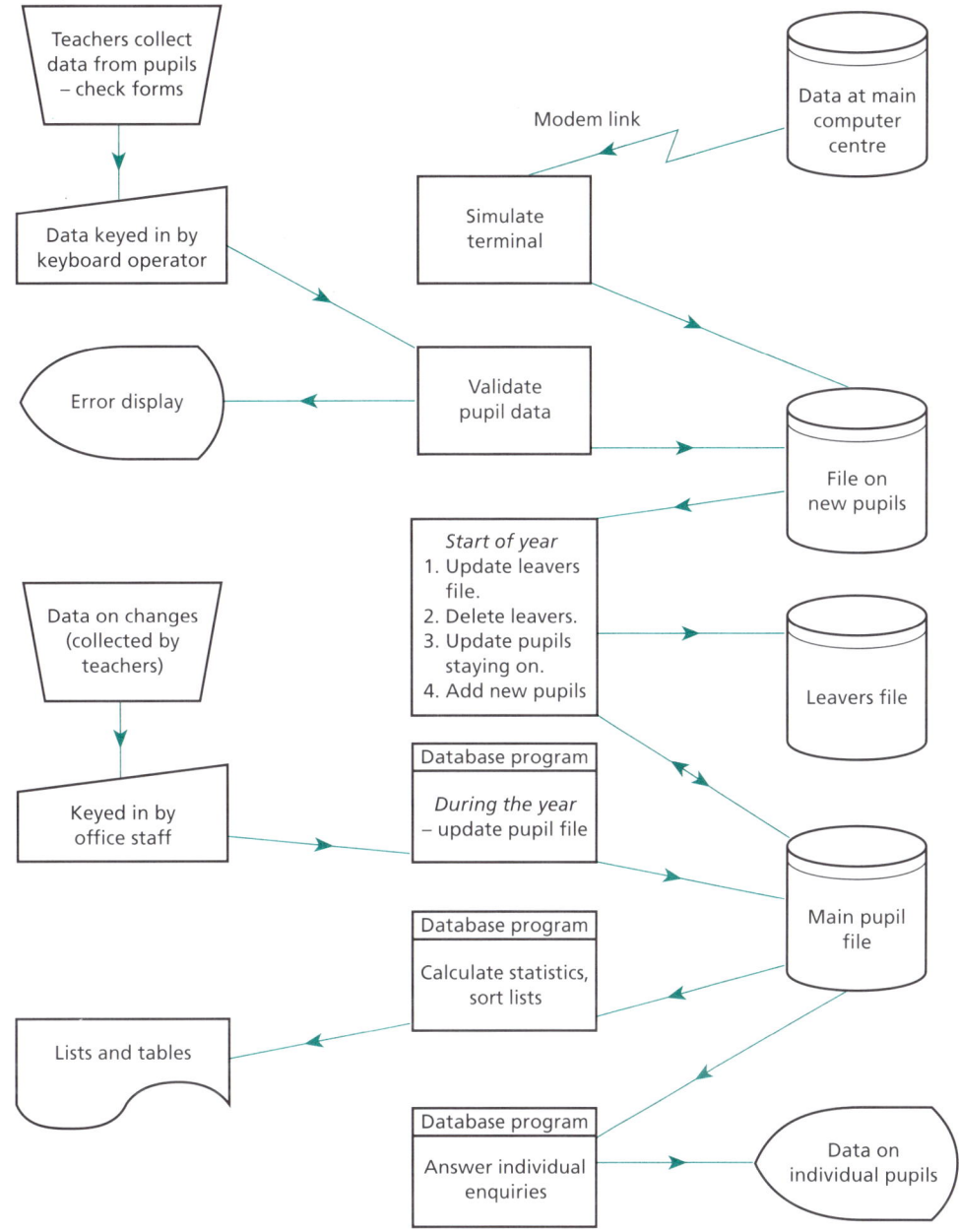

Fig. 19.3 System flowchart for a school pupil records system

Updating files
- At the start of the year:
  (a) records of leavers are copied to another file;
  (b) leavers are deleted from the main file;
  (c) the year of study, subjects studied and form tutor are changed for those staying on;
  (d) new pupils are added.
- Small changes are also carried out throughout the year by the office staff on the basis of information supplied by the teachers.

Other processing
- Calculating statistics on numbers of pupils in a particular category.
- Working out lists in a chosen order, e.g. a list of pupils in alphabetical order, lists of each tutor group.

Output
- Most lists and tables of statistics are produced on the printer.
- The screen may be used for enquiries about individual pupils.

19.3 Representing algorithms – structure diagrams

An **algorithm** is a term for any sequence of instructions, including a computer program (see Unit 9.1). There are two main types of diagram used for representing programs and other algorithms:
- **program flowcharts** – these concentrate on the order in which the instructions are carried out;
- **structure diagrams** – these concentrate on the structure of the algorithm.

KEY TERMS *A **structure diagram** is a diagram which shows how an algorithm is broken down into more and more detailed steps.*

A structure diagram is ideal when an algorithm has been designed top-down. It can then show the refinement into more and more detailed steps. (See Unit 18.2 for top-down design and stepwise refinement.)

Notation for structure diagrams

Note:
There are several methods of drawing structure diagrams. The one used here is based on the Jackson Method.

1. All steps are shown in rectangles, each containing a brief statement of the step.
   - The detailed steps making up each step are shown below it and joined to it by lines.
   - Steps which follow one another in sequence go in order from left to right across the page.
2. Selection (decision making) is shown by:
   - drawing a small circle in the top right of each of the choices AND
   - writing the condition for selecting that box just above it.
3. Repetition is shown by:
   - drawing an asterisk in the top right of the step being repeated AND
   - writing the condition for repetition just above it.

EXAMPLE: *of showing structure in a diagram*
Double rib
In knitting patterns:
- Knit and Purl are two different types of stitch.
- Knit 2 means do Knit twice.
- Double rib is a name for the sequence Knit 2, Purl 2.

1. Double rib could be represented simply in a structure diagram as Fig. 19.4.

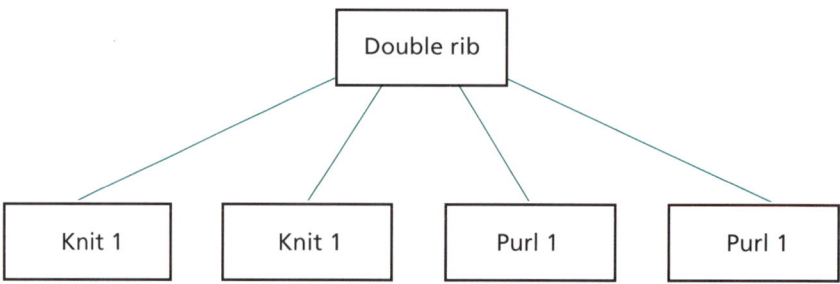

Fig. 19.4

19.3 Representing algorithms – structure diagrams

2 Double rib could also be drawn to show the structure of Knit 2 and Purl 2:

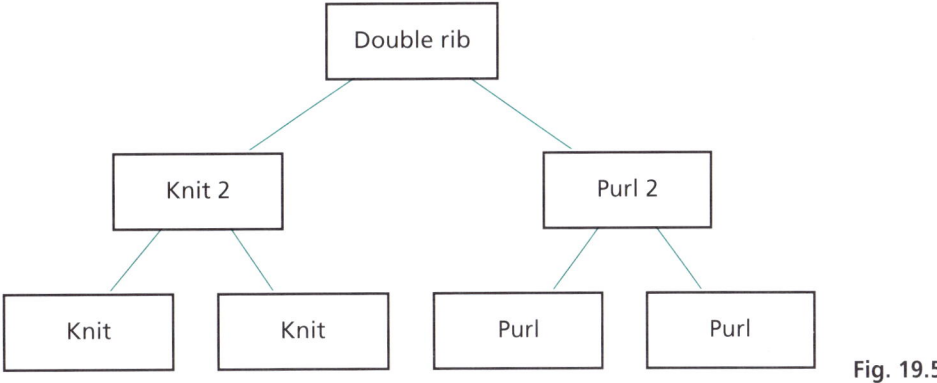

Fig. 19.5

Note:
On a structure diagram there are no STOP and START boxes. The first step is at the bottom left and the last one is at the bottom right.

EXAMPLE: *of a structure diagram showing repetition*

Second row of the knitting pattern
The **second row** is defined as:
2nd row P1, ★ K2, P2, rep from ★ to last 3 sts, K2, P1.

This means that after a **Purl 1** the sequence **Knit 2, Purl 2** has to be repeated until the last three stitches in the row. These last three stitches are then **Knit 2, Purl 1**. The sequence **Knit 2, Purl 2** has been defined as **Double Rib**. Using the ★ to indicate a repeat, the **second row** can be shown in a structure diagram as:

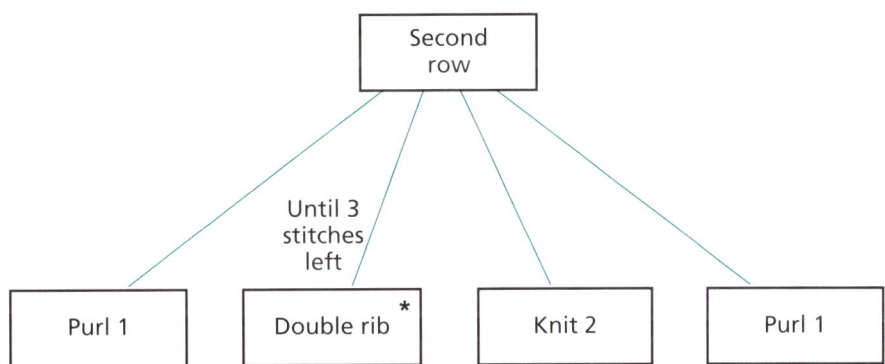

Fig. 19.6 Structure diagram for second row of knitting pattern

EXAMPLE: *of a structure diagram showing selection*

Classifying animals
If an animal has a backbone it is classed as a vertebrate. Otherwise it is an invertebrate. This can be shown as:

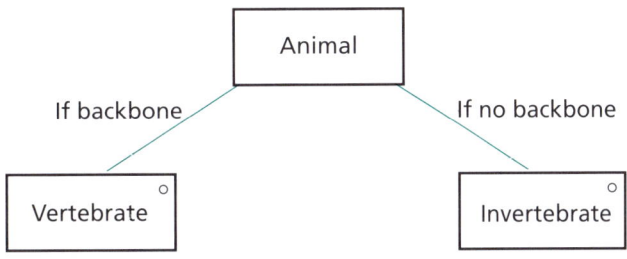

Fig. 19.7 Structure diagram for start of animal key

19.4 Program and algorithm flowcharts

Symbols used

Start or stop
The beginning or end of a program or subroutine

Connector
Link with another page or another part of the program

Input or output
Any operation to input or output data

Decision box
The box contains a decision to be made or a test to be carried out. The lines out show the result

Operation – general
Used for operations not shown by other symbols
(e.g. assignment or transfer of data)

Predefined process
Used for a sequence of instructions which is defined somewhere else
(e.g. in a subroutine)

Fig. 19.8 Standard symbols used in program flowcharts

CHARACTERISTICS: *of program flowcharts*

1. The lines and arrows show the order in which steps are to be carried out.
   - Flowlines are usually drawn in either a vertical or a horizontal direction.
   - Arrows are used where the direction is not clear. (If there are no arrows it is usually assumed that vertical lines point downwards and horizontal ones point from left to right.)
2. The boxes contain the steps – usually in ordinary English.
   - Each box has no more than one line going into it.
   - Each box has at most one line going out (except decision boxes which have more).
3. The flowchart normally has only one entry point (e.g. a START box) and one exit point (e.g. STOP).
4. Extra notes can be written in the right-hand margin.

EXAMPLE: *of a flowchart of an algorithm*

Watching a television programme
See Fig. 19.9.

19.4 Program and algorithm flowcharts

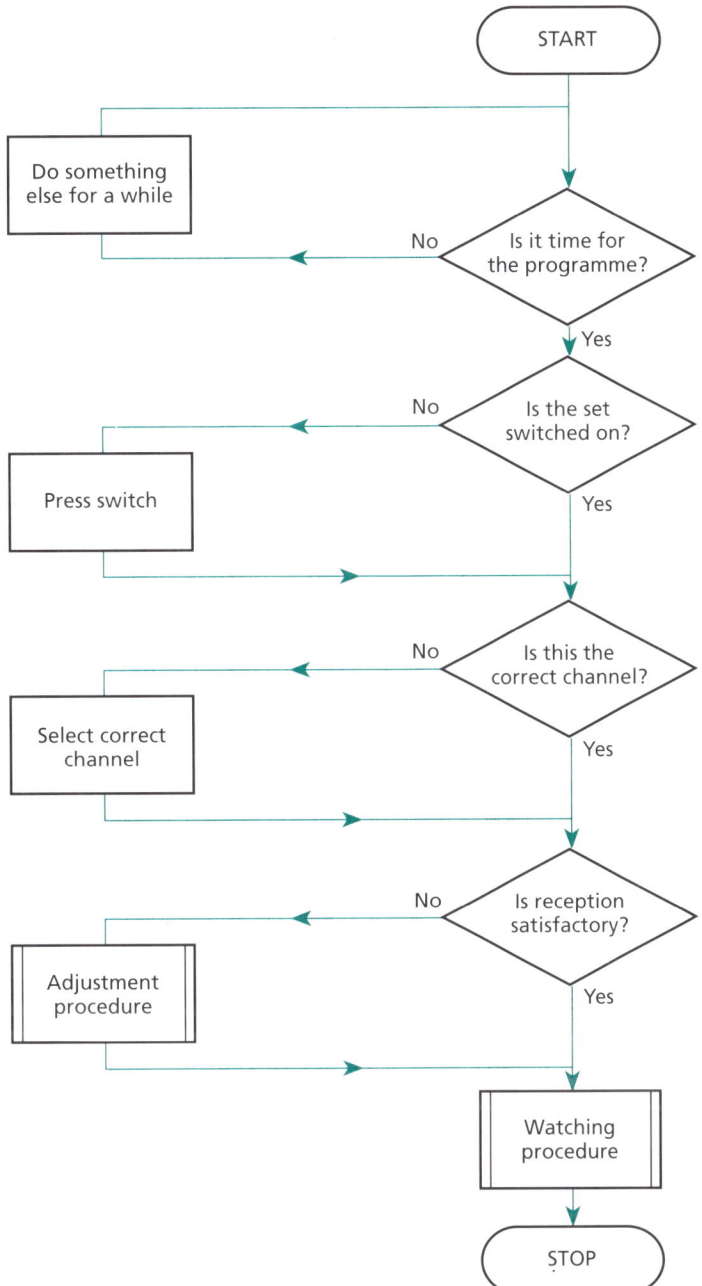

Fig. 19.9 Flowchart giving instructions for watching a television programme

Note:
What do we do if the cat wants to go out in the middle of a programme? The answer should lie in the detailed flowchart for the watching procedure (if there is one).

EXAMPLES: *of the use of decision boxes*

① **A decision**
The lines out of the box show 'YES' and/or 'NO'.

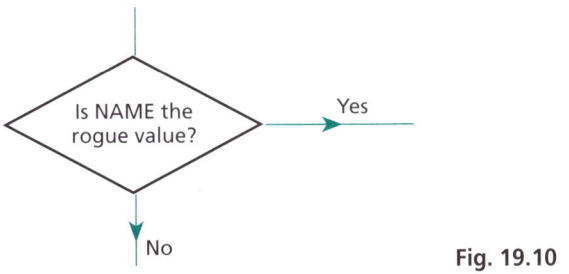

Fig. 19.10

② A test
The box contains a test. The lines out show the results of that test.

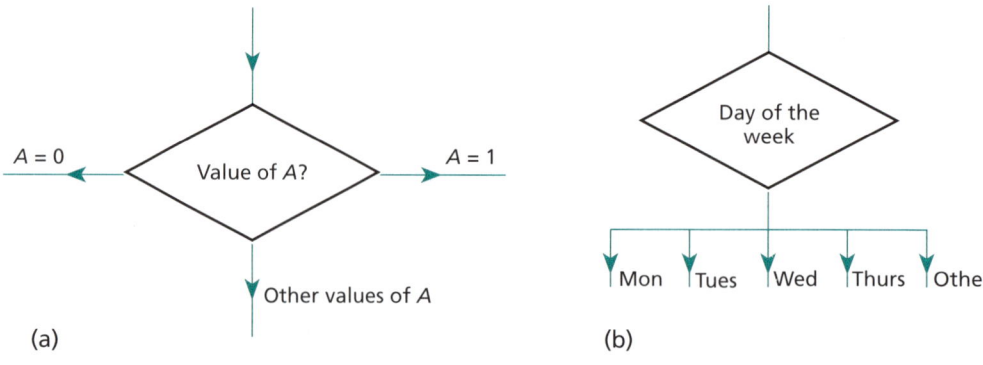

(a)   (b)

Fig. 19.11

19.5 Example comparing a structure diagram and a program flowchart

A central heating system
The house owner sets a temperature with a dial on one of the room walls. There is also a thermometer on the wall. Both of these are connected to a small processor which operates the boiler. The system works according to the following algorithm:

    REPEAT
        READ set temperature
        READ room temperature
        IF room temperature IS GREATER THAN set temperature
        THEN make sure boiler is OFF
        ELSE make sure boiler is ON
    UNTIL heating system switched OFF

Figure 19.12 shows how this program could be expressed as a **flowchart**. Figure 19.13 shows the same process as a **structure diagram**.

19.6 User documentation

Software may be accompanied by various user assistance including:
- an installation manual;
- a user manual;
- a tutorial;
- help messages.

Installation manual

This may be in the form of a small booklet containing instructions on:
- how to install the software on your computer,
- how to organise peripherals such as the printer and the mouse.

User manual

Software is accompanied by one or more user manuals. The reason why there are sometimes different manuals is that they are used for different purposes, e.g.
- to work through the steps of the program when it is first purchased;
- to look up more complex operations when you are familiar with the program;
- as a quick reference guide if you forget how to carry out a particular operation.

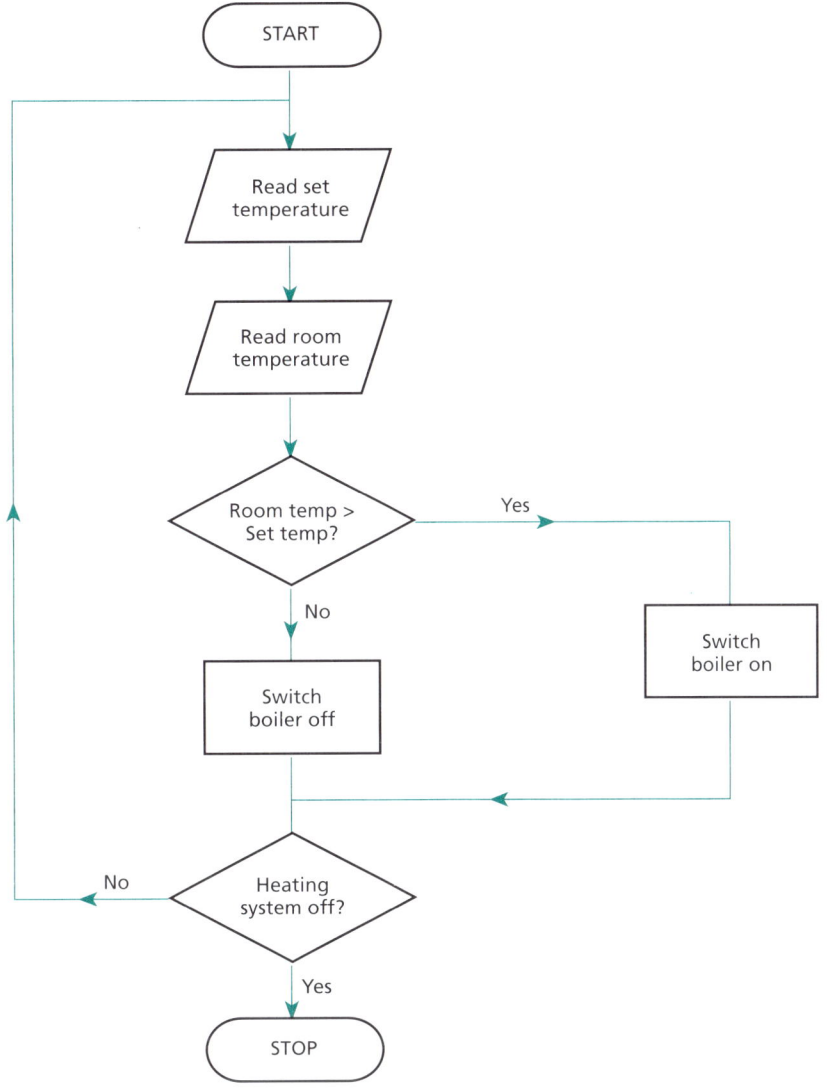

Fig. 19.12 Flowchart for a program to control a central heating system

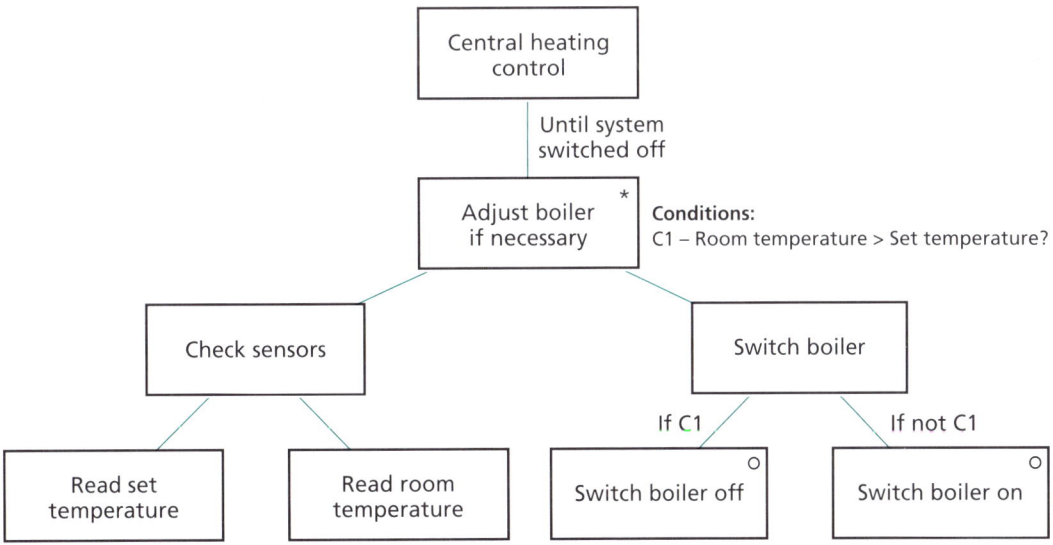

Fig. 19.13 Structure diagram for a program to control a central heating system

A user manual usually contains:
1. background information:
   - identifying the program, its author, version number, etc.;
   - hardware and software requirements for the program, e.g. computers it will run on, memory required, operating system;
   - an explanation of the system that the program is designed to work in;
   - limitations of the program – what it will not do.
2. an explanation of how to use the program:
   - how to collect and prepare data for the program. This includes instructions on how to fill in data capture forms;
   - a description of the main options on the menus;
   - sample outputs – pictures of screen displays and the data which was used to produce them;
   - a section on errors. This explains the error messages which occur and how to deal with them.

Tutorials

A tutorial usually consists of a teaching program which is supplementary to the main program. There may also be a printed manual with it. This leads the user through the main program, explaining how it works.

Help messages

Many programs have help options. These may include:
- a help screen or message dealing with the menu option which has been selected;
- a general help section which the user can search through to work out what to do.

ADVANTAGES: *of help messages compared with written documentation*
1. A help message is more immediately available than a manual.
2. The computer's search facilities can be used to find solutions quickly.
3. Selecting a help option often gives help immediately with the current operation.

DISADVANTAGES: *of help messages compared with written documentation*
1. The help information takes up storage space.
2. A written manual contains more detail.

User documentation in coursework

When doing coursework you will usually be expected to provide some of the user documentation described above. In doing this remember:
- to follow the instructions for the coursework carefully, giving the details asked for;
- instructions on how to react with a program are only a part of user documentation. A user also needs the items described under *User manual* above. Particularly important are:
  (a) background information;
  (b) instructions on how to collect data;
  (c) sample output;
- things which are obvious to you as designer of a system are not always obvious to a user of it. Ask other pupils to try out your user documentation and check that it makes sense to them. Offer to do the same for them.

19.7 Technical documentation

System documentation

When a system is developed the system designer normally documents each step carefully. This is done for the benefit of:
- **the person designing the system** – to make sure it is designed in a methodical way;
- **people working with the system designer** – as a means of communication with them. This includes:

(a) the designer's supervisor who can check that the work is being done correctly;
(b) programmers and others who are carrying out other parts of the work;
- **programmers and others responsible for maintaining or modifying the program**.

Program documentation

The documentation for a program would usually include:
- a system flowchart with notes (see Unit 19.2);
- program flowcharts and/or structure diagrams with notes (see Units 19.3 and 19.4);
- technical details of any limitations, special features, different versions, etc.;
- a program listing accompanied by a list of the variables used in the program and an explanation of their purposes;
- details of data structures used, such as files;
- a set of test data and expected output with which to check that the program operates successfully.

Use of diagrams in technical documentation

Diagrams play a large part in documentation.

1 **System flowcharts**

These can be used to describe:
- the old system as part of the analysis of the problem;
- the new system as part of the design.

2 **Structure diagrams**

These are used in design documentation and program documentation to show:
- the structure of a program;
- the detail of data structures such as arrays and files used by a program.

3 **Program flowcharts**

These are useful in explaining an algorithm or program. They can be used instead of structure diagrams or with them. Sometimes structure diagrams may be used to illustrate the overall structure of a program, while flowcharts are used for the detail of procedures.

Technical documentation in coursework

You should follow the instructions for the coursework carefully and produce the documentation which is asked for. If you have produced a program as part of the coursework then it usually requires documentation as described above. Remember:
- it is easier to write documentation for a program if it also explains itself. The program should have:
  (a) plenty of comments explaining the purpose of procedures;
  (b) variables and procedures with names which explain themselves, e.g. a variable called 'Surname' does not need explanation;
- use plenty of diagrams. These can include flowcharts and structure diagrams and also diagrams to show the layout of hardware;
- be careful not to mix up the different types of diagram:
  (a) state clearly what each diagram is, e.g. whether it is a system flowchart or a program flowchart;
  (b) program flowcharts contain decision boxes and 'START' and 'STOP' boxes but system flowcharts do not;
  (c) the sequence of boxes in a structure diagram goes across the page. You only go down the page to show detail of an operation.

Quick test

1 State the type of diagram being described:
   (a) makes clear how large tasks are split into smaller tasks,

(b) illustrates the flow of data from one operation to another,
(c) shows the sequence of operations by arrows,
(d) shows the sequence of operations across the page.

2 What boxes are rectangular in:
(a) a system flowchart, (b) a structure diagram?

3 Name *two* sources of assistance which a user may obtain from a software package other than manuals.

4 In a system flowchart what symbol would you use for:
(a) output on a printer,
(b) input using a mouse,
(c) a direct access file?

5 Choose *two* of the following which occur in user documentation:

    sample screen displays   program listing   structure diagram
    operating system   staff training   explanation of menu options

6 Choose *two* of the following which are in program documentation:

    sample screen displays   program listing   structure diagram
    operating system   staff training   explanation of menu options

Summary

1.
   - **Documentation** is information to help people use or adapt a system.
   - It consists of notes, manuals, diagrams and/or instructions.

2.
   - **Technical documentation** explains how a system or program works.
   - **User documentation** explains how to install and use software.

3. A **flowchart** is a diagram showing the operations of a process. It consists of:
   - **symbols (or boxes)** with messages explaining the operations;
   - lines connecting the symbols. These lines may have arrows.

4.
   - A **system flowchart** represents operations on data in a system. The arrows in a system flowchart represent the flow of data.
   - A **program flowchart** shows the order of operations in a program. Arrows in a program flowchart show the order of instructions.

5. Programs and other algorithms can be represented by:
   - **program flowcharts** which show the order of instructions;
   - **structure diagrams** which show the structure of the algorithm.

Chapter 20
The implications of IT

20.1 Examinations and the implications of IT

As an examination candidate you are expected to study and write about the applications of Information Technology. As part of this you need to show that you have thought about the effects of these applications on:
- efficiency and fairness of government;
- businesses, large and small;
- the environment;
- ordinary people.

For ordinary people you should consider the benefits and the drawbacks as they affect:
- enjoyment of life;
- standard of living;
- ease of living;
- privacy;
- jobs.

Even experts cannot agree on the social effects of computers. As an examination candidate you cannot be expected to be all-knowing. Just make sure that for each application you:

❶ know the facts:
- what are the effects;
- what features of the system studied give rise to these effects.

❷ keep an open mind:
- consider both benefits and drawbacks;
- be prepared to put an argument for either side. Most important issues have two sides or they would not be issues.

Consider the following question where either of two answers would be accepted.

Question:
'Gradually over the next 20 or 30 years paper money and coins will disappear in favour of electronic transactions'. State whether you agree with this statement. Give *two* different reasons to back up your answer.

Answer 1:
I agree with the statement.
(i) Electronic methods such as magnetic stripe cards are becoming more efficient and more popular.
(ii) It is dangerous to carry cash because if you are robbed or lose it, you cannot claim it back. Firms and shops do not like to deal in cash for the same reason.

OR Answer 2:
I disagree with the statement.
(i) Small shops and businesses often do not take cards because they are charged for doing so.
(ii) Cash is much more suitable than electronic methods for small transactions.

Notes:

❶ No-one knows what will happen in the next 20 or 30 years. You will not be given marks for agreeing or not. Either Answer 1 or Answer 2 should be given the marks.

❷ Reasons given need to be:
- factual;
- well thought out;
- clearly different from each other.

EXAMPLE: *of keeping an open mind*

❶ **Question:** 'Why is speech a good way of communicating with computers?'
Answer: 'It can be used by someone who cannot use their hands for keying – because they are disabled or are using their hands for their work.' (There are other correct reasons.)

❷ **Question:** 'Why is speech a bad way of communicating with computers?'
Answer: 'It does not work in a noisy environment.'

20.2 The general effect of IT on our lives

Developments in IT in the past 50 years

1940s
- The first working electronic computers.

1950s
- The first computers for sale.
- High-level computing languages are developed.

1960s
- Fairly large numbers of mainframe computers are sold.
- Stock control, payroll and accounts are the most common applications.
- Most computing is done by batch processing.
- The first interactive systems using typewriter terminals.

1970s
- The introduction of minicomputers and then microcomputers.
- Much more varied applications.
- Increase in interactive computing with the introduction of visual display terminals.
- Use of MICR by banks so that cheques can be cleared automatically.

1980s
- Dramatic increase in sales of personal computers spreads the use of computers into every part of life – shops, offices, schools, factories, our homes.
- Increased control of systems by electronic circuitry. Everyday equipment becomes 'intelligent' – cameras, washing machines, cars, central heating, lighting systems, home sound systems, televisions.
- Communication gets faster, storage larger and all for the same price.
- Software becomes more powerful and user friendly. It is no longer necessary to know anything about how a computer works to use it. Widespread use of general application packages such as word processors, spreadsheets, databases, DTP packages.
- Bar codes are used on goods to improve stock control and speed up payment for goods.
- More transactions done without paper money. Use of magnetic stripes on bank cards and credit cards.
- Widespread introduction of microcomputers in schools. Most primary schools have computers and many secondary schools have networks.

1990s
- Improvements in communications – increased use of portable telephones, fax machines; the telephone system becomes digitised and more versatile; the Internet links millions of people and organisations worldwide; linking together of information systems to use an 'Information Super-highway'.

20.2 The general effect of IT on our lives

- Gradual replacement of mainframe and minicomputer systems by networks based on microcomputers.
- Development of multimedia systems combining sound, still pictures and video. Increased used of CDs for storage – CD-ROMs for computers, photo CDs for still pictures and video CDs for television follow the audio CDs of the 80s.
- Dramatic improvements in graphics and image manipulation.
- Everyday devices become ever more 'intelligent', e.g. cars, microwave ovens and photocopiers.

General trends

1 Smaller, cheaper and more powerful computers
- During the 1970s, the introduction of microcomputers meant they could be purchased by more businesses, by people for home use and also by schools.
- During the 1980s, computers became much more powerful for the same price. All memory and storage became far cheaper.
- The use of mainframe computers and minicomputers has continually decreased as a proportion of the total usage.
- Computers are being used in an ever widening range of applications.

2 Increased reliance on communications
- People now use communication technology widely in their homes – with fax machines, portable telephones, teletext, satellite TV and widespread use of Internet.
- People are increasingly working from their homes; this improves the chances for employment of housewives, the disabled, etc.
- Companies can set up offices which are distant from one another.
- Industries can control operations automatically at a distance, e.g. water pumping stations, electricity and gas grids.
- Shopping chains can control their stock and accounts from a central computer.
- Clients of banks and building societies can handle their money from cash dispensing terminals.

3 The electronic office
The new developments in IT have made possible the **electronic office**. This is an office where most information such as documents, diagrams, finance and correspondence is handled electronically. It is stored digitally in computers, rather than on paper in filing cabinets.

An electronic office may contain:
- word processors for the input and storage of all letters and other documents;
- viewdata networks to send letters by electronic mail and for other communications;
- greater use of portable telephones and terminals by employees working in the field (such as sales representatives and engineers);
- local networks for communication within the company;
- local and national databases for the storage and retrieval of facts;
- graphics, spreadsheets and other packages for the display and manipulation of data;
- fax machines to send and receive copies of documents.

4 The decreased use of cash
A cashless society is becoming more possible technically.

KEY TERMS *EDI is Electronic Data Interchange. It is a system whereby two firms can order goods from one another without any paper transactions. The supply of goods and the payment for them are also handled electronically.*
EFT (Electronic Funds Transfer) is the moving of money from one bank account to another using data communications and without any paper transactions. People can be paid their wages and spend them without handling any actual money.
EFTPOS is Electronic Funds Transfer at Point Of Sale. Often in shops and garages customers can submit their bank card to be inserted into a reader attached to the point-of-sale terminal. The payment is then made directly from the customer's bank account to that of the shop.

EXAMPLE: *of EFTPOS*
The use of a Switch card (see under 'Magnetic stripes' in Unit 4.3).

ADVANTAGES: *of the decreased use of cash*
- Security from theft because neither buyer nor seller need to have cash.
- Simpler transfer of money between bank accounts.

DISADVANTAGES: *of the decreased use of cash*
- Many people do not have bank accounts and/or prefer to use cash.
- Cards are not practical for buying small items.
- Both buyer and seller have to pay charges for many card services.

5 Changes in shopping

Shops have used IT in a number of ways.
- Automated data capture, particularly bar codes, is being used at the checkouts and for taking stock of goods on the shelves.
- Customers are increasingly using cards for payment.
- Large shopping chains are using communications to handle their stock control and accounts automatically.

New developments include:
- **database marketing** where the shop uses information from the checkout to store in a database the shopping patterns of each customer.
- shopping from home – using a viewdata service or the telephone or mail order.

ADVANTAGES: *of increased computerisation of shopping*
- Improved turnover at checkouts.
- Shop assistants' work simplified and made more interesting.
- More accurate stock control.
- Automatic delivery of goods to the shops.

DISADVANTAGES: *of increased computerisation of shopping*
- Customers may feel their privacy threatened by database marketing.
- Shop assistants may feel threatened by computer monitoring of their work rate, e.g. their speed at the checkout.
- Small shops often cannot afford to take part in the new systems and cannot compete.

20.3 Effect of IT on work and unemployment

The introduction of IT is affecting the jobs of many people. Automation and the introduction of computers are part of a dramatic change in business and industry.

National changes in unemployment and in production

In the UK since the late 1970s:
- on average the economy as a whole has grown only slightly;
- unemployment has been high. The number of unemployed as a percentage of the whole work force rose from about 5 per cent to about 13 per cent and has remained high;
- the average number of hours worked by each person in full-time employment has hardly changed. In fact, when overtime is considered it has risen slightly;
- many more people have part-time jobs;
- there has been a movement away from manufacturing industry towards other work.

How jobs are lost through IT

- Firms which introduce computers may hope to increase their output as a result and still employ the same number of people. However, if output stays the same they have to lay workers off because they need fewer people to do the same work.
- Firms which do not introduce computers often cannot compete and they may also have to make people redundant.

20.3 Effect of IT on work and unemployment

EXAMPLES: *where jobs are lost through IT*

1. **The electronic office**
   Using a word processor and modern communications a secretary can get more work done and the work is of better quality. This has, however, led to job losses from typing pools.
2. **Automation of remote stations**
   Many workplaces, previously manned, are fully automated, e.g.
   - telephone exchanges;
   - waterworks, many of which now only need to be checked occasionally;
   - lighthouses;
   - railway stations.
3. **New computerised printing methods**
   Old typesetting methods are becoming obsolete. This has caused great problems in the newspaper industry. DTP systems are making it easier to produce publications without expert help.

New jobs created through IT

A very large industry has grown up to produce and support IT. This employs a large number of people.

EXAMPLES: *where jobs are created through IT*

1. **Hardware**
   All the new equipment has to be designed and manufactured. This creates new industries which need designers, production workers, managers, sales and maintenance staff, etc.
2. **Software**
   Someone has to produce all the computer programs. There has been a huge growth in the software industry. Jobs include:
   - **systems analyst**
     Responsible for taking a system through the stages of the system life cycle (see Unit 18.1).
   - **applications programmer**
     A programmer who writes programs to carry out specific applications for computer users. He/she:
     (a) has to have an understanding of the application itself;
     (b) usually works in a high-level language.
   - **systems programmer**
     A programmer who writes systems software (see Unit 9.2). The systems programmer:
     (a) has to be very familiar with a particular computer and operating system;
     (b) often works in a low-level language.
3. **Consultancies**
   Firms need advice on new systems. This has meant an increase in systems consultants.
4. **Operations**
   The new equipment needs staff to run it.

The effect on those in work

Many jobs are being changed as the new technology is introduced:
- staff have to be trained to use computers and other equipment;
- more people are working at keyboards and workstations and fewer on production lines;
- increasing numbers of staff at all levels and types of work spend a large part of their working day sitting at a VDU;
- there is a widespread use of word processors. Because it is easy to correct work on word processors many people who are not trained in keyboarding use them.

ADVANTAGES: *to people who work with IT*

1. Use of VDUs increases the amount of work done by each operator. The work produced by word processors is more accurate. The output is of better quality.
2. Operators can produce good quality work with relatively little training.
3. An office worker now has far more information and processing power available without leaving the desk.

4. The cheapness of equipment and the scope of modern communications enable more people to work from home.
5. For many people, computers do many of the more tedious tasks that they previously had to do so that they can concentrate on the more interesting ones.

DISADVANTAGES: *to people who work with IT*
1. VDUs may affect people's health – users of them often suffer from tiredness, discomfort and eye strain. The monitors produce harmful radiation.
2. Because operators can produce more work with a word processor they are expected to get more done. Managers often expect too much of the new technology.
3. Using a computer to monitor employees is an intrusion. They feel under continuous pressure if the machine they are using is checking up on them all the time.
4. Word processors can take away the skill that previously typists had in preparing documents. Operators may take less pride in their work.

Working from home

Modern communications make it much easier for people to work from home. Working using a remote terminal is referred to as **teleworking**. Often people doing this are employed on a freelance basis and may do work for several companies. To do this it is usual to have at least:
- a telephone,
- a fax machine,
- a personal computer,
- a modem, possibly a fax modem so that the fax machine can operate through the computer,
- electronic mail or even teleconferencing facilities - possibly by subscribing to the Internet through an access provider,
- a room to use as an office.

ADVANTAGES: *of working from home*
To employees:
1. There is no need to travel to and from work.
2. They can work at hours of their own choosing and can see more of their family.

To employers:
1. The workers are more contented.
2. There is no need to provide office space, heating and other resources.
3. The employee is easier to contact at home than in a big company or on the road.

DISADVANTAGES: *of working from home*
To employees:
1. There is a tendency for people working from home to work very long hours.
2. The teleworker has to provide equipment, office space and other resources.
3. There is no substitute sometimes for meeting colleagues in person (usually meetings have to be arranged).

To employers:
There is a security risk with confidential company information being distributed around the country in people's homes.

20.4 The effect of IT on personal privacy

KEY TERMS *Personal data* is data about people of a type which they would not necessarily want everyone to know.
Privacy of personal data refers to people's right to keep data to themselves or at least to have some control over its use.

EXAMPLES: *of items of personal data*
1. Telephone number.
2. Date of birth.
3. Income.

20.4 The effect of IT on personal privacy

④ Health record.

Personal data is stored about each of us on a large number of computers. Any British family could expect details about them to be held on numerous data files.

EXAMPLES: *of personal data files held on many people*

① Their health records on files at the doctor's surgery, and the local hospital.
② Details of their income on computers owned by their employer and by the Income Tax office.
③ The state of their accounts on bank and building society computers.
④ The amounts they spend on electricity, gas, water, etc. are stored on files by the appropriate companies.
⑤ When people buy goods or pay for a holiday or subscribe to a magazine, their name and address go on a computer file. Lists of these names and addresses can then be sold for advertising and other purposes.
⑥ Police records – the police hold records on large numbers of people. These records include:
(a) the Police National Computer, which has information on about 23 million people and includes data on:
- people with criminal records;
- fingerprints;
- stolen or suspect vehicles;
- vehicle owners.

(b) the Special Branch Computer, which stores data on over two million people. Not all of these people are criminals or even suspected of crime.
⑦ The Driver and Vehicle Licensing Centre at Swansea. Information about all drivers and their cars is now held at this centre. Uses of this data have included:
- tracing owners of a particular make of car for the manufacturer so that they can be recalled for checking;
- finding the most recent addresses of people who are dodging Income Tax.

The power of computers to use personal data

Computers can be used to carry out operations on data which could not easily be carried out when information was all on paper.

EXAMPLES: *of operations on personal data*

① **Sending data from one computer to another**
Using modern communications, data about people can be sent rapidly from one computer to another, around the world if necessary.
- All the facts stored about a given person could be brought together to provide a complete dossier.
- Records relating to financial problems or court appearances could be used by prospective employers, etc.

② **Processing data**
Lists can be produced of all people in certain categories. These could be used for political or other purposes.

③ **Targeting mail**
It is possible for companies to buy lists of names and addresses of people who are likely to be good customers. They can then send advertising material only to those people who are likely to buy it.

This process is referred to as '**targeting mail**'. Those on the receiving end often regard it as 'junk mail'.

Sources of address lists include customers with good credit accounts at stores, buyers of expensive equipment such as cars or garden machinery, lists from the electoral register.

The rights people expect

In order to maintain personal privacy people generally expect within reason to be able to:
① withhold information about themselves;
② stop data being passed from one database to another without their knowledge or consent;

Chapter 20 The implications of IT

3. find out what data is stored about them;
4. have inaccurate data corrected.

The Data Protection Act

The Data Protection Act was passed in 1984.

1. The Act refers to:
   - the **data user** – anyone who stores and processes computer data about people;
   - the **data subject** – anyone who has information about them stored by data users.
2. The Act created:
   - a Data Registrar, who is the person who sees that the Act is enforced;
   - a Data Protection Tribunal, to which people can appeal against the Registrar's decisions.
3. No-one can store and use personal data unless they have registered to do so with the Data Registrar:
   - those applying have to state what data they are storing, and what they intend to use it for;
   - if the application is accepted then the name of the data user and details of the data held goes into a data register. The register is in large public libraries and anyone can go and look at it;
   - there are some exceptions of data which does not have to be registered. This includes payroll data and data held for 'national security' purposes.
4. The Act states some important guiding principles. The main ones are:
   - data must be obtained fairly and lawfully;
   - data must only be held or used or disclosed in the way that has been registered;
   - data must be accurate;
   - people must be allowed to have information about them disclosed if they request it. If they can prove it is wrong it must be changed or deleted;
   - data users and computer bureaux must protect the data they hold.
5. There are a number of exemptions from the Act. They include:
   - Doctors, the police and the tax authorities, who do not have to show data subjects the data they hold and are exempt from the restrictions on disclosure.
   - Data can be withheld for reasons of national security.
   - People do not have to register as data users if data is to be used only for personal, family or household affairs or for recreational use
   - Companies do not have to register if data is used only for routine purposes such as calculating wages or keeping accounts.

EXAMPLES: *of effects of the Data Protection Act*
1. A loan company asks a magazine mailing company to sell its address list. The firm is only registered to use its addresses for its own internal purposes so the Data Protection Act does not allow the firm to sell them.
2. A school includes dates of birth on its pupil database but does not allow pupils general access to this part of the database.
   This is because the date of birth is considered to be personal data and should not be shown to other data subjects.

ADVANTAGES: *of the Data Protection Act*
1. It sets limits to the operation of people who use data.
2. It gives a number of basic rights to data subjects.

DISADVANTAGES: *of the Data Protection Act*
1. The Act only deals with computer data and not with paper files.
2. It is relatively difficult for people to find out who is storing data about them.
3. Data subjects cannot complain about uses or disclosures of data if the data user is registered for that use.
4. Data subjects can only complain about the inaccuracy of data if they have 'suffered damage' from it.
5. Data can be held for 'national security' purposes so that people cannot gain access to it.

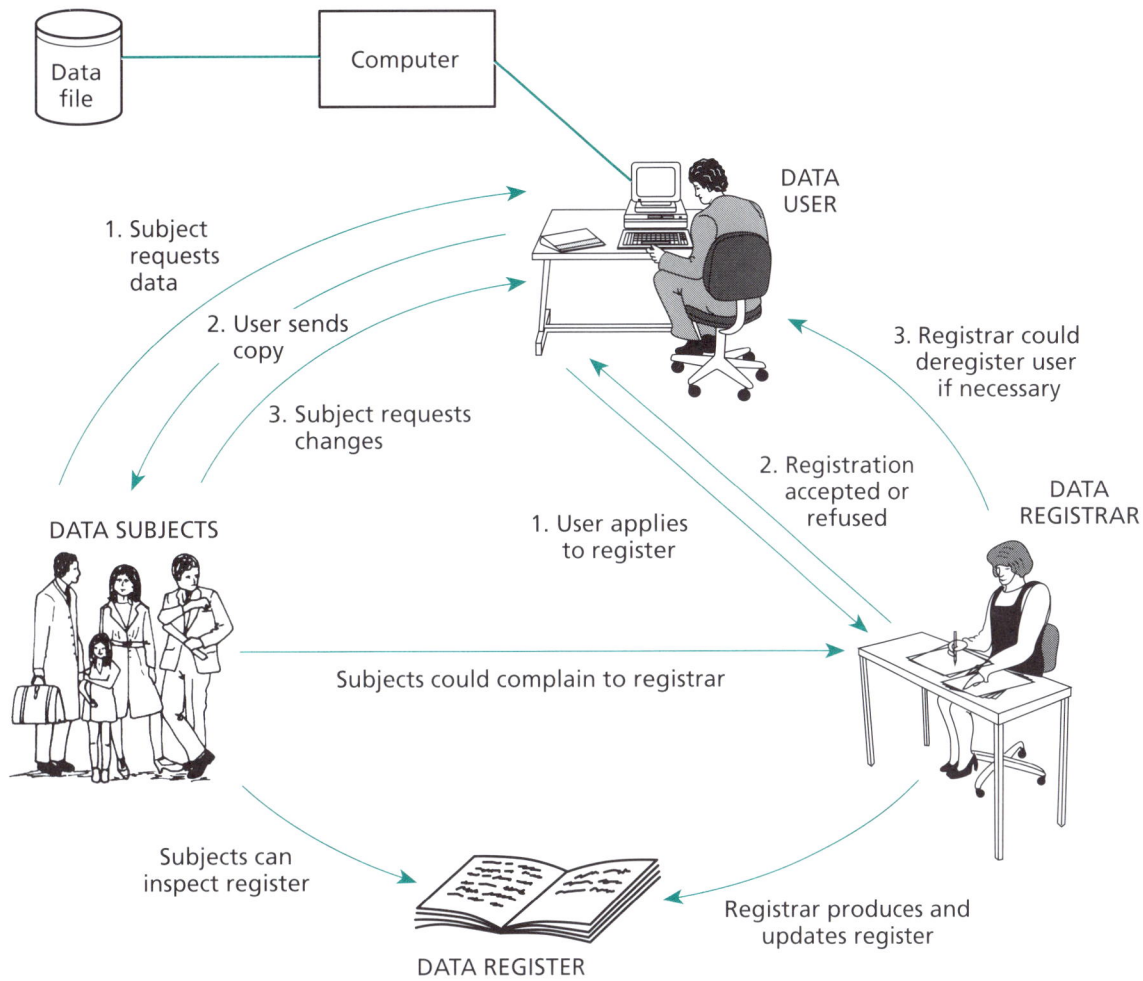

Fig. 20.1 How the Data Protection Act works

Quick test

1. Which of the following could be classed as EFT:
   (a) using a Switch card in a supermarket, (b) buying a train ticket with a cheque, (c) buying a train ticket with a credit card, (d) obtaining a discount?

2. Name *three* IT developments which have had an effect on shopping.

3. Name *three* IT developments which have had an effect on office work.

4. Give *two* reasons why we are unlikely to manage without cash altogether.

5. State *three* completely different types of effect which the introduction of IT may have on jobs.

6. State *two* different types of right which people expect to protect privacy of personal data.

7. Name *three* categories of people named or created by the Data Protection Act.

Summary

1. In answering examination questions on the implications of IT:
   - know the facts;
   - keep an open mind.

2. There have been a number of general trends in IT:
   - computers have become smaller, cheaper and more powerful;
   - there has been an increased reliance on communications;
   - the electronic office has evolved using new computer software and communications technology;
   - there has been a decreased use of cash with the use of such methods as EDI, EFT and EFTPOS;
   - shops and shopping methods have changed dramatically.

3. Increased use of information systems brings advantages and disadvantages to workers:
   - there has been a large increase in unemployment;

   But IT can also lead to:
   - new jobs being created;
   - existing jobs becoming more interesting and rewarding.

4. - **Personal data** is data about people which they may not want others to know.
   - **Privacy** refers to the right to keep data to ourselves or to have control over its use.

5. People hope for rights to:
   - withhold information about themselves;
   - stop data being passed from one database to another without their knowledge or consent;
   - find out what data is stored about them;
   - have inaccurate data corrected.

6. The Data Protection Act gives people some of these rights:
   - it defines data users and data subjects;
   - it created a Data Registrar, a Data Tribunal and a Data Register.

7. The Act says that:
   - data must be obtained fairly and lawfully, must only used in the way registered and must be accurate;
   - people must be able to have information disclosed and have it changed or deleted if necessary;
   - data users must protect the data they hold.

Questions and answers

Examination questions

This section contains a selection of examination questions. These are taken from the specimen papers in Information Technology supplied by the Examination Boards. The questions are arranged in order of the chapters of the book. Often a question uses work from more than one chapter. In this case:

1. The question has been put with the chapter which is most important in answering it.
2. The question has been referred to under the other chapters involved in it.

The questions have been chosen to represent a range of:
- the work in the book and demanded by the syllabuses,
- levels of difficulty.

After each question is given:

1. The examining board whose question has been used. The questions have all been taken from Specimen Papers for Information Technology issued by the boards for the examinations in Summer 1998. The following abbreviations have been used for the Boards and syllabuses used:
   London – Edexcel, London Examinations
   MEG – Midland Examining Group
   NEAB – Northern Examinations and Assessment Board
   NDTEF – National Design Technology Education Foundation
   RSA – RSA Examinations Board
   SEG – Southern Examining Group – Syllabus code 2436
   WJEC/CBAC – Welsh Joint Education Committee/Cyd-Bwyllgor Addysg Cymru
2. Whether the course the questions were set for is the Short Course or the Full GCSE Course (see Syllabus Analysis for an explanation).
3. The tier, Foundation or Higher, for which the paper is set (see Syllabus Analysis for an explanation).

For some examining boards the questions referred to here as 'Short Course' are actually taken by both Short Course and Full Course candidates. The Full Course candidates then have to do some more questions as well. Thus if you are a Full Course candidate you should also be able to do the Short Course questions. These Boards are: WJEC/CBAC, NDTEF and MEG.

In any case it is generally true that a Full Course candidate should be able to tackle Short Course questions as well. However, if you are doing the Short Course then tackle only Short Course questions.

There is no harm in tackling questions for other boards - there is a great deal of similarity between the different Information Technology syllabuses. You could also try some questions outside your normal range but you should concentrate on questions for your tier.

Questions and answers

Chapter 1 - information and data

1. Digital watches contain microprocessors. Describe the inputs, processing and outputs. *(MEG Short Course, Foundation and Higher Tiers)* (6)

2. The second set of history pupils is taught by Mrs Sarah Sargeant and is coded in the following way:

the first 3 letters of the subject	HIS
the set number	2
the first 2 letters of the teacher's surname	SA

   The code for the database is thus **HIS2SA**
   (a) State the code for the fourth set of Mathematics taught by Mr Ahmed Patel. (2)
   (b) Give TWO reasons why this data is coded for use by the database. (2)
   (MEG Short Course, Foundation Tier)

3. A manufacturer codes food items in the following way:

product	size	factory	year	month	day
pp	ss	ff	y	mm	dd

   for example,
   cc20br980125
   means
   200g of cheddar cheese produced in a Bristol factory on 25 January 1998.
   (a) State the code for a 500g tin of pineapple chunks produced in a Sheffield factory on the 13th May 1997. (3)
   (b) (i) Explain how the opening of a factory in Brighton would create a problem for this coding system. (1)
   (ii) State a possible solution for this. (1)
   (MEG Full Course, Foundation Tier)

   [See also Questions 5, 17 and 30 for codes.]

Chapter 2 - Information systems

4. Tick TWO applications which may use batch processing:
   Processing cheques
   Monitoring a patient's pulse
   Building a car
   Multimedia
   Producing gas bills
   Controlling traffic lights (2)
   (MEG Full Course, Foundation Tier)

Chapter 3 - Data capture

5. (a) Roger organises the spare parts and accessories department. Every three months, Roger needs to check all the accessories that he has in stock. He does a manual stock take. This involves walking round the accessories department, looking at all items in stock and counting them. He then compares his figures with those stored in the computer **Spares File**.
   Design a data capture form that Roger could use to help him in his manual stocktaking. (4)
   (b) In the computer file, accessories are given a code instead of a full description. A code for a set of mats for a Ford Fiesta Ghia is FFMAT67.
   Give THREE reasons why codes are used for computer data. (3)
   (c) All spare parts and accessories have a bar code on them. Customers take their items to the checkout and staff use computer equipment to read the barcode.
   (i) Give TWO reasons why bar codes might be used in this system. (2)
   (ii) State the names of TWO data items that may be in the bar code. (2)
   (iii) Sometimes the computer equipment does not read the bar code properly. Give ONE way in which the system could indicate that the bar code has not been read properly. (1)
   (iv) Describe what the checkout operator must do when the bar code will not read properly. (1)
   (+1 SPG)
   (London Short Course, Higher Tier)

6 Three types of user interface are:

Diagram A
```
C:> dir
```
Command driven

Diagram B
```
Menu

1. Add record
2. Delete record
3. Amend record
4. Print reports
5. Quit

Choose one of these
```
Menu driven

Diagram C

(Main window showing: Print Manager, MS-DOS Prompt, ATM Control Panel, Windows Setup)

Graphical

(a) Give ONE reason why an inexperienced user might find the command driven interface in Diagram A difficult to use. (1)
(b) Give TWO reasons why a user might find the graphical interface in Diagram C easier to use. (2)
(c) The menu driven interface shown in Diagram B is still used for many applications. Describe one advantage to the user of this interface compared with the graphical interface shown in Diagram C. (2)

(NEAB Full Course, Higher Tier)

[See also Question 22 for types of user interface and Question 54 for user friendliness.]

Chapter 4 – Input methods

7 The Crafty Fair Group is a small group of people who organise Craft Fairs across the country.

The Crafty Fair Group did a headcount on entry at their last Fair at York. It was very difficult to keep track of the large number of people walking through the entrance. They decide to give all the craftworkers a 'swipe card' to use on entry to the Fair.

(i) State what is meant by a 'swipe card'. (4)
(ii) Describe how a 'swipe card' system is used.
    Marks will be awarded for stating and explaining:
        input, (3)
        process, and (3)
        output (3)
    stages of the system.
(iii) Discuss some of the effects that the introduction of the system might have on:
    the Crafty Fair Group, (2)
    the craftworkers. (2)

(NDTEF Short Course, Foundation Tier)

8 A supermarket uses a point of sale (POS) system. All the products sold carry bar codes.
(a) Name a device used to input bar codes at the checkouts. (1)
(b) Give TWO advantages of this type of system compared with a manual system
    (i) for the shopper (4)
    (ii) for the supermarket manager. (2)

(NEAB Short Course, Foundation and Higher Tiers)

9 Direct data devices include (OMR), (MICR) and (OCR).
Name an **application** where each is used. (3)

(WJEC/CBAC Full Course, Foundation Tier)

10 Most banks now have cash machines. The banks issue plastic cards and Personal Identification Numbers (PINs) to customers so that they can get cash any time.
(a) Give TWO items of data stored about the customer on the card. (2)

(b) Describe the purpose of a PIN. (1)
(c) State ONE benefit to the bank of having cash machines. (1)
(d) State TWO benefits to the customer of having cash machines. (2)

(MEG Full Course, Higher Tier)

[See also Question 5 for bar codes.]

Chapter 5 – Output of data

11 Ring TWO devices used as output from a computer. (2)

| keyboard | mouse | data logger |
| monitor | plotter | joystick |

(MEG Short Course, Foundation Tier)

12 A dentist wants to set up a simple computer system to provide information about her patients' teeth, their appointments, treatment and accounts.
   She has a desktop computer with monochrome monitor, keyboard, mouse and a dot matrix printer.
   (a) What THREE items of hardware could the dentist buy to improve her computer system and why would they be an improvement? (6)
   (b) The dentist is considering whether to buy an 'off the shelf' package or employ a local computer bureau to write a special program to store the patients' data. Write down ONE advantage and ONE disadvantage of using an 'off the shelf' applications package rather than a specially written program. (2)
   (c) The dentist wants to protect the data in her patients' data base.
      (i) What can she do to protect her data from being lost? (1)
      (ii) What can the dentist do to prevent the wrong people changing data in the patient database? (1)

(WJEC/CBAC Short Course, Higher Tier)

Chapter 6 – Storage

13 CD-ROMs are now used to store computer games.
   Give THREE advantages and ONE disadvantage of supplying games on CD-ROM rather than on floppy disc. (4)

(NEAB Short Course, Foundation Tier and Higher Tier)

14 An advertising agency uses information systems to prepare text and graphics for brochures and other advertising material.
   (a) Which one of the following applications packages would be most suitable for this? (1)
      A communications
      B desk-top publishing
      C accounting
      D payroll.

   (b) The information system used includes four different types of storage. Two of these are CD-ROM and RAM. What TWO other forms of storage would be most suitable in this system? (2)
   (c) Explain why each of the following types of storage device is necessary
      (i) CD-ROM
      (ii) RAM (2)

(NEAB Full Course, Foundation Tier)

15 RAM AND ROM are two different types of memory found in a computer.
   (a) What do the abbreviations ROM and RAM stand for? (2)
   (b) Describe the differences between ROM and RAM. (2)
   (c) Give an example of how each is used. (2)

(WJEC/CBAC Full Course, Foundation Tier)

Chapter 7 – Data files

16 Swish Garage uses database software for keeping records and spreadsheet software for performing calculations.
   Sabina uses a computer and the Getit database package to access the Customer File. Here is part of the Customer File.

REFERENCE	SURNAME	FORENAME	TELEPHONE
156874	SMITH	DAVID	012044978564
123456	JONES	CLIFF	012544356433
342311	O'CONNOR	MAIRE	012566786754
332455	COHEN	RUTH	012576565657
436710	SABEEN	UZMA	012823467219

(a) State the number of fields for each part of the record shown. (1)
(b) Give the name of THREE more fields that could be in a record in the Customer File. (3)
(c) State what one complete record in the Customer File represents. (1)
(d) The REFERENCE field in each record is used as a key field. State what is meant by a key field. (1)
(e) When data is entered into the Customer File, it is validated using a data validation program. The REFERENCE field is checked with a field type check and a length check.
   (i) Describe how a field type check can be used to validate the REFERENCE field. (1)
   (ii) Describe how a length check can be used to validate the REFERENCE field. (1)
(f) Sabina uses a file update program when she needs to change the Customer File. The file update program has three options.
       INSERT A RECORD
       DELETE A RECORD
       AMEND A RECORD
Give, for each of these options, an example of a situation where Sabina will need to use the option. (3)
(g) Some customers are not happy giving their personal information to Sabina to be stored in a computer file.
   Describe TWO reasons why customers might not be happy to give personal information. (2)
   (+1 SPG)
   (London Short Course, Foundation Tier)

17 An estate agent keeps a file of property for sale on computer. Some of the information stored on each property is shown in the table below:

Code	Type	Class	Price	Number of Bedrooms
AXY123	House	D	91,420	4
AXY917	Bungalow	S	80,000	3
AXX134	House	S	47,500	3
AXY912	Bungalow	D	120,000	4

(a) (i) State how many records there are in the file.
    (ii) State how many fields there are in each record. (2)
(b) The CLASS field uses a single letter:
        D is a detached property;
        S is a semi-detached property.
   Suggest a helpful code for a terraced property. (1)
(c) Name the key field. (1)
(d) Every week the estate agent needs to update the file.
   (i) What does update mean? (1)

Questions and answers

      (ii) Which field is most likely to be affected when the estate agent updates the file? (1)

(e) The estate agent decides to sort the records in his file on PRICE in **ascending** order. Complete the following table to show the order after sorting: (4)

Order before sorting	Order after sorting
AXY123	
AXY917	
AXX134	
AXZ912	

(WJEC/CBAC Full Course, Foundation Tier)

[See also Question 55 for Stock Control.]

Chapter 8 – Security and integrity of data

18 (a) Describe TWO problems which can be caused by illegally accessing computers. (2)

(b) Describe TWO ways of preventing such problems. (2)

(MEG Short Course, Foundation Tier)

19 (a) Explain the term 'computer virus'. (2)

(b) State TWO precautions which should be taken to prevent viruses affecting your machine. (2)

(MEG Short Course, Foundation Tier and Higher Tier)

[Also see Question 12 for protection from hacking, Question 29 for valid data, Question 53 for changing passwords and Question 55 for check digits.]

Chapter 9 – Software

20 From the list of packages given, choose the best for each of the applications below.
    CAD
    Communications
    Database
    Desk Top Publishing (DTP)
    Spreadsheet

(a) Producing a school magazine
(b) Designing a kitchen layout
(c) Storing details of all the books in a library (3)

(NEAB Full Course, Foundation Tier)

21 The Silsden Tennis Club is having a dance to raise funds.
(a) The Secretary uses Desk Top Publishing (DTP) software to design a poster to advertise the dance.
  Complete the sentences using terms from the list.

    clip art   columns   fonts   pixels   sizes

DTP software helps the secretary lay out text and graphics in .... on the poster.
DTP software allows the secretary to use different .... and .... for the text on the poster.
The Secretary can import .... into the DTP software. (4)

(b) The Secretary prints the poster on a lazer printer. Tick ONE box to show why a laser printer is used. (1)

	Tick one box
A laser printer costs less to buy than a dot matrix printer	
A laser printer costs less to run than a dot matrix printer	
A laser printer is environmentally friendly	
A laser printer prints good quality text and graphics	
A laser printer prints good quality text but cannot print graphics	

(c) Name TWO hardware devices that are used for DTP, other than a keyboard, a disk drive, a monitor, a mouse, a printer and a processor.
  Describe what the hardware devices are used for. (2)
(d) When the Secretary bought the computer, it was supplied with an operating system and some utility programs.
  (i) Describe TWO tasks that can be done by an operating system. (2)
  (ii) Describe TWO tasks that can be done by utility programs. (2)
(e) Some Tennis Club members believe that the Secretary should not use Information Technology.
  Give a reasoned argument why the tennis club should not use Information Technology. (4)

(SEG Full Course, Higher Tier)

22 A school is setting up a new computer resource base, with 16 stand-alone computers, for pupils. The staff at the school must decide whether they should purchase a range of applications packages for each computer or a single integrated package for each machine.
(a) Give TWO reasons why the school might choose an integrated package. (2)
(b) The school has the choice of providing each computer with one of two user interfaces.
Either: a menu driven system,
or: a graphical user interface.
  (i) What is a graphical user interface? (2)
  (ii) What are the advantages of such an interface over a menu system? (2)

(NEAB Full Course, Higher Tier)

[See also Question 12 for 'off the shelf' applications packages.]

Chapter 10 – Word processing and desktop publishing

23 A school needs to send a standard letter to parents.
Ring one item which is used to do this.

digitiser   backup copy
word processor   multi media   (1)

(MEG Short Course, Foundation Tier)

24 Tick TWO advantages for using a word processor rather than a typewriter.

The ribbon is changed automatically
It is faster to correct mistakes
It never breaks down
Work can be checked on a screen before printing
There are fewer keys on the keyboard
The printing is easier to read.   (2)

(MEG Short Course, Foundation Tier)

25 Fairways School is organising a fête to help raise money. The Headteacher wants Mrs Williams to advertise the fête. She has a simple word processing package and a printer which only produces output like this:

    Fairways School Fête

She asks the IT teacher if she can use one of the new computer systems which the school has just purchased.
(a) Write down TWO advantages of a new computer system in producing a poster. (2)
(b) Explain ONE issue, other than quality of output, that the IT teacher should consider when choosing what hardware and software to give Mrs Williams. (2)
(c) Give TWO advantages and TWO disadvantages of using IT to produce a poster for the fête. (4)
(d) Describe briefly ONE piece of software which could be used to produce a poster for a fête, and discuss its effectiveness for the purpose of producing a poster. (8)

(RSA Short Course, Higher Tier)

26 Describe how mailmerge works. (3)

(MEG Full Course, Higher Tier)

[See also Question 21 for DTP, and Question 29 for standard letters.]

Chapter 11 – Handling information: database programs

27 (a) A customer comes into an estate agents and wants to buy a house in the Stanton area. The secretary loads the database and uses it to select and display the following list on the screen.

Reference Number	Name of Seller	Address	Asking Price (£'s)
713	K. Miller	14, Daisy St., Stanton	145,000
414	L. Watson	56, The Cobbles, Stanton	138,000
519	A. Skenning	15, Rose House, Stanton	175,000

Write down the instructions or steps that the secretary might have used in order to display this list on the screen. (2)

(b) A different customer tells the secretary that he wants a house in Cortley but he does NOT wish to pay more than £60,000 for the new house. The customer also asks for a printout of the list in order to go and look at any houses which suit his needs.

Write down the instructions or steps that the secretary might use in order to get the list of possible houses printed out. (3)

(c) Name ONE EXTRA item of confidential data the estate agent might have on this database. (1)

(d) Explain why the confidential data you have described would be needed by the estate agent. (2)

(e) Give an example of ONE advantage and ONE disadvantage to the estate agent of keeping the properties data on a computer. (2)

(WJEC/CBAC Short Course, Foundation Tier)

28 In a Job Centre, a database is used to hold data about jobs available. Here is one of the displays that the database can produce:

Job Ref	Employer	Minimum age	Minimum qualifications	Pay (£ per year)	Type of job	Area
Ecc/234	NEAB	23	2 GCSE	6745	Clerical	Eccles
Ecc/748	Widget	16	2 GCSE	5723	Clerical	Eccles
Liv/348	Music Inc.	25	3 years exp.	18567	Sales	Liverpool
Orp/548	Sam Travel	21	4 GCSE	10027	Driver	Orpington
Man/345	A1 Marketing	18	4 GCSE	12000	Sales	Manchester
Hal/839	JJ Racing	116	None	6440	Manual	Halifax

(a) (i) Look closely at the information shown above. Circle the ONE piece of data that is obviously a mistake. (1)

(ii) Say why this is a mistake. (1)

(b) Give THREE advantages of using this type of computer database to search for particular jobs rather than looking through all the jobs on cards pinned to the walls. (3)

Queries for this system are written like this:
    Minimum age > = 21
    Minimum age < 18 AND Area = 'Manchester'

(c) Write down the query you would use to search for all jobs which pay more than £10,000 per year. (3)

(d) Write down the query you would use to search the database for all jobs for people 18 or over in sales which pay more than £13,000. (5)

(NEAB Short Course, Foundation Tier)

29 (a) Swish Garage uses database software for keeping records and spreadsheet software for performing calculations.

Give the names of TWO other types of software they could use for producing letters and for producing charts and diagrams of sales figures. (2)

(b) Asif is in charge of used car sales. He keeps records of all used cars in the **Usedcar File.** Part of the file is shown below.

REF	MAKE	MODEL	YEAR	DOORS	PRICE
22	FORD	ESCORT	1989	4	3,500
34	ROVER	300	1990	3	4,900
13	CITROEN	AX	1992	3	5,100
11	RENAULT	19	1993	5	6,900
27	MAZDA	323	1993	5	7,400
44	ROVER	214	1990	5	4,750

Asif uses the Getit software to select records of cars that a customer wants.

(i) A customer asks for a 5-door car costing less than £5,000.
State the details of any car that Getit will find. (1)

(ii) A customer wants a 5-door car with registration year not older than 1993.
State the details of any car that Getit will find. (2)

Asif uses the Getit software to sort the cars in order of price.

(iii) Write down the reference numbers of the cars after they have been sorted by price. (2)

(iv) State how Asif should update the **Usedcar File** when a car is sold. (1)

(c) Part of a record in the **Vanhire File** is shown below.

REFERENCE   MAKE   MODEL   REGDATE   MILEAGE
NUMBER
479   Ford   Transit   010894   12327

(i) State the name of a field which contains numeric data.
(ii) State the name of a field which contains alphabetic data. (2)

(d) The REGDATE field in a record in the **Vanhire File** is supposed to be 6 characters long and is to contain only numbers. The field is considered valid if it obeys the two rules; if it does not it is invalid.

Tick the appropriate box to show whether the following examples of REGDATE are valid or invalid.

	VALID	INVALID
30NOV94		
030794		
07061995		
300294		

(4)

(e) Sabina uses the computer to send standard letters to customers. A standard letter has some pieces of data that are the same for all letters and some pieces of data that may differ for each customer.

(i) Give the names of THREE pieces of data that will be the same for each standard letter. (3)

(ii) Give the names of THREE pieces of data that may differ for each customer. (3)

(iii) Sabina uses the Customer File when she wants to send standard letters containing details of servicing and special offers.
State the names of TWO pieces of hardware that Sabina uses to do this. (2)

(f) All administration in the garage offices is now carried out using computers. Give TWO reasons why the owners of the garage decided to use computers. (4)
(+1 SPG)

(London Short Course, Foundation Tier)

Questions and answers

30 A school uses a database system to produce a variety of outputs. The database has three data tables (files). Here are some of the fields.

| Pupil | Number | Surname | Other names | Year | Form | Subject 1 | Subject 2 |

| Staff | Number | Surname | Other names |

| Subjects | Name | Code |

(a) Why do staff and pupil records have to be in different tables? (1)
(b) The subject table holds the name and code of each subject. What are the advantages of using codes for subjects? (2)
(c) One report which the system can produce is a subject list report. Part of this is shown below.

```
Subject:          French
Pupil Name                    Form        Grade Last Term

BARRY, Karen                  8L          A
EVANS, Paul                   8L          B
JONES, Amanda                 8P          E
KENNY, James                  8L          C
```

Explain how this report could be produced. (6)

(NEAB Full Course, Higher Tier)

Chapter 12 – Models of situations

31 Computer simulation can be used to test the potential performance of aeroplanes during their design.

(a) Give TWO reasons why computer simulation is used in this situation. (2)
(b) Name and briefly describe TWO other situations in which computer simulation might reasonably be used. (4)

(NEAB Short Course, Foundation Tier)

32 Information Technology is now very widely used in libraries.
(a) Describe TWO ways in which IT may be used in a library. (4)
(b) Explain TWO differences in the work of the librarian caused by IT. (4)
(c) Do you think that the readers who use the library have benefited from the use of IT? Give reasons for your answer. (4)
(d) The chief librarian could use a simulation program to explore the effects on the customers of changing the staffing arrangements.
  (i) Identify THREE variables involved in the system and explain how the chief librarian should vary them in order to gain the best results. (5)
  (ii) Discuss whether a computer simulation can accurately predict the effects on the library. (9)

(RSA Short Course, Higher Tier)

33 A computer can be used to simulate a situation such as an engine failure on a plane.
(a) Give THREE reasons why such a simulation may not always produce reliable results. (3)
(b) Why are simulators still useful in training pilots? (2)

(NEAB Full Course, Foundation and Higher Tiers)

Chapter 13 – Creating models: spreadsheets

34 The spreadsheet given is used to calculate weekly food costs at a zoo. It is also used to predict the effects of changing the number of animals.

	A	B	C	D	E	F	G
1	Animal	Number of	Cost of food	Preparations	Number of	Cost or 1	Total Cost
2	name	animals	for 1 meal	cost for 1	meals per	animal for	per week
3				meal	week	1 week	
4							
5	Zebra	12	£5.00	£1.00	21	£126.00	£1512.00
6	Lion	4	£16.00	£1.00	14	£238.00	£952.00
7	Polar Bear	2	£12.00	£1.00	21	£273.00	£546.00
8	Penguin	37	£2.00	£1.00	28	£84.00	£3108.00
9	Chimpanzee	18	£5.00	£1.00	28	£168.00	£3024.00
10	Sea Lion	8	£6.00	£1.00	14	£98.00	£784.00
11	Crocodile	3	£30.00	£1.00	3	£93.00	£279.00
12							
13							
					Grand total	for 1 week	£10205.00

(a) Shade in the ONE cell which tells you the number of lions living in the zoo. (1)

(b) Which ONE of the following statements is used to work out the values in the Total cost per week column?

    A   Cost of food for 1 meal x Number of meals per week
    B   Preparation cost for 1 meal x Number of animals
    C   Cost for 1 animal for 1 week x Number of animals
    D   Cost for 1 animal for 1 week x Number of meals per week
    E   Number of animals x Number of meals per week   (1)

(c) Which other values will be worked out by the spreadsheet? (2)

(d) The cost of food for 1 zebra meal increases to £6.50. You need to see the effect on the total food bill.
Which cell would you have to change? (1)

(e) The zoo gives 6 penguins to another zoo.
   (i) Which other cell would you have to change? (1)
   (ii) Which TWO other cells would change as a result? (2)

(NEAB Short Course, Foundation Tier)

35

	A	B	C	D	E	F	G	H
1			**ANALYSIS OF DISCO COST**					
2								
3	No. of Tickets Sold	Cost of one ticket	Income	Music Hire	BBQ Cost	Printing Cost	Total Costs	Profit
4	0	18	0	100	0	200	300	–300
5	5	18	90	100	10	200	310	–200
6	15	18	270	100	30	200	330	–60
7	25	18	450	100	50	200	350	100
8	35	18	630	100	70	200	370	260
9	45	18	810	100	90	200	390	420
10	55	18	990	100	110	200	410	580
11	65	18	1170	100	130	200	430	740
12	75	18	1350	100	150	200	450	900
13	85	18	1530	100	170	200	470	1060
14	95	18	1710	100	190	200	490	1220
15	105	18	1890	100	210	200	510	1380

Fig. 2

A hotel wants to organise a disco and wishes to know the minimum number of tickets it must sell to make a profit.

The hotel manager has created the spreadsheet shown in figure 2 in order to help him find this out.

Study the spreadsheet carefully and answer the following questions.

(a) In figure 2, how many tickets must be sold for the hotel to first make a profit? (1)

(b) The manager used formulae to work out the Total Cost and the Profit.
Write down suitable formulae which he might have used.
    (i) Formulae for TOTAL COST (1)
    (ii) Formulae for PROFIT. (1)
(c) The manager wants to increase profits by increasing the price of tickets. An existing ticket costs £18.00 and the new cost is £20.00.
  The manager makes changes in the ticket cost in Column B.
  Which column data will also change as a result of the manager's actions? (1)
(d) Give ONE other example of how a different spreadsheet can be used in the hotel. (1)
(e) State TWO advantages of using the spreadsheet in the example you have given in part (d) of this question. (2)

(WJEC/CBAC Short Course, Foundation Tier)

36 A spreadsheet is used to process data about your school's tuck shop.

	A	B	C	D	E	F
1		Choc Bar	Crisps	Minties	Chews	
2	Mon	8	12	4	5	sum(b2:e2)
3	Tues	5	11	6	3	
4	Wed	10	15	5	9	
5	Thurs	4	6	2	1	
6	Fri	7	13	3	6	
7	Total Sold					
8						
9	Cost Price	20	15	12	20	
10	Sale Price	25	20	15	24	
12	Expenditure					
13	Income					
14						
15	Weekly Profit					
16						

(a) Cell F2 contains the formula to calculate the daily total for Monday.
  Explain how the daily totals for Tuesday to Friday could be entered. (3)
(b) State the formula for cell B7 to calculate the weekly total of Choc Bars sold. (2)
(c) Name the day when you think that another tuck shop may have been open somewhere else in the school. (1)

(MEG Short Course, Foundation Tier and Higher Tier)

37 The management of a supermarket uses a computer system for various activities. Two of these activities are:
        Recording Sales on a Computer File
        Producing Publicity Material.
(a) (i) State the type of software used for each of these activities. (1,1)
    (ii) Describe how the output from the computer would be presented for each of these activities. (2,2)
(b) Otto is the manager of the supermarket.
  Otto thinks that more of a particular item is sold if more are displayed on the shelves.
  Otto decides to put his thoughts to the test.
  On odd numbered weeks he will display two full shelves of YUMYOG yoghurt but on even numbered weeks only one full shelf of YUMYOG is displayed.

Below is part of a spreadsheet that Otto uses to record the sales of YUMYOG over a ten-week period.

	A	B	C	D
1	Week No.	Number of Sales	Week No.	Number of Sales
2	1	500	2	385
3	3	456	4	410
4	5		6	
5	7		8	
6	9		10	
7	**			
8	Totals			
9	**			
10	Result =			

(i) Describe what the numbers that should appear in cells B8 and D8 mean. (2,1)

(ii) Describe what Otto should put into cells B8 and D8 to get these results. (2,1)

(iii) Otto places into cell B10 the formula B8 - D8.
Explain why Otto would be unhappy if the result in B10 is displayed as a negative number. (2)

(iv) State how Otto will display the YUMYOG in future if he sees a negative number as a result. (1)

(+1 SPG)

(London Full Course, Foundation Tier)

Chapter 14 - Presenting your work: graphics and charts

38 A CAD package is advertised as being 'mouse-driven'.
(a) Explain the terms
  (i) CAD (1)
  (ii) mouse-driven. (2)
(b) State FOUR distinct features you would expect to find and use whilst in the package. (4)

(MEG Full Course, Foundation Tier)

39 Sharon is planning to set up a business printing computer images onto T-shirts. She thinks that some of her customers will have their own pictures but others will want pictures designed on the computer. She intends to buy a graphics package to prepare the designs for printing.
Give SIX features you think she should look for in the graphics package, explaining why each is necessary. (12)

(NEAB Full Course, Foundation and Higher Tiers)

Chapter 15 - Communications

40 The Crafty Fair Group is a small group of people who organise Craft Fairs across the country.
The Crafty Fair Group were advised that they should think about networking their computer systems.
(i) State ONE reason why it might be a good idea for the group. (2)

(ii) Below are the four different homes that will each have a computer in them that could be networked.

Draw lines to show ONE method of networking these computers. (2)
Show the direction of the data flow around the network. (2)
(iii) List any special hardware and software that they would need to run a networked system. (2)
(iv) The Crafty Fair Group knows that they will be able to communicate with each other directly through their computer systems.
State what is meant by each of these methods of communication:
  Fax messages (2)
  Electronic mail. (2)
(v) State ONE advantage and ONE disadvantage of using ONE of these methods. (2,2)

(NDTEF Short Course, Foundation Tier)

41 (a) Give THREE advantages of the existence of a world-wide network such as Internet. (3)
(b) A disadvantage is that it sometimes takes a long time to find the data. Give one reason for this. (1)

(NEAB Short Course, Foundation Tier)

42 (i) Name TWO different methods of communication that make direct use of a computer system. (1,1)
(ii) Explain how ONE of these methods of communication would be used. (5)
(iii) Compare and contrast one of these methods with a method that would have been used previously. (4)

(NDTEF Short Course, Higher Tier)

43 Many medical practices and health centres now store patient information on computer files.
(a) In a particular health centre, a local area network (LAN) is used, providing terminals and local printers in each of the doctors' rooms.

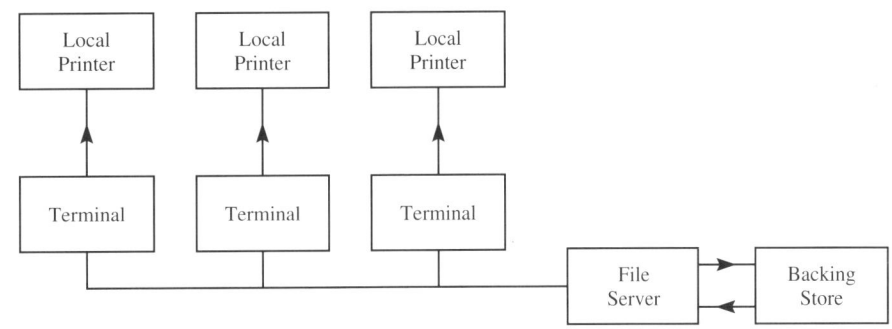

Give TWO advantages of this network instead of using stand alone machines in each doctor's room. (2)
(b) It is proposed to link the network in all the surgeries and health centres in the area to the main hospital computer system to form a wide area network (WAN).
  (i) Name an extra device that will be needed in the surgery to allow the connection to be made. (1)
  (ii) What is the function of this device? (1)
(c) Give an example of data which:
  (i) might be transmitted from a doctor in a surgery to the hospital;
  (ii) might be transmitted from the hospital to the doctor. (2)
(d) Give TWO advantages of the WAN being available:
    (i) to the patient;
    (ii) to the hospital. (4)
(e) What extra security problems might arise when the WAN is set up? (3)
(NEAB Full Course, Higher Tier)

Chapter 16 – Measurement and control

44 Burglar alarms are found in a variety of workplaces, homes and cars.
  (a) Name TWO different sensors which could be used in a burglar alarm system in the home. (2)
  (b) Describe how each of the sensors you have named could be used to prevent or warn of an intrusion by a burglar. (2)
(WJEC/CBAC Short Course, Foundation Tier)

45 An experiment is set up to investigate the rate at which boiling water cools. It has been decided to use data-logging equipment connected to a microcomputer to collect this data.
  (a) What type of sensor would be used to collect this data? (1)
  (b) A suitable time interval and period of logging have to be chosen.
    (i) What is meant by the term 'time-interval'? (1)
    (ii) What is meant by the term 'period of logging'? (1)
    (iii) From the lists below, choose the most suitable time interval and period of logging for this experiment.
      Possible time intervals: 30 sec, 30 mins, 10 hrs, 24 hrs, 48hrs.
      Possible periods of logging: 30 sec, 30 mins, 10 hrs, 24 hrs, 48 hrs. (2)
    (iv) State TWO suitable ways in which the data collected from this experiment could be displayed on the screen (VDU). (2)
    (v) Give TWO advantages of using data-logging for this experiment rather than taking manual readings with a thermometer. (2)
(NEAB Short Course, Foundation and Higher Tiers)

46 An automatic process control system is needed to mix two liquids in a heated container.
The temperature and the rate of supply of the two liquids must be kept under control.

Questions and answers

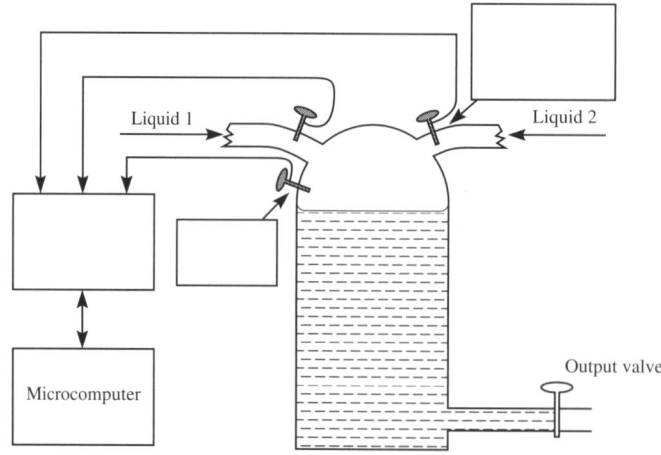

(a) Label the THREE blank boxes in the diagram. (3)
(b) Explain how feedback should work in this automatic system. (3)

(MEG Full Course, Higher Tier)

Chapter 17 – Programming for control systems

47 A floor turtle uses a set of instructions to draw shapes on paper.

PENUP	Lift the pen off the paper
PENDOWN	Lower the pen onto the paper
FORWARD n	Move n steps forward
BACKWARD n	Move n steps backward
LEFT d	Turn left d degrees
RIGHT d	Turn right d degrees

Write a set of instructions which makes the turtle draw a square with sides of 40 steps. (5)

(MEG Short Course, Foundation Tier)

48 The following set of diagrams of traffic lights show the sequence in which the lights are lit.

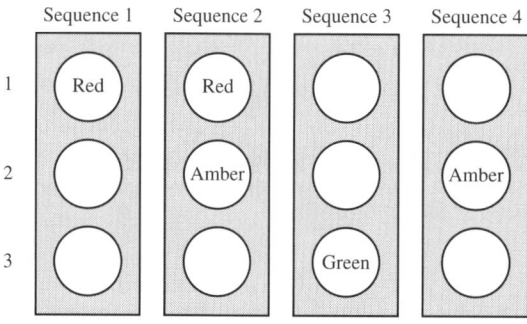

A pupil in a school is writing a control program which would simulate (copy) the sequence of the traffic lights on his screen display.

Write suitable commands the pupil would write in order to turn the appropriate lights on and off. (2)

(WJEC/CBAC Short Course, Foundation Tier)

49 Priory National is a bank.

A certain high street branch of Priory National has eight cashier service windows for customers to use.

232

Many aspects of the business of the branch are controlled by a computer system called BILL.

Above each of the cashier windows is a pair of lights:
   A green light on indicates that the cashier is available;
   A red light on indicates that the cashier is busy;
   No lights on indicates that there is not a cashier at the window.

The lights for each window are controlled by the cashier at that window.

(a) There are just four cashiers on duty.
   The cashiers at windows 1 and 5 are busy with customers.
   The cashiers at windows 3 and 8 are waiting for customers.
   On the following diagram shade in those lights which are on.

RED	O	O	O	O	O	O	O	O
GREEN	O	O	O	O	O	O	O	O
Window Number	1	2	3	4	5	6	7	8

(2)

(b) The patterns of the lights are stored in BILL.

The byte that records the pattern of the eight red lights is called R and the byte that records the pattern of the eight green lights is called G.

Each byte pattern has eight bits.

A bit set to 1 would mean that the light was **on** and a bit set to 0 would mean that the light was **off**.

   (i) The pattern stored in R for the lights displayed above would be:
         10001000
   Write down the pattern stored in G. (2)

   (ii) Complete the table below to show the state of the lights for the byte patterns given.

Colour	Byte Name	Byte Pattern	State of Lights
Red	R	11100101	--,--,--,--,--,--,--,--
Green	G	00010010	--,--,--,--,--,--,--,--

(2)

   (iii) Write down, in the table below, ONE combination of patterns of R and G that should not be allowed.

Colour	Byte Name	Byte Pattern
Red	R	
Green	G	

(2)

   (iv) Describe how BILL could validate the state of the lights. (2)

(c) BILL has been programmed recently to record how long each individual cashier spends with a customer.

   (i) Describe how BILL could 'know' which cashier is at any particular service window. (2)
   (ii) Give TWO arguments against BILL being programmed in this way. (4)
   (iii) Explain why it is very important to test any programs that are developed to run on BILL. (3)

(+1 SPG)

(London Full Course, Foundation Tier)

50 A crane is moved around a dockyard.
   It is controlled by giving a computer instructions.

Examples of instructions	What the instructions do
N2	Move the crane North for a distance of 2 units
W13	Move the crane West for a distance of 13 units

(a) The crane is at point A on the diagram.

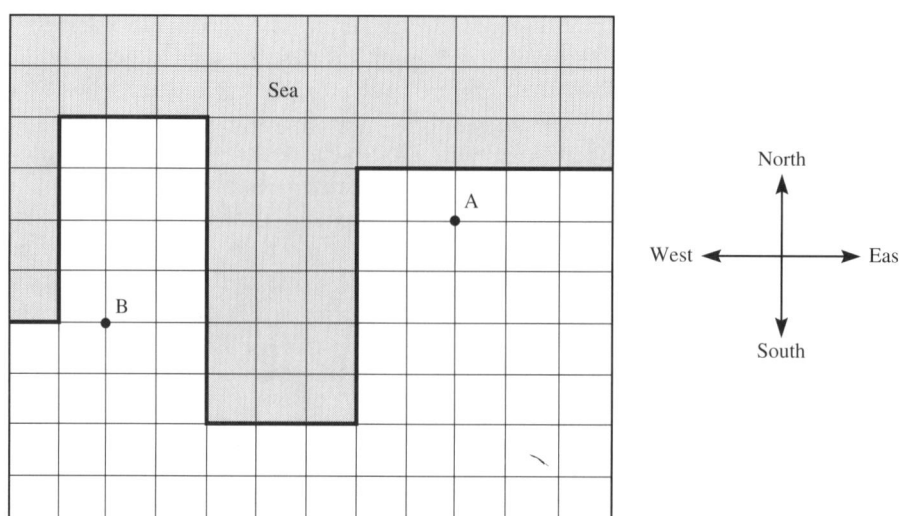

Scale: the squares have sides 1 unit in length

Write the instructions to move the crane from point A to point B. (2)
(b) A human operator gives the computer the instruction, 4 N.
Describe how the computer should respond. (2)
(c) The computer can automatically guide the crane around an object in its path.
Describe what is needed so that the computer can do this. (3)
(d) The computer automatically guides the crane around an object.
  (i) In this context describe what is meant by feedback. (2)
  (ii) Explain why feedback is an essential part of this process. (2)
(e) The computer can be given new instructions by a human operator when there is an object in its path or it can be set up to automatically guide the crane around an object.
Describe ONE advantage in having a human operator give the computer new instructions.
Describe ONE advantage in setting up the computer to automatically guide the crane around an object. (2)

(SEG Full Course, Higher Tier)

Chapter 18 – Solving problems using IT

51 The owners of a chain of video shops are considering using a computer system to handle stock records and loans of videos. You are asked to produce a feasibility report.
(a) Describe THREE ways in which you could find out about the existing system. (6)
(b) As a result of this study you are asked to design a new computerised system.
Give THREE items the design should include. (3)
(c) When the new system is installed a User Guide is provided for the shop staff.
Describe THREE topics you would expect to be covered in this guide. (3)
(d) When the system is installed the staff may not be able to use it straightaway.
Give TWO reasons why they may not be able to switch to the new system immediately. (2)

(NEAB Full Course, Higher Tier)

52 Eleanor uses a seven-year-old computer in her office which is fitted with a 20Mb hard drive and a 5.25 inch floppy drive. Her printer is a 9 pin dot matrix type, which does not produce very good quality printouts, and is noisy in operation. She has therefore decided to upgrade her system.

Eleanor has decided to carry out a Feasibility Study Report which will cover hardware, software, staffing, operating costs and the expected benefits of the new system.

(a) Explain how this study would help Eleanor choose a suitable system. (3)
(b) (i) What steps does Eleanor have to go through to produce a specification to send to prospective suppliers of the new system? (2)
  (ii) What information should the specification contain? (2)
(c) State, giving reasons for your choice, the hardware, software and peripherals you would recommend Eleanor purchases. (7)
(d) Having received a number of quotations, what should Eleanor take into account when deciding on a supplier for the new system? (2)
(e) Once Eleanor has chosen a system, what would she need to do to get it up and running in her office? (2)
(f) After using the system for a short while Eleanor finds that not all of the benefits have been achieved, and a few minor problems have occurred.
  State THREE possible reasons for these problems. (3)

(WJEC/CBAC Full Course, Higher Tier)

Chapter 19 – Documentation

53 An office worker uses this computer.

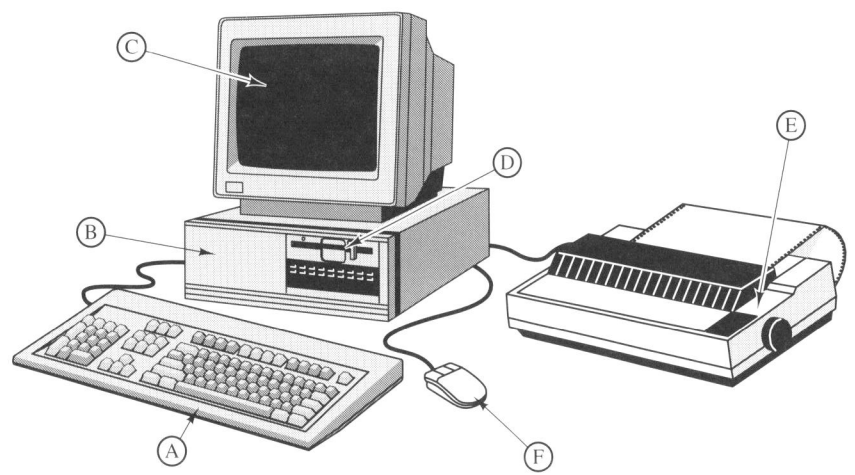

(a) (i) Write down the labels of the parts used to output information from the computer. (1)
  (ii) The computer has a hard disk.
    Write down the label of the part that contains the hard disc. (1)
(b) When the computer is switched on, the office worker has to enter a password.
  (i) Explain why passwords are used. (1)
  (ii) The office worker's password has to be changed every week.
    Explain why passwords should be changed regularly. (1)
  (iii) When the password was changed, the office worker typed in the new password. The password was typed in correctly. The computer asked the office worker to type in the new password again.
Explain why the computer asked the office worker to type in the new password again. (1)
(c) The office worker wants to access information on a computer in Australia. This is part of a flowchart that shows what the office worker has to do to access the information.
  (i) The box labelled A should contain a question.
    Write down the question that should be in the box labelled A. (1)
  (ii) The line labelled B should re-join the flowchart. Draw on the flowchart to show where the line labelled B should re-join the flowchart. (1)

Questions and answers

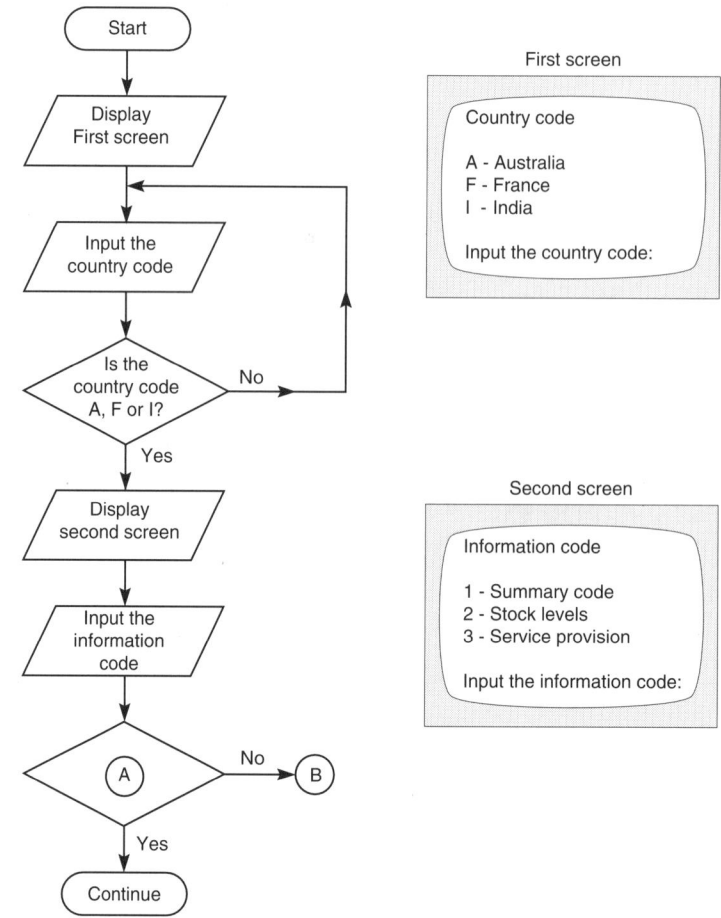

(SEG Short Course, Higher Tier)

54 (i) Explain what is meant by 'user friendly'. (1)
(ii) State THREE types of documentation that can support a system.
(3) (iii) Analyse the differences between the level and type of support offered by each type. (3,3,3)

(NDTEF Full Course, Higher Tier)

55 A supermarket uses a point of sale (POS) system. All the products sold carry bar codes.
(a) The bar code contains a check digit. Explain how this would be used to detect an error in reading the bar code. (3)
(b) The system flowchart shows how sales of goods are handled. Complete it by selecting the correct statements from the list below and entering them in the appropriate boxes. (7)

Bar codes   Error signal   Itemised receipt
Process sale   Product file   Read and validate
Sort   Stock file   Stock list
Verify

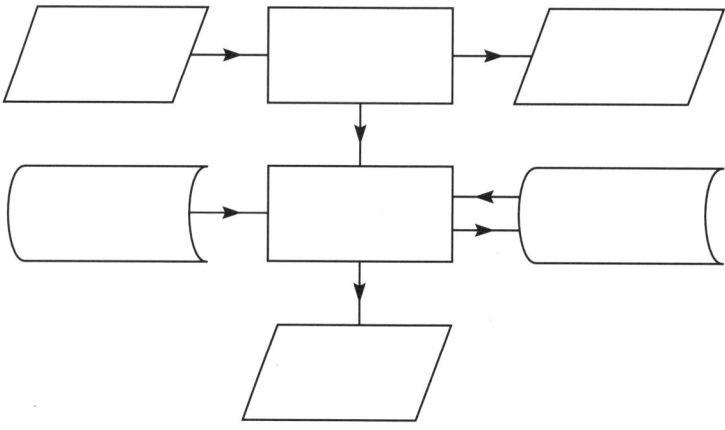

236

(c) Give ONE use that might be made of the stock file in the supermarket. (1)
(d) The system logs the number of items passing through each check-out every hour.
   Describe TWO ways in which management could use this data. (4)

(NEAB Full Course, Higher Tier)

[See also Question 51 for topics in user guide.]

Chapter 20 – The implications of IT

56 The widespread use of IT in the workplace has had a great effect on employment.
   (a) Give TWO examples of jobs which have been created by the introduction of IT. (2)
   (b) Give TWO examples of jobs which have been lost by the introduction of IT. (2)

(NEAB Short Course, Foundation Tier)

57 (i) State TWO advantages for someone who works from home.
    State ONE disadvantage for someone who works from home. (2,2,2)
    (ii) Explain why some employers would be happy to have workers based in their own homes.
    Marks will be awarded for writing about the social, economic and legal issues. (3,3,3)

(NDTEF Short Course, Foundation Tier)

58 Staff in a firm of solicitors use typewriters for all letters and forms. The firm decides to introduce wordprocessors to make the office more efficient.
   (a) Give TWO reasons why this change may worry some of the office staff. (2)
   (b) After a time most of the office staff find that the word processors make their job easier.
     Give ONE reason why their jobs are made easier. (1)

(WJEC/CBAC Short Course, Foundation Tier)

59 As the use of information technology has increased, the Government has found it necessary to provide laws to control the use of information stored in computer files and computer programs.
   One example is the Data Protection Act (DPA).
   (a) Give THREE rights that the DPA gives to the data subject. (3)
   (b) What obligations does the DPA place on a data user? (5)
   (c) Name ONE category of data which is granted complete exemption from the whole of the Data Protection Act. (1)

(WJEC/CBAC Full Course, Higher Tier)

Examination answers

This section contains hints on how to approach the questions in the previous section and suggested answers to them.

The hints are printed as Examiner's tips in the margin. Where a question is answered directly by an item in the main text no answer is given. Instead a reference is given to that item. For other questions a suggested answer is given. In these cases the answers depend entirely on the author's interpretation of the question and are his responsibility.

Examiner's tip to 1

The 6 marks and the use of 'describe' suggests writing quite a few words with at least two points made for each of the 3 answers. Inputs are actions by the owner of the watch, processing consists of operations by the watch circuits.

1   Possible inputs: a new time setting; a new date setting; an alarm setting.
    Processing: add 1 to seconds; if seconds = 60 increase minutes by 1 and set seconds to 0; if minutes = 60 increase hours by 1 and set minutes to 0; if hours = 24 set hours to 0; if alarm time = present time sound alarm.
    Possible outputs: alarm sounding; display date; display time.
    (Other answers are possible. You need 6 points with at least 1 for each section.)

2   (a) (i) MAT4PA (ii) See Unit 1.5 - 'Advantages of replacing data with codes'.

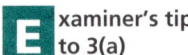

Examiner's tip to 3(a)

Make sure when you code the date that the year is first and the day last.

3   (a) pc20sh970513.
    (b) (i) There is already a '**br**' for Bristol.
        (ii) If the first and second letters have already been used, try the first and last – '**bn**' for Brighton.

4   Processing cheques and producing gas bills.

Examiner's tip to 4

Select TWO for which it does not matter if there is a delay of an hour or two before they are processed.

5   (a) Columns should be headed with at least three of: Date, Item number, Description of item, Number in stock.
    (b) See Unit 1.5 - 'Advantages of replacing data with codes'.
    (c) (i) See Unit 4.3 - 'Advantages of bar codes'.
        (ii) See Unit 4.3 - 'Bar codes'.
        (iii) Probably with a flashing light and a bleep.
        (iv) Key in the number printed under the bar code.

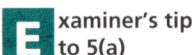

Examiner's tip to 5(a)

Make the answer look like a form by taking most of a page and drawing a rectangle for the outside of the form. Then draw a table with headings at the top of the columns. For an example of this type of form see Unit 11.2, Fig. 11.1.

6   (a) The commands have to be remembered or looked up in a manual.
    (b) See Unit 3.4 - 'Advantages of a GUI'.
    (c) It is quicker to press a number on the keyboard than to move a mouse and click.

7   (i) See Unit 4.3 - 'Magnetic stripes'.
    (ii) Input: The card is passed through a reader which reads the data stored on the magnetic stripe.
        Process: The input data is checked to see if it matches any value in a file stored in the computer.
        Output: A message is displayed saying whether the card is accepted or not. If it is accepted a control signal is sent to open the barrier.
    (iii) The Crafty Fair Group will not have to employ so many people at the entrances as they will deal only with customers and not with craftworkers.
        The craftworkers will be able to gain entrance without waiting.

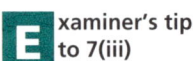

Examiner's tip to 7(iii)

Assume that the swipe cards are issued to craftworkers to gain free entrance but that customers still have to be checked – and possibly pay to get in.

8   (a) A wand OR a laser scanner.
    (b) See Unit 3.1 - 'Advantages of POS terminals using bar codes'.

9   See Unit 4.2.

10 See Unit 4.3 - 'Applications of magnetic stripes'.

Examination answers

11 Monitor, plotter.

12 (a) • Colour monitor for graphic applications.
    • Inkjet printer – for letters and generally improved output.
    • Scanner – to input documents and drawings.
    (b) See Unit 9.5.
    (c) (i) Create regular backups. (ii) Have passwords for users and files.

13 Advantages:
    • Games contain graphics, which take up a large amount of store and the CD-ROM stores far more.
    • The CD-ROM is faster so the game can use it without the program being installed on the hard disc.
    • The CD-ROM is less prone to damage.
    Disadvantage: All computers have floppy disc drives but may not have CD-ROM drives.

14 (a) B.
    (b) Hard disc, floppy disc (ROM, tape acceptable).
    (c) (i) CD-ROM to store clip-art and professional software which use large amounts of store. (ii) RAM to hold the program being run and its data.

15 See Unit 6.2.

16 (a) 4
    (b) 3 of Address, Work phone number, Car type, Car registration.
    (c) One record represents all the information about one customer.
    (d) See Unit 7.1 – 'Key field'.
    (e) (i) The REFERENCE field can be validated by checking that the data item is a number.
        (ii) A suitable length check is that there are not more than 6 characters in the REFERENCE field.
    (f) INSERT A RECORD   when there is a new customer
        DELETE A RECORD   when an existing customer leaves
        AMEND A RECORD   when an existing customer changes address.
    (g) Customers may fear that their details may be passed on leading to junk mail or they may worry about a general loss of privacy.

17 (a) (i) 4. (ii) 5.
    (b) T.
    (c) Code.
    (d) (i) See Unit 7.4. (ii) Price.
    (e) AXX134, AXY917, AXY123, AXY912.

18 (a) 1. Files may be lost or destroyed.
        2. It may be costly – security will have to be improved.
    (b) See Unit 8.1 – 'Protection against hacking'.

19 (a) See Unit 8.1 – 'Viruses' (use the definition and the notes).
    (b) See Unit 8.1 – 'Protection against viruses'.

20 (a) DTP. (b) CAD. (c) Database.

21 (a) Columns; fonts, sizes; clip art.
    (b) A laser printer prints good quality text and graphics.
    (c) • CD-ROM drive – used as a source of clip art.
        • Scanner – used to scan in pictures.
    (d) (i) See Unit 9.3 – 'Functions of the operating system'.
        (ii) See Unit 9.2 – 'Examples of utility programs'.
    (e) • If there are not many members the cost of IT hardware and software may not be justified.

Examiner's tip to 12(a)

The monochrome monitor and the dot matrix printer are low quality devices so improve on those. You don't know what storage there is so do not bother with it – it would be better to suggest a new input device.

Examiner's tip to 16

This question has an extra 'SPG' mark for spelling, punctuation and grammar so answers should be expressed in a sentence or sentences.

Examiner's tip to 16(b)

Think of other details of the customer and also details of the customer's car.

Examiner's tip to 21(c)

In this case give a very brief description, as there is only one mark for each name and description.

Examiner's tip to 21(e)

Arguments for not using IT in a small organisation usually depend on cost and access. As there are 4 marks you should try to make 4 points.

Questions and answers

- If members do not know how to use the equipment they will not be able to help out.
- Too much reliance on the Secretary will make it difficult if the Secretary leaves or is ill.
- It will be difficult to maintain security and allow members access to the computer.

22 (a) An integrated package costs less than the separate packages which make it up. Data can be transferred easily between the parts of the package.
(b) (i) See Unit 3.4 - 'Graphical user interfaces'.
(ii) See Unit 3.4 - 'Advantages of a GUI'.

23 Word processor.

24 It is faster to correct mistakes. Work can be checked on a screen before printing.

> **Examiner's tip to 25(a)**
> The term 'computer system' may not have a new type of software (such as DTP) so it would be better in part (a) to only consider improvements to the printer and word processor.

25 (a) The poster will be better printed.
It will be made more attractive by a wider range of fonts and character sizes.
(b) The IT teacher should consider compatibility of the new system with Mrs Williams' own system. She may want to improve a poster she has already done and use her old file on the new computer.
(Other answers are possible, for example ease of use.)
(c) Advantages:
- a high quality of presentation;
- designs can be stored to be edited to produce future posters.

Disadvantages:
- to use IT Mrs Williams will have to learn to use the software;
- Mrs Williams cannot edit a poster without a computer present – at home for example.

(d) A desk top publishing package.

> **Examiner's tip 25(d)**
> The description of the package should list at least four of the features (see Unit 10.7 - 'Characteristics of a DTP program').
> To discuss its effectiveness explain how these features could make it easy to produce a poster, e.g. graphics can be imported. Mrs Williams could use this facility to import an attractive border for the poster from a collection of clip art.

> **Examiner's tip to 26**
> Describe the computing steps that an operator goes through to produce a mail merge. There are 3 marks so make 3 main points – producing the letter, producing a file of personalising data, tying up the letter with the file.

26 Produce the standard letter required with gaps for the items to be filled in by the computer. Usually codes are keyed into the gaps to indicate what items have to go in them, e.g. $1, $2, $3.
Produce a database file of names, addresses and other items that have to fill in the gaps. This is usually done by reorganising an existing database so that the items are in the order required for the mail merge.
Select the merge option from the menu.

> **Examiner's tip to 27**
> For parts (a) and (b) you could explain the instructions you would carry out with the database package that you are used to. If you do this remember that the examiner may not be familiar with it, so explain what you are doing.

27 (a) Produce the query to match records for which the address ends in 'Stanton'. Select the option to list all records which match the query condition.
(b) Produce the query condition (Address ends in 'Cortley') AND (Price $<=$ 60000). Select the option to print. Select option to list matching records.
(c) Telephone number of the seller.
(d) Contact the seller if a buyer made an offer.
(e) Advantage: houses can be found very quickly to fit any conditions the buyer requests.
Disadvantage: for a small estate agent the computer system would be a large part of total costs.

> **Examiner's tip to 29**
> This question has an extra 'SPG' mark for spelling, punctuation and grammar. Where possible the answer should be expressed in a sentence or sentences.

28 (a) (i) Age of 116. (ii) Not a realistic minimum age.
(b) (1) With the computer all the jobs will be checked but with cards on walls you may miss some.
(2) Cards may have gone missing but none of the computer data will have been lost.
(3) You can search the computer data very quickly by matching a complicated query.
(c) Pay > 10000.
(d) Minimum-Age $>=$ 18 AND Type-of-job $=$ 'Sales' AND Pay > 13000.

> **Examiner's tip to 29(a)**
> A spreadsheet package may well be used for the business graphics but this answer is not allowed by the question.

29 (a) They could use a word processor for letters and a graphics package for charts and diagrams.

(b) (i)   44   ROVER   214   1990   5   4750.
    (ii) 11   RENAULT   19   1993   5   6900
         27   MAZDA   323   1993   5   7400.
    (iii) 22, 44, 34, 13, 11, 27.
    (iv) Asif should delete the record from the Used Car File or else indicate in an extra field that the car is sold.
(c) (i) Any one of REFERENCE NUMBER, REGDATE, MILEAGE.
    (ii) Any one of MAKE, MODEL.
(d)

	VALID	INVALID
30NOV94		√
030794	√	
07061995		√
300294	√	

(e) (i) Three of garage name, garage address, telephone, fax number, manager's name (other answers are possible).
    (ii) Three of customer name, customer address, car name, car registration, service date (other answers are possible).
    (iii) Two of mouse, monitor, printer, hard disc, keyboard.
(f) The owners probably decided to use computers because the management has faster access to data and they wanted to avoid having to employ extra office staff. (Other answers are possible.)

30 (a) A staff record contains different fields from a pupil record.
   (b) Any two of:
       • data takes less time to key;
       • coded data takes less storage space;
       • the data can be validated by table lookup;
       • the code forms a standard - e.g. for searches.
   (c) • Set up the headings and other text on the report form;
       • select subject and pupil tables;
       • set link between subject code and subject table;
       • set query in pupil table: search for subject code;
       • search in each subject field;
       • identify the fields of the pupil record to be printed out - surname, other names, form and grade.

> **Examiner's tip to 30(c)**
> 6 marks suggest 6 points should be made. Assume grade is in the pupil table somewhere - it would not be in either of the other two tables.

31 (a) Any two of:
       • it would be costly to make a plane to test each design change;
       • it is much quicker and simpler to change the conditions of a simulation than the actual conditions;
       • it is less dangerous to test a model than an actual plane.
   (Other answers are possible.)
   (b) See Unit 12.2 for possible simulations.

> **Examiner's tip to 31(b)**
> Assume one mark for each situation and one for the description. Also note the word 'briefly' so keep the description short.

32 (a) For example:
       (1) Bar codes can be used to organise the book loans system. A bar code is attached to each book to identify it and to each member's card to identify them. When a book is taken out or returned a wand is run across both bar codes so that the computer can record the transaction.
       (2) A catalogue of all the books in the library can be stored on the computer. Users can then find any book by author, title or subject matter and see whether it is available.
   (b) The librarian and staff will spend more time using a computer and less doing paper work.
       As searches for books and recording loans will be quicker the librarian will expect to spend less time with each user.

> **Examiner's tip to 32(a)**
> Each description need only involve a sentence stating what the application is and another sentence or two to say what happens.

Questions and answers

Examiner's tip to 32(c)

You have to answer 'yes' or 'no'. Neither answer is more correct than the other and no marks would be given for choosing. However, it is better to answer 'yes' because it is then easier to give good reasons.

(Other answers are possible.)

(c) Yes, I think the readers have benefitted.
They can find books more quickly and borrowing and return of books has been made simpler.

(d) (i) Three of:
- number of readers borrowing books,
- number of readers returning books,
- number of enquiries,
- average length of time spent dealing with a reader,
- number of counter staff.

The librarian should get the computer to produce for each variable random values which are typical of the variable. For example, if the maximum time spent is 5 minutes and the minimum is 1 minute, the simulation needs to produce a succession of times between 1 and 5.

The numbers produced should also give an average value which is the same as it is for the real times.

Examiner's tip to 32(d)(ii)

This discussion has a lot of marks so that it needs to be detailed.

(ii) The main points to make are:
- that the randomly chosen values may not be typical of the true values even if their maximum, minimum and average are right;
- there are so many variables in this situation that the simulation probably will not include them all;
- nevertheless the simulation may give some idea of what may happen – it may give the chief librarian some idea of what changes to try to start with.

33 (a) The rules governing the behaviour of the simulated plane may not accurately reflect the actual situation.
Air and wind conditions may not be simulated accurately.
The pilot knows there is no real danger and so will respond differently.

(b) It is much cheaper to fly a simulator than an actual plane.
Pilots can experience dangerous situations without real danger.

34 (a) B6.
(b) C.
(c) Column F and cell G13.
(d) C5.
(e) (i) B8. (ii) G8 and G13.

Examiner's tip to 35(b)

There is a separate formula for each of the cells under Total Cost and for each of the cells under Profit. You cannot be expected to write all of them.

35 (a) 25.
(b) (i) D4 + E4 + F4, D5 + E5 + F5 .... down to D15 + E15 + F15.
(ii) C4 – G4, C5 – G5 .... down to C15 – G15.
(c) Columns C and H.
(d) Any sensible application, e.g. staff wages.
(e) Any two sensible advantages, e.g. automatic calculation of wages, estimating costs if staff are given a rise.

Examiner's tip to 36(a)

This answer needs not the formulae but the method of entering them in the spreadsheet. You could suggest entering the individual formulae but copying is better.

36 (a) Copy cell F2 into cells F3 to F6.
(b) Sum (b2:b6).
(c) Thursday.

37 (a) (i) A database would be used for recording sales on a computer file.
A word processor OR desk top publisher would be used for producing publicity material.
(ii) Database reports would be produced from the database.
Posters OR promotional letters would be produced from a DTP package.

(b) (i) B8 contains the total sales in odd numbered weeks.
D8 contains the total sales in even numbered weeks.
(ii) Sum (B2:B6)   OR   (B2 + B3 + B4 + B5 + B6).
Sum (D2:D6)   OR   (D2 + D3 + D4 + D5 + D6).
(iii) It would mean Otto's pet theory was wrong because more had been sold on even numbered weeks.
(iv) Otto will display only one full shelf of YUMYOG.

Examiner's tip to 37

This question has an extra 'SPG' mark for spelling, punctuation and grammar so answers should be expressed in a sentence or sentences as far as possible.

38 (a) (i) See Unit 14.3 – 'Key terms'.

(ii) The user interface uses a mouse rather than some other input device such as a keyboard.
(b) See Unit 14.3 – 'Characteristics of CAD systems'.

39
- Scaling – to make designs fit the T-shirt.
- Importing of pictures – to use parts of previous designs.
- Editing facilities – to correct mistakes and improve previous designs.
- Scanning facilities – to use pictures supplied by customers.
- Adjusting colours – to fit the colour scheme suggested by the client.
- Printer control – to overcome problems with printing on T-shirts.

(Other answers possible.)

40 (i) Any member of the Group would be able to work at home on any file at any time.
(ii) Any sensible network diagram.
(iii) A file server, 4 computers with network cards to act as stations, 6 modems, a printer and the network software for file serving and print serving; also software to use the modems.
(iv) Unit 15.1 – 'Fax' and Unit 15.6 – 'Services available on viewdata networks'.
(v) EITHER: see Unit 15.1 – 'Advantages of fax' and 'disadvantages of fax'.
OR: see Unit 15.6 – 'Advantages of electronic mail over post' and 'Disadvantages of electronic mail compared with post'.

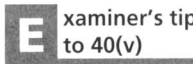

Examiner's tip to 40(ii)

You could show a file server at one of the houses, with the others each having a station connected to it using phone lines and modems. There would need to be 3 modems at the house which has the server so that the others could use it all at the same time. The member with the server could be given another computer as well as the server. The data flow arrows should be shown in both directions along the lines between the server and the stations.

Examiner's tip to 40(v)

Note that you only have to give an advantage and a disadvantage for one of these.

41 (a) Any three of:
- Vast world-wide source of information.
- People can 'meet' people from anywhere else.
- Sources of software.
- People can tell the world about their problems, e.g. from within dictatorships.
- The Internet can be accessed from anywhere.
- Goods can be sold through it.

(Other answers are possible.)

(b) America has woken up – there are sometimes too many users for the number of servers available.

42 (i) Electronic mail; fax via a computer.
(ii) Electronic mail needs a computer with modem and a communication package. The sequence is: create the document to be sent; run the communication program; dial phone number (by selecting a screen option) and log on; select E-mail and select send; send the document; log off.
(iii) See Unit 15.6 – 'Advantages of electronic mail over post' and 'Disadvantages of electronic mail compared with post'.

43 (a) See Unit 15.4 – 'Advantages of local area networks'.
(b) (i) A modem.
(ii) See Unit 15.3 – 'Communications hardware'.
(c) (i) Medical record of a patient being admitted to the hospital.
(ii) Results of tests.
(d) (i) • Test results are received more quickly.
• The hospital knows your medical history.
(Other answers are possible.)
(ii) • Staff time is saved by not having to write information.
• Saving on postage costs.
(Other answers are possible.)
(e) • Confidential information is available from more places.
• Possibility of hacking.
• Possibility of accidental corruption of data.
(Other answers are possible.)

44 See Unit 16.2 – 'Application of sensors' and Unit 17.2 – 'Example of control algorithm'.

45 (a) Temperature probe.
(b) For (i) and (ii) see Unit 16.5 – 'Key terms'.
(iii) Time interval – 30 seconds; period of logging – 30 minutes.

Questions and answers

      (iv) As a graph; as a table.
      (v) Any two of:
- The readings would be accurately timed.
- The values of the readings would be accurate.
- No calculation errors would be made.
- The whole investigation is automatic – saves anyone taking repeated readings.

46 (a) Box at left: Interface
     Middle box: Temperature sensor and/or level sensor
     Box at top right: Rate of flow sensor.
(b) Temperature: repeat of (computer samples temperature sensor; if too hot computer sends signal to put heater on – if too cold computer sends signal to put heater off).
   Rate of supply: repeat of (computer samples level sensor; if too low computer sends signal to open supply valves – if too high computer sends signal to open output valve and/or shut supply valves).

Examiner's tip to 47
The language does not have a 'REPEAT' so each side must be done separately. There is a 'PENUP' and a 'PENDOWN' so use them – they are probably worth a mark each.

47 PENDOWN
FORWARD 40
RIGHT 90
FORWARD 40
RIGHT 90
FORWARD 40
RIGHT 90
FORWARD 40
PENUP

Examiner's tip to 48
It is probably best to assume AMBER and GREEN may be on to start with. If there is a light to switch off do that before switching others on – in case there is a time delay.

48 Sequence 1: AMBER OFF, GREEN OFF, RED ON
Sequence 2: AMBER ON
Sequence 3: RED OFF, AMBER OFF, GREEN ON
Sequence 4: GREEN OFF, AMBER ON.

49 (a)

	1	2	3	4	5	6	7	8
RED	■	O	O	O	■	O	O	O
GREEN	O	O	■	O	O	O	O	■

Window Number

Examiner's tip to 49
This question has an extra 'SPG' mark for spelling, punctuation and grammar. Where possible the answer should be expressed in a sentence or sentences, i.e. from part (b) (iv) onwards.

(b) (i) 0 0 1 0 0 0 0 1

  (ii) RED   ON   ON   ON   OFF OFF ON   OFF ON
       GREEN OFF OFF OFF ON   OFF OFF ON   OFF

  (iii)
Colour	Byte Name	Byte Pattern
Red	R	10000001
Green	G	10000010

Examiner's tip to 49(b)(iii)
You could answer this with any two bytes which have the same bit 1 in both R and G. In the answer given the first bit is 1 in both.

  (iv) BILL could check R and G to see that they do not both have the same bit equal to 1.
(c) (i) Each cashier has to log on when he or she comes to the window. BILL identifies the cashier by the user identity keyed in.
  (ii) Cashiers will be worried that they are being watched and will be unhappy about it.
     Cashiers will tend to rush their work, leading to dissatisfied customers.
  (iii) Errors in the software could lead to dissatisfied customers, dissatisfied staff and possibly loss of money to the bank.

Examiner's tip to 50(b)
The instruction is not valid as instructions should be written with direction first.

50 (a) S 5 , W 7 , N 3 (other answers are possible).
(b) The computer should state that there is an error and ask for the instruction to be repeated.
(c) • Sensors to detect the object – the computer needs to know distance, direction and size of the object.
- A diversion subroutine for avoiding objects included in the software.
- Actuators to steer and drive the crane.

(d) (i) Feedback in this context consists of repeatedly sensing the object, deciding

on a course and moving.
  (ii) Feedback enables the computer to monitor whether it is successfully avoiding the object.
(e) A human operator can deal with unusual situations which the writer of a program may not anticipate.
  On the other hand, a computer can work with a minimum of human intervention so that fewer operators are necessary.

51 (a) Interview users of the current system.
  Read any manuals or instructions which are in use.
  Observe the current system in operation.
(b) Any three of:
Designs for data capture forms, input screens, output screens, validation methods, data files and programs.
(See Unit 18.2 - 'Design of a new system').
(c) See Unit 19.6 - 'User manual'.
(d) Any two of:
  • Staff may need training.
  • Data on paper from the old system may have to be keyed in.
  • The new system may prove to have bugs which were not found before.

52 (a) A feasibility study will investigate possible solutions and consider whether they are practical so that a decision can be made whether to go ahead with a new system.
  It would look at possible hardware and software costs, training needs and possible benefits and drawbacks if a new system was introduced.
  She would also have to consider compatibility between her system and IT systems used by the rest of her organisation.
(b) (i) She would have to carefully analyse her needs and design a system to fit them. She would also have to establish how much money is likely to be available for the system.
    She would then have to find out what types of hardware and software are available to satisfy these needs and within this price range. She would then write out a specification detailing hardware and software and giving a time in which an order was to be met.
  (ii) The specification should explain the purpose of the system. It should detail each piece of hardware and software and what was required of it.
    For example, printer to be of quiet operation and to produce letter quality at faster than 6 pages per minute in monochrome, more than 300 dots per inch in colour.
(c) A PC with a mid-range version of the latest processor - the fastest processor would be unnecessary and expensive.
  • Fairly large hard disc - the largest would be expensive but her data and software requirements are likely to be quite significant.
  • Floppy disc drive - as backup.
  • CD-ROM drive - for software and data received from companies.
  • Keyboard, mouse (for Windows).
  • 15inch SVGA colour monitor - SVGA for resolution, colour for Windows.
  • Laser (or ink-jet) printer - quiet, good quality.
  • Fax modem and fax - for communication outside the company.
  • The most recent Windows version pre-installed - this is now standard.
  • Office integrated software package - something compatible with other departments.
(d) Level of agreement with the system specification, cost of the proposed system, level of maintenance promised, installation and other after-sales support, reputation of the supplier.
(e) Order it, pay for installation, learn how to use the system - attend a training course if necessary; test the system herself in all the types of situation she intends to use it.
(f) • Bugs in the software, e.g. incompatibility between programs.
  • Hardware failures, e.g. incompatibility between devices.
  • Failure to anticipate all her requirements, e.g. memory shortage.

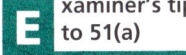

Examiner's tip to 51(a)

The techniques used later in a full analysis could be used in the feasibility study. See Unit 18.2 - 'Analysis of the problem'.

Examiner's tip to 52(b)(ii)

As there are only 2 marks for this part it is not worth going into detail for more than one piece of software or hardware - but it might be worth giving an example.

Examiner's tip to 52(c)

For maximum compatibility with other departments it would probably be best to recommend a PC. We do not know of any major speed and storage requirements and a middle range would probably help Eleanor to stay within budget.

Questions and answers

53 (a) (i) C and E (B and D are acceptable answers as data is output to discs).
  (ii) B.
 (b) (i) To make sure only authorised people use the computer.
  (ii) To make it difficult for unauthorised people to find out a password or to use it if they do.
  (iii) See Unit 8.3 – Note following 'Advice about passwords'.
 (c) (i) 'Is the information code 1,2 or 3?'
  (ii) Re-join between the first decision box and the 'Display second screen' box.

54 (i) See Unit 3.4 – 'User friendliness'.
 (ii) User manual, system documentation, program documentation.
 (iii) A user manual is for a user of the system.
  For type of support see Unit 19.6 – 'User manual'.
  System documentation is meant for people working with the designer of the system and those who maintain it. It includes a written record of the analysis, design, construction and conversion of the system. It includes system flowcharts, file, input and output structures and processing operations.
  Program documentation is for programmers who write and maintain the programs. For the contents of program documentation see Unit 19.7 – 'Program documentation'.

> **Examiner's tip to 54(iii)**
>
> By 'level and type of support' the question requires explanation of who the documentation is meant for, the purpose of it and what is included in it.

55 (a) See Unit 8.5 – 'Check digits'.

 (b)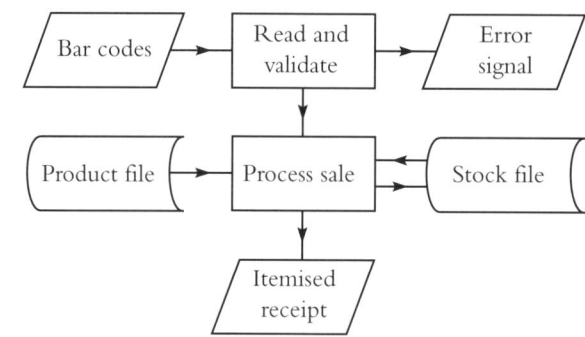

 (c) Automatic reordering of stock when stock levels fall below a set reorder level. (See Unit 7.6.)
 (d) Any two of:
  - to check the rate at which individual staff members work;
  - to keep a check on stock levels;
  - to analyse buying patterns to find out the number of checkout staff required at different times of day.

56 See Unit 20.3 – 'Examples where jobs are created through IT' and 'Examples where jobs are lost through IT'.

57 (i) See Unit 20.3 – 'Advantages of working from home to employees' and 'Disadvantages of working from home to employees'.
 (ii) See Unit 20.3 – 'Advantages of working from home to employers'.

58 (a) Fear that they might not be able to cope with the new equipment; fear that they may lose their jobs.
 (b) Errors can all be corrected before a document is printed.
 (Other answers are possible.)

59 (a) Data subjects have the right:
  - to check the data register to see who the data users are;
  - to have data stored about them disclosed;
  - to have data changed if they can prove it is wrong.
 (b) Obligations on a data user are:
  - to register their use of data;
  - to only hold, use or disclose data in the way registered;
  - to obtain data fairly and lawfully;
  - to protect the data they hold;
  - to hold only accurate data.
 (Other answers are possible.)
 (c) Data held by the police OR doctors OR the tax authorities.

Answers to quick tests

Chapter 1
1. Data
2. (a) String (or alphanumeric) (b) Integer (or numeric) (c) Integer (or numeric) (d) Real number (numeric)
3. The program instructions (OR addresses of locations, contents of the screen, part of the operating system)
4. (a) 8 (b) 1024 (c) 1024
5. Two of:
   - Codes take less time to key.
   - The code forms a standard.
   - Data takes up less storage.
   - Data is easier to validate.
6. (b) and (c)

Chapter 2
1. (a) Analogue (b) Digital (c) Analogue (d) Digital
2. Central processing unit
3. Peripherals
4. Processor (OR control unit)
5. (a) Floppy disc, printer, mouse (b) Word processing package, spreadsheet program
6. Interactive – the shop assistant interacts with the computer.
7. Real time – a computer needs to control the robot using feedback from sensors.
8. Batch – there is no need for anyone to be present when the data is processed.

Chapter 3
1. (a) and (c)
2. (a) and (c)
3. (a) and (c)
4. (a) People do not know whether to answer M, F or Male, Female.
   (b) Type is too vague – people may give all kinds of answers.
5. - Selecting an icon. - Typing a command.
6. - Using sensible icons and clear menus.
   - Having a good system of help messages.
   - Have a clear manual.

Chapter 4
1. A keyboard
2. (b)
3. (a)
4. (d)
5. (b)
6. (c)
7. Any four from:
   - bar codes; - magnetic stripe; - OCR;
   - input from sensors; - MICR; - scanning a picture.
8. MICR
9. Bar codes
10. (a) Voice recognition (b) Touch screen

Chapter 5
1. A large amount of memory is required to store it (and it takes longer to process).
2. Flatbed plotter, liquid crystal display
3. COM
4. Monitor
5. The characters are large.
6. (a) Laser (b) Dot matrix (c) Line printer
7. It is not suitable for noisy environments (OR no permanence OR if repeated, sounds exactly the same again)

Chapter 6
1. Magnetic tape, hard disc
2. Floppy disc
3. Slide the write protect tab to its read only position.
4. CD-ROM, because it would take up too many floppy discs for them to be practical.
5. ROM and CD-ROM
6. CD-ROM
7. Because they are read only and data cannot be written to them.

Chapter 7
1. By recognising the separator between one field and another.
2. Two pupils may have the same surname.
3. If you do not close a file, it may be corrupted the next time you use it.
4. A disc which has not been formatted lacks the necessary control information for accessing data.
5. Direct access.
6. Records on magnetic tape can only be accessed by reading through the tape. There is no quick method of accessing a particular part of the tape.
7. The two files are sequential. They have to be in the same order to avoid movement backwards and forwards searching for records.
8. Deleting records, adding records, changing records
9. Read each record in turn, checking whether the Present level is less than the Reorder level. If it is less, then add that item to the list.

Chapter 8
1. (b) and (d)
2. Firms still have to take precautions in case they are affected.
3. (b) and (c)
4. (a) and (e)
5. (a) Check that the month is between 1 and 12 inclusive (b) Range check OR
   (a) Check that the month is a number (b) Type check
6. (b), (d) and (e)
7. (a), (c)

Questions and answers

8. (a) Type check   (b) Length check
   (c) Type check   (d) Range check
9. Check digit
10. Virus
11. Verification
12. Password
13. Hacker

Chapter 9

1. • A desktop publisher   • A payroll program
   • A spreadsheet program
   (There are many other correct answers.)

2. • Backing up files
   • Dumping the contents of the screen to a printer
   • Sorting data
   (There are many other correct answers.)

3. Three of:
   • creating a working environment for the user;
   • controlling the use of peripherals;
   • controlling the loading and running of programs;
   • organising the use of the main store;
   • dealing with execution errors.
   (There are other correct answers.)

4. One of:
   • producing a log; • maintaining security;
   • working out the resources used by each program.

5. (a) utility   (b) robust   (c) reliable
6. • Import and export • Copy (or cut) and paste
7. Draw using standard shapes such as lines and circles.
   (Various other answers could be added.)
8. Allow calculations on cells, rows and columns using formulae.
9. Allow searches based on query conditions.
10. Produce very accurate drawings which can be enlarged without losing accuracy. (Various other answers could be added.)
11. • Word processor   • Spreadsheet
    • Database   • Graphics (or chart) program
    (Possibly also a communications program.)

Chapter 10

1. Centring, indenting
2. Emboldening, changing font, enlarging
3. (a) Embolden (OR underline OR centre)
   (b) TAB (OR set tabs)   (c) Double line spacing
4. (a) Personalising   (b) Mail merging
5. • Produce graphics as well as text (or integrate graphics with text).
   • Divide the page into columns.
6. (a) DTP   (b) word processor
   (c) DTP   (d) word processor

Chapter 11

1. (b)
2. • Surname   • Forenames   • Date of birth
   (There are many other correct answers.)
3. Data capture form
4. • Search for all records matching a query condition.
   • Sort a file for a given field.
   • Calculate statistics for records in the file.
5. A report facility allows results to be printed out together as one document with text added.
6. B (or D)

7. E
8. A
9. D
10. (a) Petra   Chaffey
     Tracey   Hinds
     Janet   Smith
     John   Smith
     Bernard   Toms
     David   Walker
    (The Smiths could also go in the reverse order but the order given uses their forenames as well.)
    (b) David   Walker   (189)
        John   Smith   (182)
        Bernard Toms   (180)
        Petra   Chaffey   (178)
        Tracey   Hinds   (176)
        Janet   Smith   (170)
    (The heights are not needed for the answer but they have been included to show that the order is correct.)

Chapter 12

1. (a), (c) and (e)
2. • To avoid a dangerous situation.
   • To save money if the real thing is expensive.
   • To save time by studying a model which runs faster than the real thing.
   (There are many other correct reasons – see Unit 12.1.)
3. (a) and (d)
4. (d), (e), (c), (b) and (a)
5. (a), (b) and (d)
6. None of them
7. (a)
8. (a)
9. (a) and (c)
10. The viewer can produce a 3-D effect. OR
    The user is not distracted by seeing other objects.

Chapter 13

1. (a) G6   (b) B4
2. (a) H7:L7   (b) G8:G11   (c) C7:F7
3. (a) SUM (G7:G11)   (b) SUM (C5:C16)
4. (b)
5. Formulae
6. • Centre • Underline • Embolden
   (Other correct answers are possible.)
7. • Integer •   Currency • Percentage
   (Other correct answers are possible.)
8. (a) The cell references (such as A5 or H7) are the variables.
   (b) The formulae are the rules of the model.

Chapter 14

1. (a) A CAD package
   (b) A chart package (OR Business graphics)
   (c) A paint package
   (d) An image manipulation package
2. • A graphics tablet   • A high resolution monitor
   • A plotter
3. • Pixel based (OR bit mapped)
   • Object based (OR vector based OR line based)
4. (a) Object based (b) Pixel based

5 • Accurate measurement
  • Scaling drawings to different sizes
  (Other correct answers are possible.)
6 Because individual objects in a drawing are stored by a CAD package using their coordinates, shape and size. In a paint package, pictures are stored as separate pixels.
7 CAD/CAM
8 From a spreadsheet (OR a database).
9 (a) A line graph (b) A pie chart
  (c) A bar chart (d) A scatter graph

Chapter 15

1 • Once you have the equipment, using it costs nothing.
  • Teletext data can be added to ordinary television pictures.
2 • There is no limit to the number of different pages available.
  • The user can interact with the computer.
3 • Keying the number of the selected page.
  • Using the coloured keys to select a page stored in memory. (This system is not available on older sets.)
4 (a) Details of radio and TV programmes (OR up-to-date news OR magazine programs).
  (b) Subtitles for the deaf.
5 • Cheap PCs • Electronic mail • Fax
6 (a) A LAN only operates on one site whereas a WAN uses external communications. (b) A WAN
7 Electronic conferencing
8 A gateway
9 Electronic mail
10 Teletext
11 Bulletin board (OR notice board)
12 • Stores messages in the appropriate mailboxes.
  • Allows a user to scan his/her mailbox to see what is in it.
  • Allows users to read their messages.
  (Other correct answers are possible.)

Chapter 16

1 (b) and (d)
2 • Signal from a pedestrian push button.
  • Signal from a traffic sensor, e.g. a pressure pad in the road.
3 (a) Between an output port and the continuous motor.
  (b) Between the thermocouple and the computer.
4 • By switching the robot into 'learn' mode and leading it through the task.
  • By inputting the sequence of operations required as a program.
5 (a), (d) and (e)
6 (a) To measure temperature.
  (b) To react to the amount of daylight.
  (c) To react to the presence of cars.
7 (a) and (d)

Chapter 17

1 PEN UP, PEN DOWN, LEFT, RIGHT, FORWARD, BACKWARD
2 PEN UP, PEN DOWN, LEFT, FORWARD (You can achieve the same effect as any RIGHT by changing the number of degrees and using the LEFT instruction. Backward can be achieved using LEFT 180, FORWARD, LEFT 180. An alternative would be to leave out LEFT and FORWARD and just use RIGHT and BACKWARD.)
3 The RIGHT 60 should be RIGHT 120.
4 A regular hexagon of side 50.
5 The AND should be an OR.
6 Two of:
  • a hardware diagram;
  • a system flowchart (showing what the system does);
  • a program flowchart or structure diagram.
7 • Test that the interface and the software has been set up correctly.
  • Test the hardware you have set up.
  • Test the whole system – software and hardware.

Chapter 18

1 (c), (d), (b) and (a)
2 (d), (b), (c) and (a)
3 • System flowchart • Program flowchart
  • Structure diagram
4 (a) and (b)
5 (d)
6 (d)

Chapter 19

1 (a) Structure diagram (b) System flowchart
  (c) Program flowchart (or algorithm flowchart)
  (d) Structure diagram
2 (a) A computer operation (process) (b) All of them
3 • Help messages • Tutorial
4 (a) A document symbol
  (b) A general input/output symbol
  (c) A disc operations symbol
  (See Unit 19.2 for the actual shapes used.)
5 • Sample screen displays
  • Explanation of menu options
6 • Program listing • Structure diagram

Chapter 20

1 (a) and (c)
2 • EFTPOS • Bar codes
  • Better communication between a store and its head office
3 • Fax • Word processors • Data communications
  (Other correct answers are possible.)
4 • Some people do not have bank accounts and prefer using cash.
  • Cash is convenient for small transactions.
  (Other correct answers are possible.)
5 • It can cause unemployment. • It can create new jobs.
  • It can change what people have to do in their existing jobs.
6 Two of:
  • be able to withhold information about themselves;
  • stop data being transported without their consent;
  • find out what data is stored about them;
  • have inaccurate data corrected.
7 • Data users • Data subjects • Data registrar

Index to applications

Each GCSE board expects candidates to be familiar with a set of applications of IT. It is not possible to include all of the required applications in this book, but many of them have been used as examples in the text. The following separate index enables you to find these quickly.

airline bookings 34
ATM 56, 57, 175

bank cheques 53
bank cards 56
billing system 36
booking system 34
book numbers (ISBN) 99
books on CD-ROM 78
burglar alarm 171, 181

camera 168, 171
car manufacture (robots) 175, 176
car parts list 89
cash issuing terminal 56, 57, 175
charity donations 52
chemical plant (monitoring) 177
cheque sorting 53
circuit testing (simulation) 137
computer aided design 151-4
credit cards 55

data logging 47, 176-7
deafness aid - sub-titles 159

engineering (design) 70, 153-4
estate agent 131-2

flight simulator 31-2, 137

Gas Board accounts 36, 72
Gas Board meter reading 40-1
gas pipeline control 173
geology (rock identification) 139
greenhouse control 171-2

home applications 32, 168

ISBN 99

lathe (computer operated) 169-70
library book loans 54-5
logo design 62

mail merge 119
map storage 95
medical diagnosis 139
meter reading 40-1
music CDs 77
multiple choice questions 51

newsagent 32
nuclear power plant (simulation) 137

Ordnance Survey 95

payroll 88
phone card 57
photo CDs 77
photograph restoration 62
POS system 39-40
prices on goods 88
process control 32, 172-4
public house bar 60

school (learning aids) 71
school (network) 69, 79, 161
school (pupil records) 196-7
school (survey) 44
service records 86
simulation 31-2, 136-7
speech recognition 62-3
stock control example 89-91
supermarket checkout 39-40
survey (by questionnaire) 43-4
Switch card 56

traffic lights 171, 181-2

virtual reality 137-8
voice recognition 62-3
voice synthesis 71

weather report 111-12

General index

absolute reference **146**
access to files 85-6
actuator **169**
A-D converter **170**
address **22**, 73
algorithm **102**, 181-3, 198-202
alphanumeric data **22**, 124
analogue (data) **28**
analogue-to-digital converter **170**
analysis (of a system) 188, 190
AND 127
android **174**
animation 149
application software **104**, 105-10
archiving (files) **95**
ATM (Automated Cash Machine) 56-7
automated data capture **39**, 39-40

backing store **73**, 75
backup **95**
bar chart **156**
bar code 39, **54**, 54-5
BASIC 103
batch processing **35**, 35-6
binary **23**
bit **23**
bit-mapped storage **149**
block (of text) 118
bulletin board **164**
business graphics 154
byte **23**

CAD 65, 149, **151**, 154-5
CAD packages 110
CAD/CAM **154**
Campus 165
cash issuing terminal 57
catalogue (of files) 83
CD-ROM **77**, 77-8
CEEFAX 159
cell (spreadsheet) **141**
cell reference 141
central processing unit **29**
centring columns 143
centring lines 115
character **22**
character printer **67**
character set **22**
charts 155-6
check digit **98**, 98-9
checking data 25, 99-100
clip art 78
clipboard 107, 120
close (file) **83**
code **24**
column (spreadsheet) **141**
COM (Computer output on microfilm) **70**, 70-1
command line interface **45**, 45-6
communications **158**, 158-67
communications software 164
compact discs 77-8
compression (of files) 95
computer **29**
computer languages **103**
computer layout 30
Computer Aided Design 149, **151**, 151-4

construction (of a system) 189, 191
control algorithms 181-3
control characters **22**, 50
control programs 179-86
control systems **168**, 168-74
conversion (to new system) 189
copy (and paste) **107**
copying (cells) 145-147
copying (files) 85, 94-5
coursework projects 190-2,
CPU **29**, 74
credit cards 55
cursor **66**
custom-designed program 106
cut (and paste) 107

D-A converter **169**, 169-170
data **21**
data acquisition **176**
data capture forms **40**, 40-2
data capture **39**, 39-49, 124-5
data communication **158**
data files **81**, 81-92
data logging **176**, 176-7
data processing cycle **25**
data type **22**, 123
Data Protection Act 214-5
database 108-9, 122-33
database creation 126
database design 123-6
database report **130**
date format 124
decode **23**
deleting (files) **87**
design (of a system) 188, 191
Desktop publishing 107-8, **120**, 120-1
digital (data) **27**, 27-8
digital-to-analogue converter **169**, 169-70
digitise **60**
direct access files **85**, 85-6
direct access store **75**
directory **83**
discs, magnetic 75-7
document readers **51**
documentation **194**
documentation, technical 204-5
documentation, user 202, 204
DOS 45
dot matrix printer 67-8
draft quality **67**
drum plotter 69-70
DTP 107-8, **120**, 120-1

EDI **209**
EFT **209**
EFTPOS **209**
electronic conferencing **164**
electronic mail **164**, 166
EMail **164**
encode **23**
encryption of data 97
evaluation of software **105**
evaluation of coursework 192
exchangeable storage 75
expert system **138**, 138-9
exporting data **107**

fax **158**
feasibility study 188
feedback **171**, 171-2
fibre optic cable 160
field **81**, 81-2
file(s) **81**, 81-92
  access **85**, 85-6
  access code 97
  organisation 85
fixed length fields 82
flat-bed plotter 69-70
floppy discs **75**, 76-7
flowcharts **194**, 194-8, 200-2, 203
fonts 115
format (disc) **83**
formulae, spreadsheet **143**, 143-5
full screen menu **46**
function keys 50-1

gateways (to networks) 164
graph plotter 69-70
graphical output 69
graphical user interface **47**, 47-8
graphics **149**, 149-57
graphics characters 22
graphics packages 109-10
graphics tablet **60**, 60-1
grid lines 152
GUI **47**

hacking **93**, 93-4
hard disc **75**, 75-6
hardware **30**, 30-1

icon **47**
image manipulation 62, 149
impact printer **67**
implementation (system) 187
importing data **107**
indenting 117
inference engine 138
information **21**
information processing **24**, 30-1
information retrieval **122**
information technology **27**, 207-16
ink jet printer 68
input methods and devices **50**, 50-64
input port **170**
installation manual 202
integers **22**
integrated package 110-11
integrity of data **97**, 97-8
interactive computing **32**, 32-5
interface **169**, 169-70
interface, user **45**, 45-8
Internet 165
IT **27**, 187-93, 207-16

job 35
job queue 35
joystick **59**
justifying text 117, 143

Kb (kilobyte) **23**
key field **82**, 124
keyboard 50-1
knowledge base 138

label (cell) 141
LAN **160**, 161-3
languages 103

Index

laser printer 68
LCD 67
letter quality 67
light pen 57, 57-8
line based storage 149
line graph 156
line printer 67
linked files 131-2
liquid crystal display 67
load files 83
local area network 160, 161-3
location 22
logging in and out 96
logical expression 127
LOGO 103, 179-81

machine code 103
macro 102, 102-3, 181
magnetic discs 75-7
magnetic stripe (or strip) 55, 55-7
magnetic tape 78-9
mail merge 119
main memory 22
main store 22, 73-4
mainframe 29
maintenance (of system) 189
manuals 202-4
margins 117
master file 87, 87-8
match (when searching) 127
Mb (megabyte) 23
memory 22, 74
menu 46
menu bar 46
merge (files) 88
MICR 53
microcomputer 29
microfiche 70-1
microprocessor 29
minicomputer 29
model 134, 134-40, 147
modem 160, 160-1
monochrome 65
monitor 29, 65
morphing 149
motors 169
mouse 58
multiaccess 33, 33-5
multimedia 77
multiprogramming 37
multitasking 37
multi-user 33

networks 33, 160-6
NOT 127
numeric data 22, 124

object based storage 149
OCR 52-3
off-line 33, 70
OMR 51, 51-2
on-line processing 33, 33-4
open (a file) 83
operating system 104, 104-5
optic fibre cable 160
optical character recognition 52-3
optical mark reading 51, 51-2
OR 127
output device 65
output (of data) 65-72
output port 168
overtype 114

page printer 67
paint packages 150, 150-1

palette (colour) 150
passwords 96, 96-7
paste 107
peripherals 29
personal computer (PC) 29
personal data 212
phone card 57
pie chart 156
pixel 65
pixel based storage 149
plotters 69-70
Point-Of-Sale (POS) terminal 39, 90
printers 67-9
privacy 212, 212-5
procedures 180
process control 172, 172-4
processing (data) 25, 213
processor 29
program 102, 102-3
program documentation 205
program flowcharts 194, 195, 198, 200-2
projects 190-2
prompt 45
protecting files 95-7
puck 60, 60-1
pull-down menu 46
pupil records system 196-7

query 127, 127-8
query language 130, 130-1
questionnaire 43, 43-4

RAM 73, 74
random access files 85
range of cells 144
real time 31, 31-2
record 81
reference (to a cell) 146
reflection (of drawings) 152
relative reference 146
relay 168
renaming files 85
REPEAT statement 180-3
resolution 65, 66
response time 33, 33-4
robots 174, 174-6
ROM 73, 74
rotation (of drawings) 152

save (a file) 83
scaling (of drawings) 152
scanner 61, 61-2
scatter graph 156
screen mode 65
search and replace 118-9
searches 88, 127
sector (of disc) 76
security of data 93, 93-4
sensors 170, 170-2
sequential access files 85, 85-6
serial access files 85
serial access stores 75
simulation 31, 136, 136-7
single-user systems 32, 33
smart card 57
software 30, 103, 103-4
    packages 103
    house 106
sort 88, 128-9
speech recognition 62-3
spell checker 116
spreadsheet 109, 141, 141-8
standalone systems 32
statistics (database) 129

stepper motor 169
stepwise refinement 189
stock control 89, 89-91
storage 73-80
storage of files 83-5
store 22
string 22
structure diagrams 194, 198-9, 203
stylus 60, 60-1
sub-directory 83, 84
surveys 43, 43-4
swipe (a card) 55
Switch card 56
system 30
system design 188-9
system flowchart 194, 195, 195-7
system life cycle 187, 187-9
systems analyst 187
systems software 103

TAB key 116-7
tape streamer 79
targeting mail 213
technical documentation 194, 204-5
telecommunications 158
telesoftware 164
Télétel 165
teletext 158, 159-60
terminal 33
testing 185, 192
top-down design 189
touch screen 59, 59-60
tracker ball 58
transaction file 87, 87-8
transistor 169
transcription error 97, 97-8
transmission error 97
transposition error 98
turnaround document 40, 40-1
turtle 179, 179-81
tutorials 204
types (of data) 22

updating files 87, 87-8
user documentation 194, 202, 204
user friendly 48
user interface 45, 45-8
user manual 202
utility program 104

validation 99-100
variable length fields 82
vector based storage 149
verification 99
videotex 158
viewdata 158, 163-6
virtual reality 137-8, 138
viruses 94
voice synthesis 71

WAN 160, 163-6
wide area networks 160, 163-6
WIMP 47
window 49
word processing 114, 114-19
word processor 107
word wrap 114
WORM 77
Write Once Read Many 77
write protection 95-6

zoom 151

252